Where Have All the Textbooks Gone?

DIRECTIONS IN DEVELOPMENT
Human Development

Where Have All the Textbooks Gone?
Toward Sustainable Provision of Teaching and Learning Materials in Sub-Saharan Africa

Tony Read

© 2015 International Bank for Reconstruction and Development / The World Bank
1818 H Street NW, Washington, DC 20433
Telephone: 202-473-1000; Internet: www.worldbank.org

Some rights reserved

1 2 3 4   18 17 16 15

This work is a product of the staff of The World Bank with external contributions. The findings, interpretations, and conclusions expressed in this work do not necessarily reflect the views of The World Bank, its Board of Executive Directors, or the governments they represent. The World Bank does not guarantee the accuracy of the data included in this work. The boundaries, colors, denominations, and other information shown on any map in this work do not imply any judgment on the part of The World Bank concerning the legal status of any territory or the endorsement or acceptance of such boundaries.

Nothing herein shall constitute or be considered to be a limitation upon or waiver of the privileges and immunities of The World Bank, all of which are specifically reserved.

Rights and Permissions

This work is available under the Creative Commons Attribution 3.0 IGO license (CC BY 3.0 IGO) http://creativecommons.org/licenses/by/3.0/igo. Under the Creative Commons Attribution license, you are free to copy, distribute, transmit, and adapt this work, including for commercial purposes, under the following conditions:

Attribution—Please cite the work as follows: Tony Read. 2015. *Where Have All the Textbooks Gone?: Toward Sustainable Provision of Teaching and Learning Materials in Sub-Saharan Africa.* Directions in Development. Washington, DC: World Bank. doi:10.1596/978-1-4648-0572-1. License: Creative Commons Attribution CC BY 3.0 IGO

Translations—If you create a translation of this work, please add the following disclaimer along with the attribution: *This translation was not created by The World Bank and should not be considered an official World Bank translation. The World Bank shall not be liable for any content or error in this translation.*

Adaptations—If you create an adaptation of this work, please add the following disclaimer along with the attribution: *This is an adaptation of an original work by The World Bank. Views and opinions expressed in the adaptation are the sole responsibility of the author or authors of the adaptation and are not endorsed by The World Bank.*

Third-party content—The World Bank does not necessarily own each component of the content contained within the work. The World Bank therefore does not warrant that the use of any third-party-owned individual component or part contained in the work will not infringe on the rights of those third parties. The risk of claims resulting from such infringement rests solely with you. If you wish to re-use a component of the work, it is your responsibility to determine whether permission is needed for that re-use and to obtain permission from the copyright owner. Examples of components can include, but are not limited to, tables, figures, or images.

All queries on rights and licenses should be addressed to the Publishing and Knowledge Division, The World Bank, 1818 H Street NW, Washington, DC 20433, USA; fax: 202-522-2625; e-mail: pubrights@worldbank.org.

ISBN (paper): 978-1-4648-0572-1
ISBN (electronic): 978-1-4648-0573-8
DOI: 10.1596/978-1-4648-0572-1

Cover photo: © Tony Read. Used with permission. Further permission required for reuse.
Cover design: Debra Naylor, Naylor Design, Inc.

Library of Congress Cataloging-in-Publication Data has been requested.

Contents

Foreword		*xiii*
Acknowledgments		*xv*
Abbreviations		*xvii*

	Overview	1
	Conclusions Related to Unit Textbook Costs	6
	Conclusions Related to TLM System Costs	9
	Conclusions Related to Textbook and TLM Availability in Schools	10
	Conclusions Related to Textbook Cost Reduction Possibilities	11
	Conclusions Related to the Main Causes of High System Cost and Low Availability	13
	Conclusions Related to School TLM Management and Usage	14
	Conclusions Related to TLM Reform Policy Options	15
	Notes	15
	References	16
PART 1	**The Current Situation**	**17**
Chapter 1	Textbooks, Teaching and Learning Materials, and Learning Achievement	19
	The Impact of Textbooks on the Quality of Education	19
	Issues in Donor-Funded Textbook Projects	21
	The Cost Effectiveness of Textbook Provision	22
	Impact Evaluations of Textbook Provision in Kenya	23
	Textbook Effectiveness and Classroom Usage	24
	Factors Affecting School Effectiveness and Student Achievement	26
	Textbook Content Research	27
	Recent Research	28
	Reading Books	30

	A Summary of Key Issues	33
	Note	33
	References	34
Chapter 2	**Current Trends in National Teaching and Learning Materials Policies in Sub-Saharan Africa**	**37**
	Trends in National Teaching and Learning Materials Provision	37
	The Transition to Private Sector Involvement in Textbook Provision	38
	The Growth in African Publishing	40
	Competing Alternative Textbooks and the Introduction of Textbook Evaluation Systems	41
	Centralized versus Decentralized Funding and Selection	43
	Enrollment Growth	45
	Comparisons between Anglophone and Francophone Approaches	46
	The Growth in Learner-Centered and Outcomes-Based Curricula	46
	A Summary of Key Issues	50
	Notes	51
	References	52
Chapter 3	**Current Textbook (and Other Teaching and Learning Materials) Availability, Costs, and Financing in Sub-Saharan Africa**	**53**
	Textbook Unit Costs at Primary and Secondary Levels in 11 Sub-Saharan African Countries	53
	Sources of Textbooks for Primary and Secondary Levels	60
	Sources of Textbook Financing for Primary and Secondary Levels	60
	Types of Supply	62
	Textbook Availability	64
	A Summary of Key Issues	67
	Notes	68
	References	69
PART 2	**A Review of the Components of the Textbook Chain**	**71**
Chapter 4	**Literacy, Curricula, Teaching and Learning Materials, Requirements, and System Costs**	**73**
	The Crisis of Literacy and Numeracy in Sub-Saharan Africa	73

	Constraints on Improved Literacy and Numeracy Performance in SSA	77
	Curriculum Design and System Costs and Effectiveness	79
	The Minimum Profile of Required TLMs and Associated Cost Implications	86
	LoI Policies and Cost Implications	89
	Regional Curricula	91
	A Summary of Key Issues	93
	Notes	95
	References	96
Chapter 5	**Teaching and Learning Materials Financing**	**99**
	Issues in Teaching and Learning Materials Financing	99
	Affordability, Sustainability, and Predictability	100
	Underfinancing	101
	Fund Diversion	109
	Fund Misappropriation and Piracy	111
	Textbook Pricing Markups	113
	Supervision and Accountability	114
	A Summary of Key Issues	115
	Notes	117
	References	118
Chapter 6	**Authorship and Publishing**	**121**
	The Textbook Publishing Process	121
	Key Characteristics of Commercial Publishing	122
	What Can State Publishing Learn from Commercial Publishing Management?	125
	A Brief Review of State Publishing in Sub-Saharan Africa	126
	The Reemergence of Private Sector Textbook Publishing	128
	Local Authorship Capacity	129
	Cost Implications of Local Textbook Publishing	129
	A Summary of Key Issues	130
	Notes	131
	References	131
Chapter 7	**Manufacturing Issues**	**133**
	Local and Regional Textbook Printing Capacity in Sub-Saharan Africa	133
	Textbook Specifications	136
	Publishers' Production Knowledge	138
	Testing	139
	A Summary of Key Issues	139
	Notes	139
	References	140

Chapter 8	What Should Textbooks Cost?	141
	Cost Components	141
	One-Year versus Four-Year Book Life—Cost Comparisons	143
	Reasons for Textbook Cost Variations in Some Approved Book Lists	144
	Textbook Costs	147
	Costs and Print Runs	148
	A Summary of Key Issues	149
	Notes	150
	Reference	150
Chapter 9	Procurement, Bidding, and Evaluation	151
	Sole Sourcing versus Decentralized Competitive Textbook Selection	151
	Evaluating and Establishing an Approved List of Textbooks and TLMs	153
	Bid Supervision	155
	A Summary of Key Issues	156
	Note	156
	Reference	156
Chapter 10	Distribution, Storage, and Management	157
	Basic Teaching and Learning Materials Requirements for Effective Distribution	157
	The Coca Cola Argument	158
	Distribution Performance in SSA—Some Case Studies	159
	Planning and Management Problems	168
	A Summary of Emerging Key Issues	169
	Notes	171
	References	172
Chapter 11	Managing and Using Teaching and Learning Materials in Schools	175
	School and Classroom Storage	175
	TLM Management Issues	176
	Patterns of TLM Usage in the Classroom	177
	Conservation and Reuse	182
	A Summary of Emerging Key Issues	183
	Notes	185
	References	185

PART 3   e-Alternatives to Hard Copy Textbooks   187

Chapter 12	The Potential Impact of Information and Communication Technology Solutions on Textbook Provision	189

	Information and Communications Technology for Education as Competition to Hard Copy Teaching and Learning Materials	189
	e-Alternatives to Textbook Provision	190
	A Summary of Emerging Key Issues	199
	Notes	204
	References	205
PART 4	**Teaching and Learning Materials Policy Issues and Options**	**207**
Chapter 13	Options in the Development of National Teaching and Learning Materials Policies	209
	Private Sector versus Parastatal Textbook Producers	209
	Centralization versus Decentralization	210
	Local Language Policies and Literacy	210
	Monopoly versus Competitive Supply	212
	Cost-Reduction Strategies	213
	Country Comparisons	214
	Annex 13A: A TLM Diagnostic Checklist	226
	Annex 13B: Critical Issues on Upgrading TLM Provision in Africa—A Decision Tree for Policy Makers	229
	Note	230
Appendix A	Statistical Summary of Country Surveys	231
Appendix B	A Summary of Issues in Information and Communication Technology Use in Schools	245
	Information and Communication Technology and Student Achievement	245
	ICT Investment and Recurrent Costs and the Total Costs of Ownership	249
	Constraints to Effective ICT Usage in Education	252
	One Laptop per Child and the Future Impact of Low-Cost Laptop Provision on SSA	262
	Notes	264
	References	265

Figures

8.1	Long Print Run Cost–Benefit Curve	149
B.1	Major Problems with ICT Use in Education	259
B.2	Means of Procuring Computers	260

Tables

O.1	The Links in the TLM Chain	4
O.2	Potential Impact of Print Run Fractionalization on Unit Textbook Costs (4 Colors)	8
O.3	Implications of Moving Text from Textbooks to Teachers' Guides and Readers	12
2.1	Textbook Provision Systems in Francophone and Anglophone Africa—A Comparison	47
3.1	Textbook Costs for Grade 1	54
3.2	Textbook Costs for Grade 6	55
3.3	Textbook Costs for Grade 8	55
3.4	Textbook Costs for Grade 11	56
3.5	Median, Maximum, and Minimum Unit Textbook Costs	58
3.6	Average Annual Amortized Maximum and Minimum Costs of Provision	59
3.7	Median Amortized Costs per Student of TLM Provision	59
3.8	Sources of Authorship, Publishing, Manufacturing, and Raw Materials for Grades 1, 6, 8, and 11	61
3.9	Types of Textbook Funding	62
3.10	Adequacy, Regularity, and Predictability of Government TLM Budgets	63
3.11	Types of Textbook Supply	64
3.12	Estimated Primary TPRs in Urban, Rural, and Remote Locations	65
3.13	Primary Textbook Availability in Rwanda, 2007	65
4.1	Percentage of Grade 4 Pupils Who Attained the Minimum (MML) and Desirable (DML) Levels of Mastery Learning	75
4.2	Estimated Average Score of Pupils' Achievement in a Sample of African Countries	76
4.3	PSLE Pass Rates, 2000–09	82
4.4	Textbook Ownership in Cameroon, 2007	85
4.5	Costs of Basic Textbook Provision for P1, 2008	88
4.6	Costs of Alternative Approach to TLM Provision for P1, 2008	88
5.1	Average Annual US$ Midpoint Exchange Rates, 2000–09	108
8.1	Commercial Textbook Price Components	142
8.2	State Publishing Textbook Price Components	142
8.3	Comparative Prices for One- and Four-Year Textbook Specifications	143
8.4	One- and Four-Year Price Comparisons	144
10.1	Annual Textbook Rental Fee Collection Rates in Lesotho	165
13.1	Country Comparisons	219
A.1	Textbook Costs for Grade 1	231
A.2	Textbook Costs for Grade 6	231
A.3	Textbook Costs for Grade 8	232
A.4	Textbook Costs for Grade 11	232

A.5	Dictionary Costs for Grade 1	232
A.6	Dictionary Costs for Grade 6	233
A.7	Dictionary Costs for Grade 8	233
A.8	Dictionary Costs for Grade 11	234
A.9	Atlas Costs for Grade 1	234
A.10	Atlas Costs for Grade 6	234
A.11	Atlas Costs for Grade 8	235
A.12	Atlas Costs for Grade 11	235
A.13	Reader Costs for Grade 1	235
A.14	Reader Costs for Grade 6	236
A.15	Reader Costs for Grade 8	236
A.16	Reader Costs for Grade 11	236
A.17	Summary of Annual Amortized TLM Costs for Grade 1	237
A.18	Summary of Annual Amortized TLM Costs for Grade 6	237
A.19	Summary of Annual Amortized TLM Costs for Grade 8	237
A.20	Summary of Annual Amortized TLM Costs for Grade 11	238
A.21	Average Annual Amortized TLM Costs per Student by Grade Level	238
A.22	Types of Textbook Funding	238
A.23	Types of Atlas Funding	239
A.24	Types of Dictionary Funding	239
A.25	Types of Reader Funding	239
A.26	Types of Textbook Supply	240
A.27	Estimated Primary Textbook–Pupil Ratios in Urban, Rural, and Remote Locations	240
A.28	TLM Distribution Methods	240
A.29	Distribution Performance	241
A.30	Distribution Characteristics	241
A.31	Sources of Authorship, Publishing, Manufacturing, and Raw Materials for Grades 1, 6, 8, and 11	242
A.32	Adequacy, Regularity, and Predictability of Government TLM Budgets	243

Foreword

This study was commissioned as part of the World Bank's effort to support universal availability of textbooks in Sub-Saharan Africa (SSA). It examines the cost and financing barriers to universal textbook provision in the region, and is a compilation of the author's rich and multifaceted experience, across several decades working in the education sector in Africa. It covers a wide range of education issues including curriculum development and review, teaching and learning materials (TLM) provision, literacy and numeracy, language of instruction policy, procurement systems, distribution challenges, print manufacturing, materials development and design, and TLM management and usage in schools. Recent issues raised by attempts to embed information and communications technology (ICT) and other educational technologies within national education systems are also covered, as is the growing recognition that improved TLM system management is a critical component in achieving affordable and sustainable TLM provision to all students.

The study examines the rationale behind the national TLM policies and the many TLM projects funded by different donor agencies in many African countries over the years in an effort to understand why permanent solutions for the adequate and sustainable provision of TLM in support of curriculum objectives and specified learning outcomes have been so elusive.

The study is an excellent source of institutional memory of both good and bad practices, and of what has worked and what has not with regard to textbook policies in Africa and the support provided by development partners. A good example of this is the continuing emphasis on reducing the manufacturing costs of textbooks as a means of achieving better levels of provision and sustainability while other issues have been paid relatively less attention, including the cost and provision consequences of inefficient distribution and storage of TLMs, the high levels of stock losses in district and school storage and management, and the widespread problems of nonuse by teachers of the TLM stock provided. The study has adopted an evidence-based approach using—and, where necessary, quoting extensively from—documents published by government and development partners, international reports, national TLM policy documents, project design documents, consultant and project implementation reports, evaluation and project completion reports, and academic research studies. These source documents have been drawn from more than 40 anglophone, francophone, lusophone, and Arabic-speaking countries and cover every aspect of TLM provision, from national curriculum and language-of-instruction policies (the starting points) through budgeting and financing, system management, authorship, origination and publishing, manufacturing, distribution and storage, and finally school-based management and usage of materials.

Over the years, there have been a number of consistent policy themes that have strongly influenced TLM policies and system planning. These include the tensions between state and private sector publishing and the pros and cons of each; the difficulty in achieving consistent financial allocations for TLMs; monopolistic versus competitive supply systems; the widespread failure of state-organized distribution; the evolving relationships among international, regional, and national publishing industries; the trade-offs between higher quality and lower priced international manufacturing and the desire to support local manufacturing industries; international, regional, or national and local language of instruction policies; and the centralization versus decentralization debate in decision making on the selection of TLMs. The study examines these issues through national examples, but draws wider conclusions based on the evidence of outcomes.

The study will be particularly useful for policy makers, development partners, and other stakeholders attempting to understand the wide range of issues surrounding the complexity of textbook provision in SSA.

Peter Nicolas Materu
Practice Manager
Education Global Practice, World Bank (GEDDR)

Acknowledgments

I am particularly grateful to Birger Fredriksen and Sukhdeep Brar, who read several versions of the evolving manuscript and provided many insightful comments and suggestions. Sukhdeep also came up with the original idea for this study and provided the necessary funding, determination, and moral support to take it through to completion. Brian Jones, formerly CEO of Evans Bros Publishers (United Kingdom), provided much practical costing data and read the manuscript for accuracy from the point of view of a commercial publisher involved in textbook and supplementary reader publishing for Africa. His viewpoints embraced all of the international, regional, and national aspects of teaching and learning materials (TLM) publishing via his involvement with the Evans companies in Kenya, Nigeria, and Sierra Leone. I have benefitted greatly from the opportunity to debate frequently and at length every aspect of the TLM provision problem in Sub-Saharan Africa (SSA) countries with Amanda Buchan, my colleague and friend for more than 30 years. Amanda also provided up-to-date information on the TLM situation in Cameroon, the Democratic Republic of Congo, and Rwanda. Passionate debates long into the night on TLM problems and potential solutions have always characterized my long-established working relationship with Mike Kiernan, and Professor Alan Penny's wide and extensive knowledge of education in Africa has been inspirational for me over many years. Nicholas Read provided most of the expertise and input into the sections on alternatives to printed TLMs, the rapid (and expensive) developments and investments in Information and Communication Technologies for Education (ICT4E) and also to TLM system management and the development and use of digital management systems as a major issue in SSA countries. Tony Ashe made his technical expertise freely available in the section on print origination and manufacturing and also provided the up-to-date assessment of the possibilities of print on demand for textbook provision in SSA in response to a query from a World Bank project task manager. Vincent Bontoux identified knowledgeable researchers for TLM issues and provided opinions and advice on TLM usage and policies in some of the francophone countries included in this study. Over the years I have been very fortunate to work on TLM provision problems in very many SSA countries, and I have learned a great deal from local experts, authors, publishers, printers, booksellers, distributors, consolidators, Ministry of Education (MOE) officials and ordinary classroom teachers, including a number of innovative and committed teachers who managed to achieve extraordinary learning outcomes for their students in often very difficult circumstances. I have made many valuable and lasting personal and professional friendships as a result. The names of most of these are too numerous to mention here, but it is important that I acknowledge particularly the support provided by Iris Uyttersprot of United Nations Children's Fund (UNICEF), Sophie Waterkeyn of Belgian Technical Cooperation (BTC), and Richard Arden of the Department for International Development (DFID) who provided the opportunities and support to work on many of the issues raised in the text. I am also grateful for the contributions to a greater understanding of the many aspects of TLM provision issues in Africa made by Alice Ibale, George Kalibbala, and Samuel Enyutu in Uganda, David Muita in Kenya, Abdullah Saiwad in Tanzania, Charles Sehlabi in Lesotho, and the charismatic and inspirational Murietta Olu-Williams in Sierra Leone, who started me out on the long road to this study more years ago than I care to remember. Eating rock lobster late at night in the Atlantic restaurant on Lumley beach in Freetown with red land crabs the size of dinner plates waving enormous claws silhouetted against the phosphorescent breaking waves and covering every inch of sand as far as the eye could see between the coconut palms, while furiously debating every aspect of the textbook project that she was managing, is a memory I shall always cherish!

This study was financed by the Norwegian Pre- and Post-Primary Education Trust Fund (NPEF) and the Multi-Donor Education and Skills Fund (MESF), which are gratefully acknowledged.

Abbreviations

3G	3rd Generation, as applied to mobile phones
4G	4th Generation, as applied to mobile phones
4/1	One side of a printing sheet printed in 4 colors and the reverse in 1 color (also 1/1, 2/1, and so on)
ADB	Asian Development Bank
ADEA	Association for the Development of Education in Africa
AEO	Assistant education officer
AfDB	African Development Bank
AIF	Agence Internationale de la Francophonie
APNET	African Publishers Network
AT	Advisory Teacher (Namibia)
BOLESWA	Botswana, Lesotho, and Swaziland
BTC	Belgian Technical Cooperation
CAI	Computer aided instruction
CDN	Confirmed delivery note
CDSS	Community Day Secondary School (Malawi)
CEO	Chief education officer
CEQUIL	Cameroon Equity and Quality Improvement Project (World Bank funded)
CF	Coopération Française
CfSK	Computers for Schools Kenya
CIDA	Canadian International Development Agency
CLIL	Content and language integrated learning
CONFEMEN	Conference of Ministries of Education Using French as a Language of Instruction
CPMD	Curriculum and Pedagogic Materials Department (Rwanda)
CRT	Criterion referenced tests
CSS	Conventional Secondary School (Malawi)
DANIDA	Danish International Development Agency
DD	Digital divide

DDD	Domestic digital divide
DEC	Distance Education Centres (Malawi)
DEO	District education office(r)
DFES	Department for Education and Skills (United Kingdom)
DFID	Department for International Development (of the British Government)
DFIDEA	Department for International Development East Africa
DGIS	Dutch Government International Aid Agency
DIMPP	Decentralised Instructional Materials Procurement Project (Uganda)
DML	Desired Mastery of Learning (MLA)
DP	Development partner
DPOD	Digital print on demand
DRC	Democratic Republic of the Congo
DSA	District Schools Auditor (Kenya)
DTP	Desktop publishing
EAC	East African Community
EAEP	East African Educational Publishers (Kenya)
EALB	East African Literature Bureau (colonial predecessor of Kenya Literature Bureau)
EAPH	East African Publishing House (Tanzania)
EC	European Community
ECOWAS	Economic Community of West African States
EFA	Education for All
EGRA	Early Grade Reading Assessment
EGMA	Early Grade Maths Assessment
e-learning	Learning using digital technology and materials
ELT	English language teaching
EMAC	Educational Materials Approval Committee (Tanzania)
EMIS	Education Management Information System
EO	Education officer
ERfKE	Education Reform for the Knowledge Economy (Jordan)
FCUBE	Free Compulsory Universal Basic Education (Ghana)
FDSE	Free Day Secondary Education (Kenya)
FLT	French language teaching
FOSS	Free Open Source Software
FPE	Free Primary Education (Kenya)
FQUPE	Free Quality Universal Primary Education (Dakar EFA, 2000)

FUPE	Free Universal Primary Education
GEQUIL	General Education Quality Improvement Loan (Ethiopia—WB)
GER	Gross enrollment ratio
GOE	Government of Ethiopia
GOG	Government of Guinea
GOK	Government of Kenya
GOM	Government of Malawi
GOT	Government of Tanzania
GOU	Government of Uganda
GPA	Grade point average
gsm	Grams per square meter—a measure of paper weight
HD	High definition
IADP	International Association for Digital Publications
ICR	Implementation completion report
ICT	Information and communication technology
ICT4E	ICT for Education
IEA	International Association for the Evaluation of Educational Achievement
IFLA	International Federation of Library Associations
IGCSE	International General Certificate of Secondary Education
IIEP	International Institute for Educational Planning
IMMH	Instructional Materials Management Handbook (Liberia)
INSETT	In-service teacher training
iPad	Tablet computer manufactured by Apple Inc.
IRA	International Reading Association
ISP	Internet service provider
IWB	Interactive white boards
JEI	Jordan Education Initiative
JKF	Jomo Kenyatta Foundation (Kenya)
KIE	Kenya Institute of Education
KBSA	Kenya Booksellers Association
KLB	Kenya Literature Bureau
KPA	Kenya Publishers Association
KSES	Kenya School Equipment Scheme
KISA	Kenya Independent Schools Association
Ksh	Kenya shilling
L1	1st language

L2	2nd language
LAMP	Literacy Assessment & Monitoring Programme (UNESCO successor to MLA)
LAN	Local area network
LoI	Language of instruction
LOLE	Language of limited extent
LOS	Line of sight
LPO	Local purchase orders
MAL	Main area language
MBS	Malawi Book Supplies
MDG	Millennium Development Goals
MESF	Multi-Donor Education and Skills Fund
MIE	Malawi Institute of Education
MIITEP	Malawi Integrated In-Service Teacher Education Programme
MINEDUC	Ministry of Education (Rwanda)
MK	Malawi kwacha
MLA	Monitoring Learning Achievement
m-learning	Learning using mobile communication devices
MLMP	Minimum Learning Materials Profile
MML	Minimum Mastery Learning
MOE	Ministry of Education
MOES	Ministry of Education and Sports (Uganda)
MOESS	Ministry of Education, Science, and Sports (Ghana)
MOEST	Ministry of Education, Science, and Technology (Malawi)
MOEVT	Ministry of Education and Vocational Training (Zanzibar)
MOF	Ministry of Finance
MSCE	Malawi Secondary Certificate of Education
NAPE	National Assessment of Primary Education (Uganda)
NBER	National Bureau of Economic Research (United States)
NCDC	National Curriculum Development Centre (in Uganda and Rwanda)
NCERT	National Council for Educational Research and Technology (India)
NCF	National Curriculum Framework
NCHRD	National Center for Human Resource Development (Jordan)
NEA	National Education Assessment (Ghana)
NER	Net enrollment ratio

NGO	Nongovernmental organization
NPEF	Norwegian Pre- and Post-Primary Education Trust Fund
OLPC	One laptop per child
OMCQ	Objective multiple choice questions
PARSE	Projet d'Appui au Redressement du Secteur de l'Education (World Bank project in the Democratic Republic of Congo)
PASEC	Programme d'Analyse des Systèmes éducatifs de la CONFEMEN
PASEF	Projet d'Appui au Secteur Éducation Formation (World Bank Project in Côte d'Ivoire)
PC	Personal computer
PDA	Personal digital assistant (usually applied to a handheld computer or "palm top")
PEDP	Primary Education Development Project (Tanzania)
PEO	Provincial education officer
PETS	Primary Expenditure Tracking Survey
PIRLS	Progress in International Literacy Study
PISA	Programme for International Student Assessment
PLC	Primary Leaving Certificate
PLE	Primary Leaving Examination
ppi	Pixels per inch
PRESETT	Pre-service teacher training
PRIMR	Primary Math and Reading Initiative (Kenya)
PRISM	Primary School Management (DFID-funded education project in Kenya)
PSIMP	Primary School Instructional Materials Project (Kenya)
PSLC	Primary School Leaving Certificate (Tanzania)
PSLE	Primary School Leaving Exam
PTA	Parent Teacher Association
PTC	Primary Teacher Training College
PTR	Pupil–teacher ratio
PwC	PricewaterhouseCoopers
PWD	Public Works Department
RCT	Randomized controlled trial
REB	Rwanda Education Board
RNE	Royal Netherlands Embassy
RwF	Rwanda franc
SACMEQ	South and East African Consortium for Monitoring Educational Quality

SAU	Schools Audit Unit (Kenya)
SD	Secure digital (when applied to memory cards, etc.)
SEDP	Secondary Education Development Project (Tanzania)
SES	Socioeconomic status
SIDA	Swedish International Development Agency
SMC	School Management Committee (Kenya)
SMS	Short message service
SPRED	Support for Primary Education (World Bank/DFID-funded project in Kenya)
SSA	Sub-Saharan Africa
SSU	School Supplies Unit (Lesotho)
STSC	School Textbook Selection Committee (Kenya)
SUPER	Support for Ugandan Primary Education Reform (USAID-funded project)
SWAp	Sector-wide approach
TAC	Teachers' Advisory Centres (Kenya)
TCO	Total cost of ownership
TDA	Teachers' didactic aids
TES	Tanzania Elimu Supplies (parastatal distribution company, now defunct)
TIE	Tanzania Institute of Education (curriculum development and sometime textbook publisher)
TIMMS	Trends in International Maths and Science Study
TLM	Teaching and learning materials
TMC	Textbook Management Committee (Guinea)
TPR	Textbook–pupil ratio
TRF	Textbook Revolving Fund
TRS	Textbook Rental Scheme
TSh	Tanzania shilling
UNAM	University of Namibia
UNESCO	United Nations Educational, Scientific, and Cultural Organization
UNEB	Uganda National Examinations Board
UNICEF	United Nations Children's Fund
UPE	Universal Primary Education
UPS	Uninterrupted power supply
USAID	United States Agency for International Development
UV	Ultraviolet (as in UV varnish—a textbook cover finishing process)

VLE	Virtual learning environment
VFM	Value for money
WB	World Bank
WEO	Woreda Education Office (Ethiopia)
ZIS	Zonal Inspector of Schools (Kenya)

P1 refers to (primary) grade 1; P2 refers to grade 2, and so on. However, in some Sub-Saharan African countries grades are referred to by level of schooling; hence, S1 refers to the first grade at the secondary level; S2 refers to the second grade at the secondary level, and so on.

Overview

This study is based on the multiple experiences of more than 50 years of working in the education sector in many Sub-Saharan Africa (SSA) countries—initially as a teacher in state secondary schools, further education, and adult education classes in Ghana in the 1960s and then as an educational publisher and finally as a researcher and development consultant on a wide range of African education issues covering curriculum development and review, teaching and learning materials (TLM) provision, literacy and numeracy, languages of instruction (LoI) policy, procurement systems, distribution challenges, print manufacturing, materials development and design, TLM management and usage in schools, and, more recently, the wide range of issues thrown up by current attempts to embed information and communications technology (ICT) and other educational technologies within national education systems and the growing recognition that improved TLM system management is a critical component in achieving affordable and sustainable TLM provision to all students.

The study has attempted to make sense of the rationales behind many different national TLM policies and the many TLM projects funded by different donor agencies in many African countries over more than 40 years and, as a result, to understand why ministries of education (MOEs) and development partners (DPs) have found it so difficult in so many countries over so many years to find permanent solutions to the adequate and sustainable provision of TLMs in support of curriculum objectives and specified learning outcomes.

At least part of the problem is the difficulty in achieving effective institutional memory in DPs and in (MOEs) and ministries of finance and in ensuring that information on both good and bad practices and on what works and what doesn't is widely and effectively disseminated. A good example of this is the continuing and almost obsessive concern with reducing the manufacturing costs of textbooks as a means of achieving better levels of provision and sustainability, while largely ignoring the much greater cost and provision consequences of inefficient distribution and storage of TLMs and the high levels of stock losses in district and school storage and management and the widespread problems of nonusage by teachers of the TLM stock provided. This study consciously addresses these issues by attempting to draw together in one volume all of the lessons learned from multiple TLM provision policies and projects over the past 40 years. The study has adopted an evidence-based approach using as source documents—and, where necessary, quoting extensively from—published government and DP policies, objectives and priorities, international reports, national TLM policy documents, project design documents, consultant and project implementation reports, evaluation and Project Completion Reports, and academic research studies. These source documents have been drawn from more than 40[1] anglophone, francophone, lusophone, and Arabic-speaking SSA countries and cover every aspect of TLM provision from national curriculum and LoI policies (the starting points) through budgeting and financing, system management, authorship, origination and publishing, manufacturing, distribution and storage, and finally school-based management and usage of materials.

Over the past 40 to 50 years there have been a number of consistent policy themes that have strongly influenced TLM policies and system planning. These include the pros and cons and the tensions between state and private sector publishing; the difficulty in achieving consistent financial allocations for TLMs; monopolistic versus competitive supply systems; the widespread failure of state organized distribution; the evolving relationships between international, regional, and national publishing industries; the trade-offs between higher quality and lower priced international manufacturing and the desire to support local manufacturing industries; international, regional, national, or local LoI policies; and the centralization versus decentralization debate in decision making on the selection of TLMs. These issues are covered in the text through national examples but wider conclusions have been drawn based on the evidence of outcomes. These major policy issues recur again and again in country after country and one of the associated problems is the constant shift in TLM policies in many SSA countries that make it so difficult for individual schools and teachers to become thoroughly familiar and comfortable with any system. It is sometimes depressing to see how often previous policies that have failed have been reintroduced a few years later as "new" policies by MOEs or DPs, usually with the same outcomes.

Inevitably, the study is influenced by personal observations based on many years of working and school visiting in urban, slum, rural, and remote (and sometimes very remote) locations covering thousands of schools and education offices in many different African countries encompassing all types of environments from lofty mountains, to high forests, to deserts, grasslands, and marshlands.

The key role of textbooks and other TLMs in enhancing the quality of learning is almost universally recognized. This role is especially important in low-income countries where textbooks and other TLMs can help compensate for adverse factors such as large class size, substandard classrooms and facilities, poorly trained teachers, reduced contact hours between teachers and students, high levels of illiteracy among parents, and a lack of reading materials in homes or in schools. However, despite decades of funding by governments and DPs, few low-income SSA countries have been able to establish sustainable systems for providing textbooks and other essential TLMs on a regular basis. As a result, TLMs remain inadequately supplied—and used—in most SSA countries.

This study explores the background to this situation and seeks to explain why adequate and effective TLM provision has remained so elusive and what needs to be done to make quality TLMs sustainably available to all pupils and well used in primary and general secondary education. The achievement of this objective takes on added importance given that the poor quality of instruction in most SSA countries and its impact on the early achievement of literacy and numeracy, is considered now to be among the most important constraints on achieving universal completion of primary education. Furthermore the strong growth in primary school enrollments in SSA over the past 10 to 15 years has resulted not only in increased budget demands for primary education but also in student and parental demand for increased access to secondary schools where textbooks and other TLMs are even more costly than in primary education.

Each link in the TLM Chain is studied in order to identify the cost and supply implications of different policies and the links most likely to fail or create high costs. Examples of both good and bad practice are provided. Longer-term trends in TLM provision policies are also reviewed in order to identify the policy impact on affordability and equity for urban, rural, and remote schools. The study reviews strategies that can reduce costs and improve affordability.

The main reason for the failure to solve the TLM provision issue is probably a widespread misunderstanding among MOEs and DPs of the nature and complexity of the problems to be solved. Effective TLM provision requires a number of different activities and inputs to operate efficiently in correct sequence. These activities are often referred to as the Book Chain or, more accurately, the TLM Chain.[2] If just one of the links in the chain is dysfunctional there is a risk that the whole system will not function effectively. Thus, TLM reform should always be conceived of as the review of a whole system rather than a concentration on single factor solutions only. The basic links in the TLM Chain with explanatory notes are provided in table O.1, below.

Different policies can be applied to each of the links in the chain and these can have a profound impact on TLM prices and TLM system costs, equity of supply, and sustainability. Policies are not always based on educational concerns or on sensible cost control practices, but often may be driven by political/economic considerations. The ongoing debate over the use of national, regional, or international manufacturing sources for textbook printing is a good example of the face-off between educational and political/economic concerns. Also, there are few, if any, national curriculum development organizations that take into account the cost implications of their curriculum designs. Few MOEs have

Table O.1 The Links in the TLM Chain

The links in the chain	Notes on the links
Curriculum and syllabus design	This has a significant impact on the system cost and thus the affordability and sustainability of TLM provision because it determines the number of subjects that require textbooks and teachers, guides. Overloaded syllabus content can also impact on unit textbook costs. It should also specify what other TLMs (including e-materials) are needed to deliver curriculum objectives. Ideally the cost implications of all curriculum-related proposals should be a core part of any curriculum review. Unfortunately, very few national curricula are subjected to any kind of cost analysis. Because of the potential impact on costs, LoI policies should also be part of the curriculum/LoI/TLM trio of key policies, which ideally need to be developed simultaneously.
The minimum profile of TLMs	This is the specification of the minimum set of TLMs for each grade level required to deliver grade level curriculum objectives and the specified learning outcomes. This also has an impact on system costs because it often specifies not just textbooks and teachers' guides but also reading books, atlases, dictionaries, teaching aids, teachers' reference books, and increasingly digital learning materials as well.
Supply assumptions	These cover supply ratios (target textbook/student ratio, number of reading books per grade level, atlas/student ratios, etc.); these also cover target classroom life, assumed annual loss and damage rates, and enrollment growth rates. Thus, the supply assumptions also have a significant impact on system cost.
Production specifications	These include number of colors, extent, page formats, text paper, cover card, binding style, finishing style, etc. Basically they break down into presentational specs and durability specs. They have an impact on the unit costs of TLMs and thus on system costs—but enhanced durability and thus longer classroom life enables costs to be amortized over longer periods and thus unit production costs can be significantly reduced when calculated as annual amortized costs.
Key policy decisions	These include: • Who pays? (government or parents) • How are TLMs paid for? (free supply to schools, school capitation grants, parental purchase, rental fees, etc.) • Monopoly or competition • Centralization or decentralization? • Who selects—government, district, or school? • Who publishes (see below)? • Who distributes (see below)? • Who manufactures (see below)? These decisions will have an impact on system cost and sometimes on unit production and annual amortized costs.
Pricing	To what extent is pricing controlled for example—as a condition of approved list status? Pricing policy can have a profound impact on both unit costs and system costs. Failure to achieve a degree of price predictability can lead to recurrent TLM costs running out of control.
Authorship and publishing	Who authors and who publishes (MOE or private sector publishers)? With MOE authorship and publishing it is often difficult if not impossible to accurately determine unit production costs because so much of the publication investment (for example salaries, rent, equipment, maintenance, author payments, prepress) is often buried in inaccessible government budget lines.
Procurement	Procurement documentation contains basic specifications, pricing policies, print runs, and evaluation methodologies and instruments. Good competitive procurement can have a significant impact on both unit and system costs.
Manufacturing	Includes prepress, raw materials, printing, binding, and finishing. Has an impact on unit costs and thus system costs as well, but always a less important component of total TLM pricing than is generally assumed by MOEs and DPs. There is frequently a policy tension between local, regional, and international manufacturing sources.

table continues next page

Table O.1 The Links in the TLM Chain *(continued)*

The links in the chain	Notes on the links
Distribution and storage	State distribution has a poor record in many SSA countries and annual loss and damage rates through poor storage and distribution can be very high—up to 65 percent per year has been recorded. This is a very major factor in system costs. With private sector supply there will be considerable differences in the distribution component of unit costs according to the specified final distribution point—school, district, or MOE central store. But if the publisher or bookseller is required to deliver to schools there is no additional cost to the MOE, whereas private sector distribution to the MOE requires the MOE to pay for onward delivery to schools. The delivery from districts to schools is usually the most critical storage and distribution problem.
School management and conservation	Has a great impact on TLM classroom life and thus is often a critical component of system cost. Very high rates of loss and damage in schools are common in many SSA countries, leading to either reduced TLM availability or increased and expensive replacement rates.
Using TLMs in class and at home	The total cost of TLM provision is negated if TLMs are not used when they get to schools. This is a common problem and pre- and in-service training in TLM usage is a critical issue, which will increase system costs.
Supervision and monitoring of implementation	Lack of good quality supervision and monitoring leads to higher losses of TLM stock in schools and thus increased system cost.
Managing the TLM provision system	TLM provision is a complex system, which needs professional management supported wherever possible by sophisticated, custom-designed, computerized management systems.

Source: Read 2010.
Note: LoI = language of instruction ; MOE = Ministry of Education; TLM = teaching and learning materials.

a clear idea of the annual budget allocations needed to maintain their TLM provision in healthy condition and to ensure that the basic TLM requirements are available and well used in every school. Even if all the right decisions are taken up to the manufacturing stage and books of good content, presentation, and manufacturing quality at affordable prices are produced, the whole process can be negated if TLMs don't get to schools or if they are not used—or badly used—when they get there.

When all the links in the chain have been reviewed and reformed the issue of system management remains. The combination of large numbers of schools and students located in different regions, often with different facilities and operational environments, with large numbers of titles supplied in differing quantities (and sometimes in different languages) is very difficult to manage on a manual basis; and sophisticated computerized management systems are needed to ensure that good management decisions can be made based upon good information, sound future planning, and adequate financial allocations to maintain TLM supplies at target levels for every school in the country.

> For many countries, from the 1960s through to the mid-1980s, monopolistic textbook supply and state publishing, printing and distribution appeared to offer the cheapest and most cost-effective routes to affordable and sustainable textbook provision. However, the dominance of state-owned facilities did not solve the fundamental financing problems … the discrepancies between urban and rural levels of provision (still exist) in all SSA countries … but there is no evidence to suggest that

state systems have performed any better than commercial systems in solving the most basic textbook provision problems. (Da Cruz et al. 1998)

At a textbook roundtable conference in 1994 when future policy options were being debated, the Tanzanian Minister of Education commented,

> There is no guarantee that the operation of a commercial market-based system, per se, will automatically solve equity and availability problems. The private sector cannot be expected to solve all educational textbook supply issues by itself. Government funding and clearly articulated and widely circulated support policies are also necessary. (MOEC 1994)

Governments and DPs have sought over many years to find long-term, sustainable solutions to the fundamental problem of providing good quality and relevant textbooks and other TLMs at affordable prices equitably and on time to all students in all locations. Examples of the different strategies to achieve these objectives are provided in the text below and a consideration of the successes and failures of the different approaches is also provided in the expectation that they will help to identify more realistic and more effective solutions in the future.

In the past 10 years the demand for the provision of ICT to SSA schools has added another very expensive education budget line for government and schools (and parents) and there is a growing recognition that ICT and print-based TLMs may soon be in direct competition for available funding in the future. Some policy makers see e-materials as potential replacements for printed textbooks and reading books. Thus, this study also reviews ICT provision and other educational technology and e-alternatives to printed TLMs as potential rivals for available finance. The study concludes with a set of tools that should facilitate evidence-based policy dialogue between DPs, national policy makers, and TLM professionals (printers, publishers—both print and digital—booksellers, other distributors, etc.) on the design of appropriate and affordable systems.

The main conclusions from the study are provided below.

Conclusions Related to Unit Textbook Costs

a) The usual components of unit textbook costs are:
- Prepress—a fixed origination cost comprising typesetting, artwork, film/electronic disk, and so on
- Manufacturing—a variable running cost comprising raw materials, printing, binding, and finishing;
- Royalties or fees for authorship;
- Publishers' overheads comprising salaries, editorial, marketing, administration, storage and systems, rent, utilities, financing and borrowing costs, and so on
- Distribution costs; and
- Publisher's profit.

b) Quoted national textbook costs often contain different combinations of the above components and are therefore often not easily comparable. For example:
    - *Manufacturing cost* includes only raw materials and printing (for example, Burundi);
    - *Procurement cost* (that is the cost of delivering to an MOE, which will undertake its own distribution to schools) does not include the full distribution cost to schools but only distribution to the MOE (for example, Uganda);
    - *Delivered cost* (that is the cost of the publisher delivering direct to schools) contains the full distribution charge (for example, Rwanda); and
    - *Retail price* for supplying to schools through a retail bookshop and thus requiring a full distribution discount to a third party supplier[3] (for example, Kenya);
c) Before textbook cost comparisons are attempted between different countries it is critical that the components of each quoted "price" or "cost" are clearly identified.
d) On a "rule of thumb" basis the manufacturing cost (including raw materials) is usually considered to represent between 15 and 20 percent of the retail price of a textbook or the full cost of delivering direct to schools.
e) Raw materials may comprise 30 to 60 percent of the cost of manufacturing (depending on print runs, production specifications, and sources of supply) but they do not comprise the same percentage of the retail price or the total costs of provision. This distinction has led to great confusion in past attempts to identify the causes of the perceived costs of textbook supply when raw materials and manufacturing costs alone have often been perceived by MOEs and DPs as the benchmark for supply costs.
f) Most of the costs of textbook supply have to be paid for somewhere. Even if the MOE publishes itself and only quotes raw materials and manufacturing costs, the real costs of authorship, editorial, financing, distribution, overheads and so on are always incurred and have to appear somewhere in MOE budgets. Alternatively they may simply not be funded at all, which is often the case of distribution costs and in this scenario the materials do not arrive in schools at all and therefore the investment costs are wasted.
g) Distribution charges as part of textbook costs vary significantly according to the required delivery location (MOE central warehouse, district offices, or individual schools) and to the complexity and difficulty of national distribution networks. These cannot be "averaged" and require calculation for each country.
h) Distribution costs will also vary according to the level of risk: for example confirmed bulk supply to a single MOE warehouse location in the capital city supported by payment via an irrevocable letter of credit is a low-risk requirement for a publisher; competitive supply through the local retail book trade can be speculative with risks of unsold stock, late payment, or nonpayment by the bookseller.

Table O.2 Potential Impact of Print Run Fractionalization on Unit Textbook Costs (4 Colors)

Language	Uzbek	Russian Federation	Karakalpak	Kazakh	Tajik	Kyrgyz Republic	Turkmen	Totals
Print runs ('000s)	600	30	25	20	15	2	1	693
Fixed costs US$ '000s	30	30	30	30	30	30	30	210
Running costs US$ '000s	600	30	25	20	15	2	1	693
Total costs US$ '000s	630	60	55	50	45	32	31	903
Unit costs US$	1.05	2.00	2.20	2.50	3.02	16.45	31.95	1.31

Source: Read 2003.

i) The financing cost component of textbook prices is also affected by the speed of payment: for example in Ghana textbook publishers have sometimes been required to wait for two years or more for payment from government and the costs of financing this cash flow gap have to be built into the quoted prices. When local bank interest rates are high this can represent a significant additional cost component. Ghana is by no means the only SSA country where payments can be slow or long delayed by disputes over deliveries and in some countries publishers have declined to supply because they cannot afford the credit costs.

j) The main factors that determine unit textbook costs are the following:
- Print runs—unit costs decrease with increased print runs until a cost plateau is reached (see chapter 8, Costs and Print Runs).
- The impact of multiple LoIs in fractionalizing print runs—where multiple languages of instruction are specified in national education systems (for example, Eritrea, Ethiopia, Namibia, South Sudan, Uganda, and others) print runs can be reduced below cost-optimization plateaux thus increasing unit costs (see table O.2). The situation can be ameliorated by printing local language textbooks in one or two colors where the cost optimisation plateaux are much lower.
- The impact of textbook–pupil ratios (TPRs) in reducing print runs—1:1 TPRs requiring supply to the total grade level enrollment. 2:1 or 3:1 TPRs reduce print runs by 50 percent and 66 percent respectively but also may reduce print runs below the cost optimization plateaux;
- Textbook extent—longer textbooks require more raw materials and more typesetting and design and layout costs.
- Textbook formats—larger textbook formats provide more opportunities for user-friendly design and presentation but larger page sizes require more text paper and thus additional cost. Large format books may be more easily damaged thus increasing system costs through stock losses.
- Use of color—four-colour printing is significantly more expensive than one-or two-colour printing, although the cost impact can be reduced by printing four-colours on one side of the printed sheet and one-colour on the reverse side (4/1 printing). However, this approach requires considerable authorship, editorial, and design skills and may be beyond the technical capacity of many new local publishers, particularly when tight production deadlines have to be met.

- Sourcing of raw materials—big international textbook printers often buy paper and card stocks direct from the mill and thus achieve significantly lower raw materials costs for their clients. They can also generally offer a wider range of raw materials options and qualities in sheet sizes that are conformable with their own printing machine sizes, thus achieving lower levels of wastage on the machines. Buying from national or regional merchants is likely to be more expensive and the range of raw materials options and sheet sizes will also tend to be more restricted. Paper sizes may not be exactly conformable with machine sizes, thus leading to higher wastage levels.[4]
- Printing and binding—international textbook printers frequently work three shifts per day and amortize plant costs more effectively as a result. They typically invest in modern, well-maintained, high-efficiency plants producing lower costs and with lower levels of wastage on the machine. Many national printers work one or two shifts often on less efficient reconditioned older plants with higher levels of down time and wastage.
- Import duties on raw materials and printing plant are common in SSA countries whereas finished books are usually imported duty free under the terms of the Florence Agreement and the Nairobi Protocols on the Free Flow of Books and Information. This makes local printers more expensive than external printers.
- Durability and long book life—specifications for long book life require more expensive raw materials and manufacturing processes, which increase unit costs. As a rule of thumb the costs of a four-year specification are around 20% higher than for a one-year specification (see chapter 8, One-Year versus Four-Year Book Life—Cost Comparisons). Four-year specifications allow for effective cost amortization but can appear to be more expensive in direct country-to-country cost comparisons.

k) Unit textbook manufacturing costs are very rarely the main determining factor in high-cost textbook provision systems.

l) The concept of annual amortized unit costs is more useful as an indicator of affordability and sustainability than simple unit costs.

Conclusions Related to TLM System Costs

TLM system costs are determined by the following factors:

a) Curriculum specifications comprising the following:
- Number of required textbooks and teachers' guides per grade level (see chapter 4, Literacy, Curricula, Teaching and Learning Materials Requirements, and System Costs); large numbers of required textbooks per grade level significantly increase the costs of TLM provision;
- Other specified required TLMs (for example, readers, teachers' aids, dictionaries, atlases, and so on)
- Subject content specifications, which determine textbook extent and therefore have an impact on production costs (more raw materials, increased printing and binding costs)

b) Supply targets and assumptions comprising the following:
   - TPRs
   - Other TLM supply targets
   - Book life assumptions
   - Annual loss and damage (wastage) rates
c) LoI policies, which determine the number of different textbook language variants
d) Unit costs of TLMs, which are determined by the factors affecting TLM unit costs (see (j) above)
e) The requirement to provide consumable workbooks, which need annual replacement where the costs cannot be amortized and where annual distribution costs are incurred
f) Financial policies relating to free TLM provision and parental contributions
g) Effective control of input prices through the use of price as one of the key factors in textbook evaluation and contracting
h) Nature of local distribution
i) Stock losses in distribution and storage
j) Stock losses in schools via lack of conservation, poor stock management, theft and damage, and so on.
k) Enrollment growth rates

TLM system costs are generally a more significant indicator of system affordability and sustainability than simple unit textbook costs.

Conclusions Related to Textbook and TLM Availability in Schools

The main factors affecting levels of textbook and other TLM availability in classrooms are the following:

a) The adequacy, reliability, and predictability of TLM system financing.
b) The availability of good information on TLM needs in schools as the basis for calculating stock requirements and thus financing levels; a majority of SSA countries have no clear idea of the level of TLMs in schools at any moment in time and thus TLMs are often supplied on the basis of available funding, which may not be sufficient, rather than need. Many of the Education Management Information Systems (EMIS) operational in many developing or transitional countries (not just in SSA) do not provide accurate or timely information and many do not provide the basic data required for TLM policy making and are often not fit for purpose for TLM planning.[5]
c) The availability of good TLM management systems, which can control TLM supply, provide reliable information, and project forward financing requirements accurately; TLM supply is ideally suited to computerized database management systems but few, if any, SSA countries have invested in this kind of management technology. Rwanda and more recently Namibia are notable exceptions.

d) Effective national TLM distribution systems to ensure that TLMs actually reach the schools in the required quantities, undamaged, and on time; in general, commercial distribution paid on the basis of proven delivery performance is usually more successful than ministry systems that are frequently unsupported by budgets, trained and motivated staff, transport, storage facilities, effective systems, good monitoring and supervision, Education Management Information Systems and so on.
e) Good standards of TLM management, conservation, and usage in schools. TLMs in schools often suffer from poor storage, care, and management leading to high levels of loss and damage. Annual stock losses of 50 percent or more have been reported in schools in some countries.
f) Poor usage skills mean that the TLMs provided are often not used properly or sometimes are not used at all.
g) The main requirements to achieve good usage and conservation in schools are:
   - Good school and classroom storage;
   - Simple but effective TLM management, record keeping and conservation systems in schools;
   - Training in TLM usage;
   - Training in TLM management; and
   - Regular and informed inspection and supervision.

Conclusions Related to Textbook Cost Reduction Possibilities

There are a number of standard textbook cost-reduction strategies that can be considered in order to make textbook (and other TLM) costs more affordable and thus sustainable to either government or parents. They are the following:

a) Require fewer curriculum subjects and thus fewer textbooks (this requires a curriculum review but generally provides the greatest system cost saving).
b) Reduce page extents (review syllabus content requirements; many syllabuses are overloaded in comparison with typical student-teacher contact hours and as a result textbooks can provide too much content that often cannot be completed in the time available).
c) Turn textbooks into books of core content by shifting material into teachers' guides (supplied at one book per class rather than one book per one, two, or three students) or into library books (supplied in small multiples to school libraries rather than in class sets). This strategy will depend for its effectiveness on consistent library funding but it is clear from the research evidence (see chapter 1, Recent Research) that school or classroom libraries and core content textbooks are potentially much cheaper and more effective in terms of learning outputs than no school libraries and overlong textbooks (see table O.3 for a hypothetical example).
d) Extend book life to achieve maximum cost amortization (review minimum physical production specifications to ensure that they meet minimum durability standards).

Table O.3 Implications of Moving Text from Textbooks to Teachers' Guides and Readers

Compare the paper usage (and thus the cost) of 15 Grade 7 textbooks each with an average page extent of 400 pages printed in editions of 100,000 copies each. The total page extent required is **600 million pages**. A hypothetical alternative approach could be as follows:

- 15 Grade 7 textbooks each of 300 pages in print runs of 100,000 copies for the "average student" = 450 million pages
- 15 extension books (one to support each textbook) for the 15 percent of elite students each containing 100 pages but printed in editions of 15,000 copies (one per elite student) = 22.5 million pages
- 60 library books each of 48 pages printed in editions of 20,000 copies (one book per five students) and based on specified curriculum topics, which provide opportunities for further individual reading and research by the students = 57.6 million pages

The total page requirement of the alternative approach is only **530.1 million pages** compared to the existing comprehensive textbooks (a saving of approximately 12.5 percent in paper and printing) but a far wider range of learning resources have been provided that caters for the average student in the basic textbook, the elite student in the extension materials, and all students in the provision of a new generation of library books which can be used to encourage active research, information management skills, and enhanced learning for all students.

Source: Author's calculations.

e) Introduce book sharing and thus reduced TPR (for example, 3:1 rather than 1:1);
f) Reduce use of four colors.
g) Reduce wastage in manufacturing.
h) Reduce wastage in warehousing and distribution (this can be very substantial; annual loss rates of up to 50 percent or more have been recorded in some countries).
i) Reduce wastage in school storage and school usage (this can be very substantial; annual loss rates of up to 50 percent have been recorded in some countries and 20 percent annual loss and damage is not unusual).
j) Use textbook loan or rental schemes and revolving fund systems to support lower cost and affordable parental contributions.
k) Reduce page formats (large formats use more paper and are frequently less durable).
l) Offer short-term rather than long-term student textbook loans in order to reduce annual rates of loss and damage (short-term loans provide more control than long term loans but require more teacher management time).
m) Offer tax exemptions for book manufacturing raw materials (finished books are usually imported duty free under the terms of the Florence Agreement on the Free Flow of Books and Information, but printing equipment and paper often attract duty, thus making local printers more expensive than external printers).
n) Maintain greater control over input costs from publishers and printers (review evaluation and approval mechanisms and conditions to ensure that price is

a significant factor in evaluation and approval and that pricing is closely monitored in parent purchase situations).
o) Increase use of teachers' guides only in some subjects as opposed to the use of textbooks.

Very few countries have explored the full range (or even a limited range) of the cost reduction possibilities available to them.

Conclusions Related to the Main Causes of High System Cost and Low Availability

This study concludes that there are multiple causes of poor TLM system performance in SSA. However, the most common causes of poor performance are considered to be the following:

a) Lack of good, accurate, up-to-date, reliable, and accessible information on schools, grade level enrollments, TLM availability in schools and classrooms, current prices, wastage levels, book life, and so on. In many countries the basic information needed to plan and manage an effective TLM system either doesn't exist or isn't readily available when required.
b) Poor TLM system management—usually lacking trained manpower resources, simple but effective management systems, adequate hardware, good communication facilities, and an adequate annual operational budget. TLM system management is ideally suited to the design and operation of database management information systems but very few SSA countries have considered this as a realistic or priority investment.
c) Unaffordable TLM system costs—often based on unrealistic curriculum design and TLM specifications and supply policy assumptions; few SSA countries have developed—and costed—a minimum profile of the TLMs needed to deliver curriculum objectives as the basis for forward cost projections.
d) A continued dependence, particularly at upper secondary grades, on imported textbooks carrying developed world overheads and profit expectations.
e) The failure to make use of basic cost-reduction strategies (see above) to achieve affordable annual amortized unit costs.
f) Inadequate, irregular, and unpredictable financing of TLM needs—often resulting from the lack of any clear idea of the realistic costs of meeting TLM policy targets.
g) Lack of control over TLM input prices, often resulting from the failure to include price as a key factor in the evaluation of publisher submissions for approved book status.
h) Dysfunctional TLM distribution systems resulting in unacceptably high levels of loss and damage to textbook and other TLM stocks.
i) Dysfunctional school storage and school TLM management systems resulting in unacceptably high levels of loss and damage to textbook and other TLM stocks.

j) Inadequate training and supervision of schools in TLM management, conservation, and usage.
k) The reluctance of many teachers to actually use class sets of the materials provided.

Conclusions Related to School TLM Management and Usage

School level management and use of TLMs is seriously sub-standard in many SSA countries and is responsible for potentially large percentages of TLM loss and damage, which in turn reduces the effectiveness of TLMs in schools and increases the costs of effective provision.

In order to reduce the TLM loss levels in schools and to ensure the proper use of the TLMs provided, the following actions are suggested:

- Upgrade storage facilities in schools to meet minimum criteria of security, weatherproofing and cleanliness (that is freedom from infestation by vermin, insects,[6] and fungus).
- Provide secure and weatherproof classroom-based storage in primary schools and in particular in lower primary classrooms.
- Design simple TLM management systems for schools using Stock Registers and Stock Issue registers, which should be provided free of charge to schools every year in the same way that student attendance registers are provided free in many school systems.
- Produce and publicize loss and damage policy guidelines to all schools.
- Produce a TLM Management Handbook to all schools, teachers in training, district education officers (DEOs), and the inspectorate.
- Produce a simple guide to the effective classroom use of all TLMs.
- Provide in-service and pre-service training and ongoing regular support to teachers and inspectors in the use of TLMs in the classroom and school TLM management systems.
- Ensure that a review of TLM management systems should be a requirement of all inspection visits to schools.
- Where decentralized financing mechanisms for TLMs are in use, ensure regular auditing of school accounts.
- Undertake regular surveys (every three to four years?) of TLM availability in schools to ensure that provision targets are being met and maintained and take corrective action on the results of the surveys as required.
- Provide better and more precise textbook and TLM specifications when publishers are invited to submit for evaluation and approval; these should include clear and unambiguous definitions of standards, concepts, skills, and competencies that are required to be achieved and guidance on how these should be measured and assessed.
- Ensure more rigorous textbook evaluation mechanisms before textbooks are approved for use in schools.

- Reconsider the issue of the additional help required by second language (L2) students in subject content and skills learning.
- Provide clear guidance to publishers on how to handle variations in national contact hours.

Conclusions Related to TLM Reform Policy Options

Full details of the various TLM policy options are provided in the body of the text. The most significant policy options to consider are the following:

a) Invest in national computerized TLM management systems to provide good information, system control, and accurate forward cost projections.
b) Work to develop local system management capacity through the creation of a professional TLM system Management Unit.
c) Shift from state to private-sector authorship, publishing, production, and distribution operating in a public private partnership with government.
d) Shift from monopoly single-source textbooks to competing alternative textbooks based on the establishment of approved lists of competing books selected by rigorous evaluation systems in which price is a key criterion for approval.
e) Apply effective but fair input price control as a condition for award of approved status in order to achieve stable forward pricing.
f) Decentralize from supply-side policies to demand-based school selection and ordering against annual per capita TLM budgets. All available evidence suggests that schools can select and order efficiently if provided with the opportunity and basic training. School-based selection provides school ownership of the materials selected and individual schools know their own TLM needs better than any MOE department.
g) Apply appropriate cost-reduction strategies to make the TLM system affordable and sustainable. Computerized database management systems can support the application of affordable supply options and thus the calculation of the TCO.
h) Invest in an effective commercial performance-based distribution system.
i) Invest in school and classroom storage and simple school management and usage systems and provide regular training and supervision.
j) Opt for high production specifications and long book life to achieve maximum cost amortization and minimum distribution costs.
k) Seek high quality, competitively priced raw materials and manufacturing.

Annex 13A provides a Diagnostic Checklist as a tool for establishing TLM policy parameters.

Notes

1. Angola, Benin, Botswana, Burkina Faso, Burundi, Cameroon, Chad, Côte d'Ivoire, Djibouti, the Democratic Republic of the Congo, Eritrea, Ethiopia, The Gambia, Ghana, Guinea, Kenya, Lesotho, Liberia, Madagascar, Malawi, Mali, Mozambique,

Namibia, Niger, Nigeria, Republic of the Congo, Rwanda, Senegal, Sierra Leone, South Africa, South Sudan, Sudan, Tanzania, Togo, Uganda, Zambia, Zanzibar, Zimbabwe. The experiences of many other developing and transitional economy countries outside Sub-Saharan Africa (SSA) that have been involved in textbook and TLM reform programs—in North Africa and the Middle East, Central Asia, and the countries of the Former Soviet Union, East and South Asia, Oceania and Latin America—have also been taken into account wherever relevant.

2. Some of the components of the TLM Chain are included in textbook prices and some are not. Thus some links are MOE policy decisions that have an impact on pricing and system costs but are not included in publishers' costs and prices. Some links are MOE operational costs to ensure that TLMs are well looked after and well used. See tables 8.1 and 8.2, for a more detailed presentation of the textbook price components commonly used by textbook publishers.

3. The normal trade distribution discount in most SSA countries is 25 percent; higher discounts can be awarded to large customers or wholesalers. Where direct distribution to schools by publishers is required, the distribution cost is often between 10 and 15 percent; where supply to districts only is required, the distribution charge may be six to seven percent; and where supply only to a central MOE warehouse in the capital city is specified the charges are often only five percent or less—even when supplied from international printing sources.

4. Kenyan and Ugandan publishers have claimed in the past that cover card specifications in Rwanda cannot be sourced from regional merchants or printers.

5. As an example, in South Sudan current curriculum policy is to provide education for lower primary classes in 51 local languages. But the EMIS data on which print runs will have to be based has no information on either the grade level numbers of local language students or their location in the states and counties of the country. The lack of good EMIS data will inevitably make print runs and delivery schedules largely a matter of guesswork and thus increase the likelihood of waste.

6. Antitermite paint is widely available and cheap and provides good protection for a reasonable period against termites if applied for 30 centimeters above ground level to walls and the legs of bookcases and cupboards used for TLM storage.

References

Da Cruz, A. J., T. A. George, F. Z. Gnahare, F. Z. Kouakou, P. Mendonca, C. Schlabi, M. Simao, and A. Read. 1998. *Financing Textbooks and Teacher Training Materials*. Perspectives in African Book Development Series. Paris: Working Party on Books and Learning Materials, Association for the Development of Education in Africa.

MOEC (Tanzanian Ministry of Education and Culture). 1994. *School Textbook Provision in Tanzania: Roundtable Conference on Textbooks*. Dar es Salaam, Tanzania: MOEC.

Read, T. 2003. *Language, Development and Education in Uzbekistan*. Tashkent: British Council.

———. 2010. "Guidance Notes on Learning and Teaching Materials." DFID Education Advisors CEC for DFID.

PART 1

The Current Situation

CHAPTER 1

Textbooks, Teaching and Learning Materials, and Learning Achievement

The Impact of Textbooks on the Quality of Education

Since the 1960s there has been considerable research by academics and development partners (DPs) into the factors affecting school effectiveness and improved student achievement in both developed and developing countries. In 1978 Heyneman and Farrell reviewed and summarized a number of earlier research studies from different countries and drew the following broad conclusion:

> From the evidence that we have so far, the availability of textbooks appears to be the single most consistently positive factor in predicting educational achievement. In 15 out of the 18 studies (83%) it is positive. This is, for example, more favourable than 13 out of 24 (54%) recently reported for teacher training.

More work on student achievement by Habte et al. in 1983 confirmed the earlier conclusions:

> Since the 1960s social scientists have been trying to isolate the characteristics most closely associated with achievement in basic learning skills; though technical caveats abound they have come to one conclusion; in wealthy countries much of the learning in schools is accounted for by factors not connected with the school environment, implying that additional physical facilities, teaching equipment and textbooks only help the acquisition of new knowledge a little. But the quality of the physical environment and particularly the classroom tools in low income countries is shown to explain three and even four times the difference in achievement than it can in high income countries. In fact the poorer the country in economic terms, the larger the impact on achievement school quality seems to have. One conclusion is consistent: higher achievement is always associated with the availability of textbooks and other printed materials.

In 1984 Heyneman and Jamieson in a randomized evaluation of textbook provision in the Philippines found large gains in learning associated with textbook availability in classrooms.

Fuller in 1985 also surveyed the available research into factors affecting student achievement. He divided the factors into those that consistently related to educational achievement and those that did not. Among the most important of the factors that were most consistently associated with measurable improvements in student learning was the adequate availability in the classroom of textbooks for student use.

Verspoor (1986) confirmed Fuller's findings a year later.

> Without quality improvement many of the benefits associated with the tremendous growth of enrollments in developing countries may never come about. Research evidence and (World) Bank experience indicate the considerable potential contribution that textbooks and other instructional materials can make to effective teaching and the improvement of the quality of education.

In 1990 Verspoor and Wu in another World Bank study again re-confirmed the importance of textbooks for student achievement gains.

> Textbooks are the educational input most consistently associated with gains in student learning.

Research into the factors affecting student achievement continued throughout the 1990s without challenging the central role of textbook provision as a key determinant of educational quality and improved student achievement. Another World Bank report published in 2001 commented specifically that

> Teaching and learning materials are critical ingredients in learning and the intended curriculum cannot be easily implemented without them. Over the past forty years the importance of adequate teaching and learning materials provision (including textbooks, teachers' guides and supplementary materials) to support educational development and quality upgrading has been recognized by governments throughout the developing world and by most development partners. There is now substantial research evidence which shows that textbooks are one of the most important inputs that have a demonstrable impact on student learning.

Up to this point much of the research into student achievements had either been commissioned by, or reviewed and summarized by, the World Bank. However, other donors now conducted their own studies and came to similar conclusions, for example that

> the impact of textbooks is greatest in the poorest countries where teacher quality may be low and where facilities and resources are scarce and generally of poor quality. (DFID 2003)

Issues in Donor-Funded Textbook Projects

The growing body of research evidence confirming the critical role of textbooks in upgrading student achievement in poor countries quickly percolated down into practical World Bank strategies, and between 1980 and 1990 the number of World Bank education projects with textbook components increased from five percent to 55 percent. Despite this increase in activity and investment in textbooks the practical implementation of effective textbook provision remained problematic. In 1990 the World Bank commissioned a General Operational Review of Textbooks, which identified many critical problems in previously uncharted territory (Searle 1990). One of the most fundamental conclusions reached by the Review was that textbook development and delivery systems for sustainable teaching and learning materials are never purely educational systems. The complexity of the textbook-related systems was summed up in the 1991 African Book Sector Study as follows:

> Books require large quantities of industrial raw materials, which are subject to national industrial policy and often to import tariffs and quotas. Book manufacturing requires heavy industrial plant, spare parts, regular maintenance, reliable power sources and skilled labour and there are wide variations from country to country in the quality, capacity, reliability and cost of book manufacturing. Distribution and warehousing of books are vital support services and if they are not performed well and consistently the total investment in textbook provision can be negated. The quality of textbook content and its effectiveness in the classroom depends upon perceptive curriculum and syllabus development, good and experienced authorship, illustrations, design and publishing skills and the availability of trained and committed teachers—all of which can vary considerably from country to country. Textbooks, once delivered to schools must be well-managed, stored and conserved. In schools textbooks may not be well-used, or may not be used at all. Key policy decisions have to be made on complex issues such as subsidies, cost recovery, free supply, book loan or book purchase, the nature and degree of state involvement and control, the relationship between state and private sector interests, the languages of instruction and textbook provision (they are not necessarily the same) and local, regional and multi-national involvement in writing, publishing and manufacturing. (Buchan, Denning, and Read 1991)

The World Bank's 1990 Operational Review of Textbook Projects recognized also the complexities and difficulties of achieving adequate, high-quality, and comprehensive textbook and other teaching and learning materials (TLMs) provision systems on a national scale on a sustainable basis (Searle 1990). As a result, by the end of the 1980s many donor-funded textbook projects started to shift away from single factor projects (a curriculum project or print upgrading or publishing development or distribution project, and so on) into more comprehensive projects covering a variety of critical inputs. Searle (1990) commented on this trend as follows:

> But there is a danger in the more comprehensive approach as well. It may even be the case that the more comprehensively the project attempts to address the provision problems, the more likely the difficulties because more comprehensive solutions require greater coordination and more high level involvement in approvals. Thus, a serious attempt to establish a well-functioning book provision system, particularly when it involves book publishing should be seen as a long term effort, probably lasting as long as a decade or more.

The 1991 Ministers of Education Conference held in Manchester focused on textbook provision issues as the main conference theme. The Conference Proceedings summed up the role of textbooks in Africa as follows:

Textbooks in Africa fulfil three important purposes simultaneously:

a) They provide the main vehicle for the curriculum;
b) They are the main, if not the only source of information for the teacher and students;
c) Examinations and student assessments are derived heavily from them.

In this situation the textbook is effectively the curriculum. (British Council 1992)

The Cost Effectiveness of Textbook Provision

In 1990, the issue of *effective* interventions to upgrade student achievement was raised by Lockheed and Verspoor:

> There are some interventions that are quite effective, but their costs are too high to make them cost effective. Two examples of this type are small class sizes and computer-aided instruction. For both, the level of expenditure required to demonstrate an effect is too great to be practicable in developing countries.... Interventions for which there is clear evidence of both cost-effectiveness and feasibility of implementation are most desirable, since they are those that give the most learning for the resources spent.... Research and practice suggest that there are five principal areas in which policy intervention to improve student learning should be considered:
>
> a) Improving the curriculum
> b) Increasing the supply of learning materials
> c) Increasing instructional time
> d) Improving teaching
> e) Increasing the learning capacity of students. (Lockheed and Verspoor 1990)

This report emphasized the *cost effectiveness* of textbook provision as a means of increasing student performance because it combined maximum beneficial impact on student achievement with relatively low and affordable cost. In this context it is interesting that the high cost implications of the use of information and communication technology (ICT) in education, which was specifically identified in this paper as not cost effective and thus unaffordable for developing countries, have not inhibited increasingly significant investments in ICT in schools in Sub-Saharan Africa (SSA) in the past decade (see Part 3).

In 1999 Pritchett and Filmer emphasized the cost effectiveness of investments in learning materials.

> Although teachers are often underpaid there are sometimes too many of them. A common pattern is that much more is spent on teachers' salaries (a convenient vehicle for political patronage) than on textbooks, paper and pencils. …(S)pending on school materials has a rate of return ten to one hundred times larger than additional spending on teachers, which means that school materials are very scarce relative to teachers. (Pritchett and Filmer 1999)

Impact Evaluations of Textbook Provision in Kenya

In 2006 the Department of International Development (DFID) funded an impact evaluation for the Kenyan Ministry of Education on the Primary School Instructional Materials Project (PSIMP), which had provided free textbooks to all primary school students between 2003 and 2005.

> In this study we have concluded that the Instructional Materials and INSETT programmes have had a huge positive impact on teaching and learning in all primary schools in Kenya…. We have found dramatic changes in the practice of assigning homework to children in both upper and lower primary. We attribute this expanded, child-centred learning directly to the increased availability of textbooks in primary schools…. In 1999 only 3% of classroom time involved reading compared with 46% in 2006. In live observations undertaken in 159 classes, 84% of teachers made use of textbooks in their lessons, while group-based reading activities were observed in 46% of lessons…. When asked about how textbooks had improved learning for the poorest children teachers reported their increased motivation, performance and opportunity to learn, as well as an increase in retention and completion rates. Free textbooks were seen as equalizing learning opportunities for the poorest pupils by making schooling more affordable and accessible…. Parents were asked to explain how the provision of Instructional Materials had improved the teaching and learning in their school. Regarding teaching, parents cited better planning, improved commitment from teachers, and wider syllabus coverage. With respect to learning, parents said that:
>
> - Pupils are able to do assignments easily and in good time;
> - Pupils are able to read more on their own;
> - Pupils are able to explore new knowledge on their own;
> - Pupils are able to read ahead of the teacher; and,
> - Pupils are able to engage in discussions on their own. (DFID 2006)

However, in 2007, the National Bureau of Economic Research (NBER) in the United States published a research paper with a dissident view of the impact of textbooks on student achievement in Kenya resulting from the Instructional Materials Project.

> A randomized evaluation suggests that a program which provided official textbooks to randomly selected rural Kenyan primary schools did not increase test scores for the average student. In contrast, the previous literature suggests that textbook provision has a large impact on test scores. Disaggregating the results by students' initial academic achievement suggests a potential explanation for the lack of an overall impact. Textbooks increased scores for students with high initial academic achievement and increased the probability that the students who had made it to the selective final year of primary school would go on to secondary school. However, students with weaker academic backgrounds did not benefit from the textbooks. Many pupils could not read the textbooks, which are written in English, most students' third language. (Glewwe, Kremer, and Moulin 2007)

The NBER conclusions are not necessarily surprising in the sense that textbooks will probably inevitably be better used in good schools by good students than in poor schools by underperforming students. It is interesting that recent research on the use of ICT in schools has tended to reach the same conclusions—that ICT is likely to be more effectively used in good schools by good students than in poor schools by poor students. Additionally, adding the language of instruction and basic literacy as qualifying factors related to the impact of textbooks emphasizes the complexity of the textbook provision process referred to above and underlines the fact that textbooks to be fully effective need to be part of a well-designed student and teacher support system, which must incorporate as well an appropriate language of instruction policy and effective usage of materials in schools.

Textbook Effectiveness and Classroom Usage

Virtually all research into textbook impact on student achievement has been based only on the physical availability of the textbooks in the classroom. There is an implicit assumption in the research that the textbooks are actively used in class and that students have sufficient literacy in the language of the textbooks to be able to read and understand them. An EdQual research review in 2007 emphasized that process in textbook usage was as important as inputs.

> The abundance or lack of school resources may play a less important role than the efficiency in the use of such resources. (Guoxing 2007)

The nonuse situation implied above has been noted in many other textbook project reports in SSA countries over many years. For example, see Little (1995) and Vere (1993). It has also been reported in a 2012 report on textbook provision in Sierra Leone (Sabarwal et al. 2012) and in Cameroon (Buchan 2013) and in South Sudan (Jones and Sayer 2013; Read 2014). Uncertainty over future textbook supplies leading to hoarding is reported to be the main reason for the nonissue of textbooks to students in Sierra Leone.

Research has also revealed that the delivery of textbooks to schools does not necessarily imply that textbooks are used in the classroom. The 2006 Department for International Development (DFID) study on the impact of the PSIMP on student achievement in Kenya highlighted the increase in the use of textbooks in class as one of the main factors in upgrading student achievement. Kalibbala, writing on the implementation of the USAID-funded Support for Primary Education Reform (SUPER) in Uganda in 1999, commented,

> Current textbook utilisation levels in schools are very low. It was erroneously assumed by the past textbook provision programmes that textbook provision was synonymous with utilisation and that once books were delivered to schools they would be read by students. However, many new books remain unused in school cupboards and stores. Many reasons are given for the non-use of the books. This is perhaps the most contentious of all book related issues. (Kalibbala 1999)

Self-evidently, textbooks cannot be effective if a significant proportion of students do not have access to them or if they have not achieved basic literacy in the language of the textbooks, which, unfortunately, is a common problem in many SSA countries. For example, the 2005 Education for All (EFA) Global Monitoring Report expressed concern about student performance as follows:

> The Report monitors progress towards the 6 EFA goals set by over 160 countries at the World Education Forum in Dakar (2000). It finds that significant efforts are being made to increase resources, broaden access to schools and improve gender parity. However, exhaustive analysis of research data shows that the quality of education systems is failing children in many parts of the world and could prevent many countries from achieving EFA by the target date of 2015. More children are going to school than ever before, but many drop out before grade 5 of primary school or graduate from primary school without even achieving a minimum set of cognitive skills. (UNESCO 2005)

The indirect learning benefits of textbook provision were identified by Hoxby in 2000:

> The availability of textbooks among classmates may affect one's own learning through a variety of channels. The conventional peer effects argument asserts that students with books learn faster and that these more knowledgeable peers are then beneficial for one's own learning because of enhanced motivation or competition or sharing of knowledge. This peer effect should increase with the share of classmates having books, and this increase could be more or less than proportional depending on whether homogeneous or heterogeneous classes provide a more efficient learning environment.

In 2005 Frolich and Michaelowa confirmed the importance of the indirect benefits of textbook provision and also suggested that the impact of textbooks on student achievement would be under estimated if the indirect benefits were ignored. This finding seems to contradict the Kremer, Glewwe, and Moulin conclusion that the benefits of textbook provision are overestimated (see above). Among the most important of the indirect benefits was the teacher's ability to use textbook sets in class as an active teaching and learning tool, which only became possible when textbook–pupil ratios (TPRs) reached a minimum level (probably 1:3). The use of class sets of textbooks changes classroom methodologies and the classroom dynamic between teacher and pupil. It is also widely perceived to be the most effective use of classroom contact hours between teacher and student, which is an important issue when there is so much evidence of lost contact hours (see "Underfinancing" section in chapter 5).

> The flexibility involved … allowed us to explore … the related issue of different channels through which textbook possession may affect other classmates' learning, e.g., book sharing, knowledge sharing and changes in teachers' instructional methods… if externalities are neglected in the empirical analysis (and all other sources of… bias are eliminated), the overall benefits of textbooks will generally be underestimated…. Primarily, it turns out that textbooks do have a positive and very large externality on other students in the class. With respect to French proficiency, the externality is as much as 9 times larger than the direct effect of textbooks and this result is remarkably robust across different specifications. For mathematics, results are less robust, but equally point to the prevalence of strong externalities. Any individual student still has a higher benefit from his own book because the overall peer effect has to be shared by an average of 47 other students in the class. Nevertheless, such a large externality cannot be explained by book sharing alone, and other transmission channels such as knowledge sharing of students possessing a book or change in teaching methods have to be at work. (Frolich and Michaelowa 2005)

Factors Affecting School Effectiveness and Student Achievement

A review of research studies on student achievement and school effectiveness in 1994 found positive associations with student achievement for textbook availability in 26 out of 39 studies (67 percent), for school libraries in 19 out of 22 studies (86 percent), for instructional time on task in 27 out of 33 studies (82 percent), and for homework frequency in 11 out of 13 studies (85 percent). The impact of other popular factors on student achievement had fewer positive associations as follows; class size (11 out of 48 studies or 23 percent), child nutrition and feeding (Six out of 13 studies or 46 percent), teacher qualifications (29 out of 51 studies or 57 percent), in-service teacher training (11 out of 17 studies or 65 percent), teacher experience (14 out of 35 studies or 40 percent), and teachers' salaries (six out of 22 studies or 27 percent). The high-level impact of school libraries on student achievement identified by the Fuller and Clarke review (1994) echoed the findings of the Heyneman and Farrell research review in 1978, which also identified the consistent association of school libraries with student achievement. Under the circumstances it is surprising that DPs and SSA ministries of education

(MOEs) have given so little priority to the provision and development of school and classroom libraries over the past 50 years.

In 2006 a study by the Association for the Development of Education in Africa (ADEA) found that

> the critical characteristics found most consistently in schools with good Primary Leaving Examination (PLE) results centre around the interactions within the school and the classroom. The role and performance of the Head Teacher in teachers' preparation and coverage of the syllabus and on pupil participation in the classroom was highly significant. Teachers' preparedness for class, regular assessment of pupils' work and emphasis on the use of instructional materials, and particularly textbooks, and on pupils' reading and writing are critical to stimulating pupil participation. (ADEA 2006)

Textbook Content Research

To date, relatively little research has been directed towards the qualitative impact of good as opposed to bad textbooks or to the use of color in textbooks, which has significant cost implications. Verspoor and Wu (1990) recognised that these were neglected areas and Lockheed and Verspoor addressed some of the issues of curriculum and textbook content.

> Children who enter schooling in developing countries often spend more than one year in first grade and progress slowly through the early grades. Why is this the case? One explanation is that the level of instruction in early grades in developing countries may be too difficult. (Lockheed and Verspoor 1990)

A 1989 textbook content analysis on a range of textbooks published for African primary grades confirmed the impression that, at that time, many textbooks published for developing countries were too demanding for their target audiences and that this was a particular problem in the early grades of primary school.

> In general, the maths books required pupils to undertake work, which was above expectations for the grade. Books written at curriculum centres were no better than other books.... The analysis of the reading/language arts books revealed unrealistically high expectations of the level of work pupils were able to tackle, particularly in view of the paucity of pre-reading activities and of the later stage of "immersion in books," typical of poor countries.... The books written at curriculum centres were, again, no more suitable for pupils than other books. (Cope, Denning, and Ribeiro 1989)

More recent research on a comparative analysis of national curricula and textbooks by Benavot (2010) notes that textbooks tend to be more specific than national curriculum guidelines in specifying topics, activities, and performance targets and that this discrepancy is more pronounced for reading and literacy than math at primary school levels.

The advent of competency-based curricula in many SSA countries has caused problems for many authors and publishers who often do not have practical experience of competency-based teaching and learning in an SSA context. Many teachers find the teaching, management, and organizational implications of competency-based curricula alarming and difficult to deliver in practice; and the problem is intensified by textbooks, which more often than not do not provide teachers with the level of support required to deliver competencies in the classroom. Textbooks also have to cope with widely differing contact hours in which to deliver the curriculum and widely differing equipment provision and school facilities as well.

Recent Research

In recent years the research results on the importance of textbooks as a factor in student learning have shifted from a generally widespread acceptance that textbooks are critical to student achievement, to a more skeptical approach that suggests that textbooks in their current form (however this can be defined as a generality) do not improve learning for many students. New research methodologies (for example the use of randomized controlled trials—RCTs) claim to have improved the ability to test and understand the relationship between textbooks and learning outcomes. RCTs do, however, have limitations because many RCT studies, which focus on test scores alone may ignore other benefits related to textbooks. Three studies—Evans and Ghosh (2008), McEwan (2013), and Glewwe et al. (2011)—found evidence that the availability of textbooks improves learning across a broad range of countries. Evans and Ghosh explored the cost effectiveness of various inputs comparing data from 40 experimental and quasi-experimental studies across a broad range of contexts. The study found that textbooks were one of several low-cost and effective interventions which improved learning, but the authors also noted weaknesses in the research that undermined this finding to some extent.

McEwan's meta-analysis of 76 RCTs on 110 inputs similarly found evidence that there is a positive relationship between "instructional materials"[1] (including textbooks) and test scores. However, the author also reported that findings were not robust to checks from study moderators, perhaps suggesting that other variables might explain the observed relationship between instructional materials and outcomes. Glewwe et al. suggested that textbooks and similar materials improved student learning. However, when less rigorous studies were excluded from the analysis, the evidence that textbooks improved learning was considered to be quite weak. This was corroborated by Glewwe et al.'s (2011) summary of the results from 13 RCTs, which found that textbooks had no statistically significant impact on learning.

Two studies have disputed any positive relationship for most students. Glewwe, Kremer, and Moulin (2007) and Kuecken and Valport (2013) considered evidence across 12 countries in SSA. Both studies found that textbooks *in their current form* do not improve learning for the majority but only impact those who already have high levels of learning. Furthermore, Kuecken and Valport found that only one form of textbook access—sharing, not ownership—had a positive impact on test scores for students in the highest percentile of achievement.

Four other studies found that textbooks improved learning. Khaniya and Williams (2004) evaluated the impact of a multiyear reform project on Nepal's primary education system. While the whole reform project was not found to improve learning, when isolating the variables, the study found that the availability of curriculum and textbooks for teachers was systematically related to student achievement. Second, Tayyaba (2010) explored the impact of multiple inputs on test scores in math in 770 schools across Pakistan. It was found that the availability of learning resources, including but not limited to textbooks, increased test scores significantly. Similarly, Fehler, Michelowa, and Wechtler (2009) found positive correlations between achievement in test scores and textbooks in studies across SSA. Finally, Shollar (2001) found positive learning gains from a "whole school approach" intervention in South Africa that included textbooks, teacher training, and regular monitoring.

Other research suggests that textbooks are more likely to be linked to improvements in student learning if they are linked to changes in pedagogy in the classroom, but this is surely dependent on other factors that are almost certainly more significant than textbooks in affecting the transformation of classroom pedagogy. There is also concern that textbooks are more likely to have a beneficial impact if they are easily understood by the pupils and that this militates for more textbook publishing in mother tongue language and a greater concern for the language levels used in textbooks.

In the final analysis, experience and research suggest that textbooks will have a significant and relatively low-cost impact on student learning if certain conditions exist. These can be summarized as follows:

- Textbooks should be based on a curriculum, which can be delivered successfully to all schools and students. This requires that curricula should not be overloaded with too many subjects and too much content that teachers have to "rush" to complete in the school year, which leaves many children behind; that they should take full account of the wide differentials in contact hours, facilities, and teacher quality between urban and rural schools in many countries, and that they should not specify curriculum outcomes that cannot be adequately tested and that are often beyond the knowledge and skill sets of the majority of the teachers.
- Textbooks should be in a language that pupils and teachers can easily comprehend—but the issue of mother tongue is much more complex than is widely understood and the choice of the textbook language(s) must be handled with considerable care.
- Language levels used in the textbooks must be suitable and comprehensible for the students and for the teachers. Insufficient guidance on language levels is provided to authors and publishers by MOEs and there is a widespread tendency to write at too high a level. Authors are predominantly sourced

from curriculum developers and teachers working in good (often private) schools and too often assume that the language levels of their own schools are typical nationally, when experience suggests that this is very rarely so.
- Textbooks should be efficiently distributed so that they arrive on time in all schools. It is often not appreciated how inefficient, wasteful, and slow textbook distribution can be in many countries. Studies from SSA have recorded annual loss levels during distribution of between 25 and 65 percent of printed stock; many textbooks are stuck in unsuitable district warehouses and never get to schools at all; and there are often great differences in stocking levels and TPRs between different schools.
- Textbooks when delivered to schools must be issued to the students. Many countries in SSA have reported recently that many teachers do not issue textbooks to their students for a wide variety of reasons.
- When textbooks are issued for class use they are often used inexpertly by teachers so that the main benefits of textbook use are not developed. It is claimed that long years without textbook supplies have left many teachers with little or no practical experience in the correct and creative use of textbooks and associated teachers' guides. Pre-service teacher training only rarely has courses in the use of textbooks and other TLMs.
- School management and conservation must ensure that textbook supplies to schools can be maintained. Studies have shown that loss and damage rates for textbooks in schools can be up to and above 25 percent per year.

If all of the above conditions are met then textbook provision can be an important and cost-effective factor in improving student learning.

Reading Books

Despite the widely recognized links between student achievement, early literacy, the development of a lifelong reading habit, and the availability of good collections of reading books in both primary and secondary schools, relatively little research has been undertaken on the significance of reading book availability in primary schools and school libraries in secondary schools in poor countries, although much of the research referred to above claims that it is as relevant for other TLMs as it is for textbooks. Both Heyneman and Farrell (1978) and Fuller and Clarke (1994) reported that the availability of school libraries had a more consistently positive impact on student achievement than any other input, including textbooks. In Africa, a good part of the reasons for the lack of research has been the widespread failure in many countries over many years to invest in reading book provision and school and classroom libraries. The previously well-developed school libraries and national school library services typical of many anglophone SSA countries in the 1960s have now deteriorated or disappeared completely as a result of lack of funding and neglect. However, the importance of access to reading books has been underlined by a number of research studies, including the 2006 Progress in International Literacy Study (PIRLS) report, which noted that

> there was a positive relationship between students' reading achievement at the fourth grade and parents having engaged their children in early literacy activities before starting school (e.g., reading books, telling stories, singing songs, playing with alphabet toys, and playing word games). The presence of children's books in the home also continued to show a strong positive relationship with reading achievement. The average reading achievement difference between students from homes with many children's books (more than 100) and those from homes with few children's books (10 or fewer) was very large (91 score points, almost 1 standard deviation).... [F]or most students textbooks were the foundation of reading instruction, supplemented by other materials. (Mullis 2006)

Access to stimulating collections of attractive and relevant reading books—even though the collections may be small—is clearly an important determining factor in the achievement of early literacy, which is in turn a key determinant of student achievement in succeeding grades. In SSA very few homes have any children's reading books and relatively few parents have the skills, resources, or the time to engage actively with their children in preschool reading support at home. This is a particular issue in rural and remote areas. Lee, Zuze, and Ross (2005) found that, in all 14 South and East African Consortium for Monitoring Educational Quality (SACMEQ) countries studied,

> student socioeconomic status was strongly and positively associated with their literacy achievement.

In other words, the poorer the school the lower the level of literacy with the consequent knock-on effects on student achievement. Under these circumstances the availability of reading books—both fiction and nonfiction—in school or classroom libraries and the ability to borrow reading books for home use are clearly of critical importance and most particularly in rural and remote areas where these materials are unlikely to be available from any other source.

The positive relationship between reading book availability and literacy has been demonstrated by the results of the various Book Flood projects. The book floods were very simple in concept. They

- Targeted lower primary—"start young with reading";
- Provided many reading books to provide immersion in *meaningful* text;
- Encouraged children to read often—frequent silent reading sessions were specified;
- Used shared reading methodologies, which aimed to integrate oral and written language;
- Encouraged teachers to read stories to children on a regular basis; and
- Avoided language drills and tests.

The research results produced the following conclusions (Elley 1992):

- Book floods require less teacher training than other methods.
- They show consistent and dramatic impact on reading and other language skills.
- They generate enthusiasm and positive attitudes in teachers and children.
- They produce effects that transfer to other subjects.
- They assist teachers whose competence in the target language is often limited, by providing them with good language models.
- They are easy to justify to local governments.

The International Association for the Evaluation of Educational Achievement (IEA) produced a list of the inputs most often correlated in both developing and developed countries with differences in literacy levels (Elley 1992). The most important factors were

- A large school library;
- Frequent silent reading;
- More instructional time;
- Large classroom libraries;
- Frequent reading tests.

In terms of literacy, the availability of textbooks scored at the bottom of the list of positive factors. This doesn't invalidate previous research on the importance of textbook provision in student achievement; it simply means that textbooks are not the most important input for early literacy and that the provision of school or classroom libraries has a more marked impact on early literacy achievement. Once literacy has been achieved, textbooks are important in upgrading achievement in other subjects. The consistent provision of textbook sets to P1 students entering school for the first time, frequently from rural environments where there has been little or no print sensitization, is very frequently a waste of scarce resources compared to the provision of a good supply of appropriate reading books for young children.

The importance of the school library in the delivery of new student-centered and skills- and competency-based curricula has been summed up as follows:

> It has been demonstrated that, when librarians and teachers work together, students achieve higher levels of literacy, reading, learning, problem-solving and information and communication technology skills. (IFLA 2010)

The following quote sets out the case for the development of school library services in both developed and developing countries:

> The characteristics of 21st century education have been articulated by many and continue to evolve. However, in order to achieve within this developing context and beyond, it is accepted that students need:
>
> - Reading literacy
> - Information literacy

- Technological literacy
- Skills for personal knowledge building
- Oral literacy and numeracy

Research evidence from the USA, Canada and Australia shows that where school libraries are resourced effectively and managed by a qualified librarian with educational expertise, all of the above are fostered and student academic achievement on standardised tests is higher than in schools where these conditions do not exist. Studies over the last 50 years have supported this conclusion, but increasing numbers of investigations and improved methodology over the past decade have brought new credence and immediacy to this positive relationship. (Barrett 2010)

A Summary of Key Issues

The conclusions from a review of the research evidence provided above are as follows:

- The evidence for the impact of textbook provision on student achievement in repeated research studies over the past 40 years is overwhelmingly positive. Even the few dissident studies accept that textbooks have a positive impact for good students in good schools.
- For textbooks to be effective they must be not only available but also regularly used in class and they must be in a language that is widely understood by students and teachers.
- Textbooks are the most cost effective of all education inputs on student achievement because they provide significant impact at a relatively modest cost; relatively small investments in textbooks and other TLMs have a disproportionately large impact on achievement compared to marginal investments in, for example, teachers.
- Textbooks are less significant in lower primary grades where the early achievement of literacy should be the highest priority. In these grades the provision of well-conceived and designed teachers' manuals with well-selected, stimulating, and attractive reading materials has been demonstrated by research studies to be the most important input correlating with early literacy achievement.
- Book flood projects need to be reconsidered by DPs and MOEs as a fast-track methodology to improved literacy in lower primary grades.
- Investments in school and classroom libraries have an even greater correlation with increases in student achievement in lower primary grades than investments in textbook provision.

Note

1. As with other studies, this study measures the impact of "instructional materials" and does not isolate the effect of textbooks on learning outcomes.

References

ADEA (Association for the Development of Education in Africa). 2006. *Critical Characteristics of Primary Education*. Paris: ADEA.

Barrett, L. 2010. "Effective School Libraries: Evidence of Impact on Student Achievement." *Librarian* 65 (3).

Benavot, A. 2010. *Education for All Global Monitoring Report*. Paris: UNESCO.

British Council. 1992. *Proceedings of the Ministers of Education Conference on Textbook Provision and Library Development in Africa*. Manchester, United Kingdom: British Council.

Buchan, A., C. Denning, and A. Read. 1991. *African Book Sector Studies Summary Report*. Windsor, United Kingdom: International Book Development for World Bank African Ministers of Education Conference.

Buchan, A. 2013. "Preparation Report for Textbook Component of World Bank-Funded Cameroon Equity and Quality Improvement Project (CEQUIL)." Windsor, United Kingdom: International Education Partners for World Bank/CEQUIL.

Cope, J., C. Denning, and L. Ribeiro. 1989. *Content Analysis of Reading and Maths Textbooks in Fifteen Developing Countries*. London: Book Development Council for the World Bank.

DFID (Department for International Development). 2003. *The Multi-Site Teacher Education Research Project*. London: DFID.

———. 2006. *Delivering Quality and Improving Access in Primary Education: An Impact Evaluation of the IM and INSET Programmes*. MOES, Nairobi. London: DFID.

Elley, W. B. 1992. *How in the World do Students Read?* Hamburg, Germany: Institute for Educational Achievement.

Evans, D. K., and A. Ghosh. 2008. "Prioritizing Education Investments in Children in the Developing World." RAND Working Paper, RAND Corporation, Santa Monica, CA. http://www.rand.org/content/dam/rand/pubs/working_papers/2008/RAND_WR587.pdf.

Fehler, S., K. Michelowa, and A. Wechtler. 2009. "The Effectiveness of Inputs in Primary Education: Insights from Recent Study Surveys for SSA." *Journal of Development Studies* 45 (9): 1545–78. http://www.tandfonline.com/doi/abs/10.1080/00220380802663625#.Ut_uFNLFLn4.

Frolich, M., and K. Michaelowa. 2005. *Peer Effects and Textbooks in Primary Education: Evidence from Francophone Sub-Saharan Africa*. Bonn, Germany: Institute for the Study of Labor.

Fuller, B. 1985. *Raising School Quality in Developing Countries: What Investments Boost Learning?* A World Bank Study. Washington, DC: World Bank.

Fuller, B., and P. Clarke. 1994. "Raising School Effectiveness while Ignoring Culture—Local Conditions and the Influence of Classroom Tools, Rules and Pedagogy." *Review of Educational Research* 64: 119–57.

Glewwe, P., E. Hanushek, S. Humpage, and R. Ravina. 2011. "School Resources and Educational Outcomes in Developing Countries: A Review of the Literature from 1990 to 2010." NBER Working Paper 17554, National Bureau for Economic Research, Cambridge MA. http://www.nber.org/papers/w17554.

Glewwe, P., M. Kremer, and S. Moulin. 2007. *Many Children Left Behind? Textbooks and Test Scores in Kenya*. Cambridge, MA: National Bureau of Economic Research.

Guoxing, Y. 2007. *Research Evidence of School Effectiveness in Sub-Saharan African Countries.* Bristol, United Kingdom: University of Bristol Graduate School of Education.

Habte, A., G. Psacharopoulos, and S. Heyneman. 1993. *Improving the Quality of Education in Developing Countries.* A World Bank Study. Washington, DC: World Bank.

Heyneman, S., and J. Farrell. 1978. *Textbooks and Achievement: What We Know.* A World Bank Study. Washington. DC: World Bank.

Heyneman, S., and D. Jamieson. 1984. "Textbooks in the Philippines: An Evaluation of the Pedagogical Impact of a Nationwide Investment." *Educational Evaluation and Policy Analysis* 6 (2): 139–50.

Hoxby, C. 2000. *Peer Effects in the Classroom: Learning from Gender and Race Variation.* Cambridge, MA: National Bureau of Economic Research.

IFLA (International Federation of Library Associations). 2010. *The School Library in Learning and Teaching for All.* Paris: UNESCO.

Jones, B., and N. Sayer. 2013. *Annual Review of DFID Textbook Project in South Sudan.* Juba: DFID.

Kalibbala, G. 1999. *Sustainable Textbook Provision and Utilization in Uganda.* A World Bank Study. Washington, DC: World Bank.

Khaniya, T., and J. Williams. 2004. "Necessary but Not Sufficient: Challenges to (Implicit) Theories of Educational Change; Reform in Nepal's Primary Education System." *International Journal of Education Development* 24 (3): 315–28. http://www.sciencedirect.com/science/article/pii/S0738059304000069.

Kuecken, M., and M. Valfort. 2013. *When Do Textbooks Matter for Achievement? Evidence from African Primary Schools.* Paris: Paris School of Economics.

Lee, V. E., T. L. Zuze, and K. N. Ross. 2005. "School Effectiveness in 14 Sub-Saharan Countries: Links with 6th Graders Reading Achievement." *Studies in Educational Evaluation* 31: 201.

Little, A. 1995. *Education in Zanzibar: Classrooms, Quality and Costs.* Stockholm: Swedish International Development Agency for the Ministry of Education.

Lockheed, M., and A. Verspoor. 1990. *Improving Primary Education in Developing Countries.* A World Bank Study. Washington, DC: World Bank for the World Conference on Education for All in Jomtien.

McEwan, P. 2013. *Improving Learning in Primary Schools of Developing Countries: A Meta-Analysis of Randomized Experiments.* Cambridge MA: Center for Education Innovations. http://academics.wellesley.edu/Economics/mcewan/PDF/meta.pdf.

Mikulska, A. 2014. "School Teaching and Learning: The Challenge of Education in South Sudan." *NORRAG News.*

Mullis, V. S. 2006. *IEA's Progress in International Literacy Study in 40 Countries.* Boston, MA: PIRLS.

Pritchett, L., and D. Filmer. 1999. "What Educational Production Functions Really Show: A Positive Theory of Education Spending." *Economics of Education Review* 18 (2): 223–39.

Read, N. 2014. *Annual Review of DFID Textbook Project.* Juba: DFID.

Sabarwal, S., D. Evans, and A. Marshak. 2012. "Textbook Provision and Student Outcomes— the Devil in the Details." World Bank, Washington, DC.

Schollar, E. 2001. "A Review of Two Evaluations of the Application of the READ Primary Schools Program in the Eastern Cape Province of South Africa." *International Journal* of *Education Research* 35 (2): 205–16. http://www.sciencedirect.com/science/article/pii/S0883035501000179.

Searle, B. 1990. *General Operational Review of Textbooks*. A World Bank Study. Washington, DC: World Bank.

Tayyaba, S. 2010. "Mathematics Achievement in Middle School Level in Pakistan: Findings from the First National Assessment." *International Journal of Education Management* 24 (3): 221–49.

UNESCO (United Nations Educational, Scientific, and Cultural Organization). 2005. *The Quality Imperative—EFA Global Monitoring Report 2005*. Paris: UNESCO.

Vere, J. 1993. *Zanzibar Primary School Curriculum Review*. Geneva, Switzerland: UNICEF for the Ministry of Education.

Verspoor, A. 1986. *Textbooks as Instruments for the Improvement in the Quality of Education*. A World Bank Study. Washington, DC: World Bank.

Verspoor, A., and K. Wu. 1990. *Textbooks and Education Development*. A World Bank Study. Washington, DC: World Bank.

———. 2001. *A Chance to Learn*. A World Bank Study. Washington, DC: World Bank.

CHAPTER 2

Current Trends in National Teaching and Learning Materials Policies in Sub-Saharan Africa

Trends in National Teaching and Learning Materials Provision

Since the early 1990s the most significant trends in national teaching and learning material (TLM) provision policies in Sub-Saharan Africa (SSA) have been the following:

- The development of public-private partnerships (PPPs) to replace state textbook provision systems. In these PPPs the private sector operates as authors, publishers, and manufacturers (and sometimes distributors) of textbooks and other educational materials while the state establishes the system and rules of provision, evaluates submitted textbooks against agreed qualitative criteria, creates approved lists of textbooks and other TLMs, determines the nature and point of choice and selection, specifies the supply assumptions, monitors and supervises system performance, and provides funding (if free or subsidized textbooks are part of government policy).
- The rapid growth of local African-owned educational publishers operating on both a national and regional level. This is most marked in anglophone countries but even in francophone countries there is a shift towards more local private sector involvement in textbook provision and the growth of local educational publishing and authorship.
- The introduction of competing alternative textbooks to replace monopoly textbook provision, which is closely associated with the introduction of textbook evaluation systems that combine physical, content, presentational, and price factors (for example Kenya, Namibia, Malawi secondary, Rwanda, Uganda primary.) Wherever these systems have been properly applied and price has been a critical factor in evaluation, they have tended to improve production and presentational standards and reduce prices. The widespread use of minimum physical production specifications as a condition of approval

for sale to schools has created durable textbook production in an increasing number of countries, and the potential for long textbook life in the classroom allows for cost amortization and reduced costs of textbook and TLM provision systems. Unfortunately there has been a tendency for durability testing systems to lapse in many countries.
- A significant increase in the physical and content quality of textbooks and teachers' guides resulting from competitive pressures as publishers have sought to study the strong points of their rivals and to produce better textbooks for commercial reasons.
- The decentralization of textbook selection based on choices made at the level of individual schools. Once again, this has tended to be a movement most marked in anglophone countries. Some countries have experimented with district-based choice (for example Tanzania and Zambia), and Ghana and Cameroon (for lower primary) maintain choice from alternative approved textbooks for selected districts at a national level.
- Primary and secondary school enrollments have continued to grow significantly in most SSA countries in terms of real numbers but also in terms of percentage gains in gross enrollment ratios (GERs) and net enrollment ratios (NERs).
- There are an increasing number of national curricula that specify competency-based and child-centered approaches to learning and the development of concepts and higher-order thinking skills.

The Transition to Private Sector Involvement in Textbook Provision

A majority of African countries on independence sought to take control of their own education systems. As a consequence the 1960s were characterized by a wave of national curriculum development activity and the introduction of new subjects and new content, which reflected national and pan-African history, culture, environment, and aspirations. In a number of cases (for example, Tanzania) this resulted in enlarged primary and secondary curricula with multiple subjects, each of which required a textbook, which in turn considerably increased the system costs of textbook provision. This period was also characterized by the introduction of monopolistic state publishing houses, printing plants, and distribution systems, based on socialist models, although it should be noted that the previous colonial governments had sometimes introduced parastatal textbook publishing houses as well.[1] A good example is the East Africa Literature Bureau founded in the 1950s by the colonial government in Kenya to originate and publish textbooks for the countries of East Africa; the Bureau still exists now in the modified form of the successor Kenya Literature Bureau, which in 2013 remains active as a textbook publisher and is still in state ownership although operating in a competitive free market environment.

A review of the outcomes of the state textbook provision systems in Africa (and elsewhere in the world and particularly in the Former Soviet Union) isn't encouraging. Despite the creation of monopolistic state-owned companies initially strongly supported by state and sometimes by donor funding, very few of these companies developed into effective or sustainable operations. Nor were state companies any better supported by government financing than private sector operations. However, the advent of state textbook provision had a devastating impact on local commercial publishing, printing, and bookselling; and while private sector textbook publishing has tended to recover quite rapidly when provided with access to national textbook markets, textbook printing and bookselling have taken much longer to reestablish themselves (see "Comparisons between Anglophone and Francophone Approaches" and "A Summary of Key Issues" sections, below). This has a particular impact on current textbook provision systems because the highly developed internal bookselling networks (often run by church organizations) that existed prior to the advent of the state distribution monopolies in many SSA countries were largely destroyed by state intervention and have proved very difficult to recreate, thus severely limiting current textbook distribution options. There have been attempts to regenerate national wholesale and retail bookselling networks but this has proved to be far harder than the reestablishment of good quality local publishing. Experiments such as Uganda's Decentralized Instructional Materials Procurement Project (DIMPP) failed largely because the process of decentralization was pushed through by the Ugandan Ministry of Education and Sports (MOES) too rapidly for underfunded, inexperienced, and fledgling provincial booksellers to learn how to manage their finances in order to make adequate profits and to pay their publisher suppliers. This has been a common problem in many developing countries where the local book trade has been used for textbook distribution (for example in Malawi, Tanzania, Uganda, and Zambia). However, in Kenya a strong local book retail sector managed fully to reestablish itself after the collapse of the state-owned textbook distributor, the Kenya School Equipment Scheme (KSES) in 1984. But this is a rarity and very few other SSA countries have had the benefit of a comprehensive national bookselling network of experienced and professional suppliers.[2]

Similarly, local printing has largely failed to achieve genuine international (or even regional) competitiveness in price, reliability, and quality and equally often hasn't managed to develop adequate capacity in key processes for durability, such as thread-sewn binding or high-quality cover finishing. There are exceptions and Kenya, Nigeria, and South Africa all have well-established, competent textbook printing capacity although it is probably true even in these countries better prices could be achieved using international printing sources. Prepress and printing quality may be adequate in many countries but price, reliability, and process availability often have been problematic. Where there are only a few local printers with suitable equipment, textbook printing has to be organized *in sequence* (that is printing one book at a time in one—or a limited number—of printers), which requires the early preparation of materials ready for printing and thus increased investments in early prepress and in storage until the books are ready for distribution in time for the beginning of the school year, which in turn has an impact on the cash flow of local publishers and frequently is a significant factor in cost increases if local bank loan or overdraft interest rates are high. The great advantage of sourcing printing regionally or internationally is the possibility of printing *in parallel* (that is in using a number of different printers simultaneously), which greatly reduces the printing lead time thus avoiding the need to tie up investment capital for long periods. While many governments have been keen to develop their local printing industries and have sometimes put pressure on procurement systems to favor local printing (for example in many countries in the Middle East) this is only practical if the local printing industry has

- The plant, processes, raw materials, and skills required for good quality textbook manufacture;
- Sufficient capacity in the key processes (for example, binding and finishing in support of durability standards are often critical bottlenecks);
- Easy access to raw materials and plant at competitive prices;
- The management capacity and financial resources to guarantee reliable, on-time delivery without manufacturing flaws and errors, which can be very expensive for the publishers, particularly where competitive bidding is involved; and
- Competitive prices or a government or development partners (DPs) who can afford and are prepared to pay the (frequently) higher costs associated with local manufacturing.

Educationalists and publishers generally argue that local printing industries shouldn't expect to be developed on the basis of higher costs and inferior quality to the detriment of national education systems and that if they want to be able to participate actively in local textbook manufacturing they need to invest in the necessary plant, staff training, and quality assurance systems to enable them to compete on equal terms with regional and international printers.

The Growth in African Publishing

The shift from state provision to private sector access to the key national textbook markets started to gain momentum in anglophone countries from the 1980s. One of the first donor-funded projects to actively encourage and support textbook publishing by private sector publishers to meet specific local curriculum requirements was the World Bank–funded Sierra Leone Education III project in 1983, closely followed by similar World Bank funded projects in Liberia and the Gambia.[3] In these early days the beneficiaries were largely British multi-national publishing companies. In Nigeria educational publishing was indigenized in 1976/77[4] and it was indigenized in Ghana in the 1980s. The local branches and subsidiaries of foreign publishers became majority-owned local companies. In one case a wealthy local board member of the Nigerian subsidiary of the U.K. publisher Evans Bros actually bought out the U.K. parent company and acquired the 40 percent shareholding that the U.K. company owned in the Nigerian subsidiary.

The indigenization of foreign companies in anglophone West Africa was paralleled by a growth in locally owned African publishing companies such as Fourth Dimension Publishing House in Nigeria. In East and Central anglophone Africa the indigenization process was also paralleled by the rapid growth of local publishing companies that were 100 percent African owned. In the 1990s Longman sold off its local Kenyan company and locally originated copyrights to a new Kenyan-owned company called Longhorn, and Heinemann similarly sold its local company to local management using local capital. The local company was renamed East African Educational Publishers (EAEP).[5] Both of these companies were still very active in regional textbook publishing in 2013. At the same time new locally financed private sector publishing companies emerged in response to market access in Kenya, Malawi, Tanzania, Uganda, and Zambia among others. In Uganda, the successive textbook bids organized first by the Support for Ugandan Primary Education Reform (SUPER) project and then by World Bank–funded projects were competed for by up to 14 local (Ugandan) and regional (Kenyan) publishing companies and the awards were certainly not dominated by the remaining multinationals. In fact, in 2014 only Oxford University Press of the U.K. based multinationals is still operational in East Africa.[6] Most textbook publishing for Kenya, Rwanda, Tanzania, and Uganda is now in the hands of regional African-owned publishers.

The same process has not been as pronounced in francophone Africa where state publishing and the multinationals have continued to dominate textbook provision in many countries up to the present. However, although state textbook origination and copyright ownership are still common in francophone countries, monopolistic supply has been abandoned in Cameroon, Côte d'Ivoire, Mali, and Senegal, and this has provided opportunities in the last 10 years for the emergence of locally owned textbook publishing companies, which are prepared to compete with metropolitan French companies.

Competing Alternative Textbooks and the Introduction of Textbook Evaluation Systems

The demise of state textbook publishing and the emergence of private sector textbook publishers operating in partnership with local ministries of education (MOEs) has been supported by a parallel shift from monopolistic textbook provision to systems of competing alternative textbooks. The competing textbooks are typically selected for an MOE-approved list through submission and evaluation processes which varied in their degree of rigor, objectivity, and effectiveness. The period of approval generally lasted for a complete curriculum cycle (typically five years) but in some cases there were no time limits imposed. Ideally the textbook evaluation methodology always should include rigorous content, presentational, durability, and price criteria to produce the best result; but some of the evaluation methodologies omitted price considerations (for example Namibia and Tanzania) and thus failed to achieve the best cost-reduction outcomes; others failed to specify minimum production standards, which frequently led to unacceptably low classroom life expectations. The SUPER project In Uganda and the interventions in Tanzania by the Swedish International Development Agency (SIDA) and the World Bank had no limits on the number of textbooks that could be added to the approved lists, no time limits for approved status, and no mechanisms for removing textbooks once they were on the list. As a result the number of approved titles expanded every year and teachers were often confused by the extent of the choice available; many of the potential cost benefits were lost through fractionalized print runs or lack of control over pricing.[7] Experience suggests that somewhere between three and six titles per subject and grade level—depending on the grade level enrollments—provide satisfactory outcomes. As a general rule private-sector publishers don't like restrictions on the number of approved titles (in case their own titles don't make the cut) and would generally prefer higher rather than lower approved list ceilings. However, reduced numbers of approved titles generally means fiercer price competition and thus reduced costs. The use of effective and rigorous evaluation methodologies and criteria using price as a significant (but not overwhelming) factor in evaluation scoring has tended to result in textbooks and teachers' guides of improved manufacturing and content quality as well as significantly reduced costs. A report on the impact of the introduction of rigorous textbook submission, evaluation, and approval systems associated with World Bank–funded primary textbook procurements in Uganda in 2001 found as follows:

> Overall, the decrease in price in pupils' books annihilates the inflationary price increases and beyond: it's as if the publishers were now working 15% under 1998 nominal prices! The two most impressive cuts were obtained in Social Studies and Science, and these lower prices have been achieved whilst maintaining stability in the extent of the books:

Subjects	Increase/Decrease in extent 98→01	Decrease in price 98→01
Social Studies	+3%	55%
Science	−15%	45%

> As far as the use of color is concerned, the situation has improved in these two subjects: all 3 Social Studies books reviewed in 2001 offer 4-colour printing (against 1 out of 4 in Cycle 6); in 1998, two Science books were in four-color printing out of four publishers, whereas in 2001 the proportion was 2 out of 3.
>
> - English and Science were the only subjects to reduce their extent: not only are Math books much cheaper now in constant terms (−39%), but the number of pages has gone up by 31% (with similar color patterns as in 1998 throughout all of the approved publishers).
> - Social Studies follow yet another pattern: very slight increase in extent (+3%), but an impressive improvement in the use of color (the two reviewed books were 4-colour + pictures, whereas only one out of 4 books was in 4-colour in

1998, the three remaining ones then only offering two-color printing); all this with a record 55% average cut in prices in constant currency.
- It should also be noted that Cycle 8 books all come with varnished covers, which provides an important improvement in durability, whereas only one third of Cycle 6 titles had varnished covers.
- Conclusion: the success of the new competitive textbook evaluation process in reducing prices is impressive, with an average 44% gain in purchasing power for the schools, relatively evenly spread throughout the subjects. Mathematically, it means that within the same budget the schools would be able to go from a 1:3 book:student ratio to a 1:2 ratio and even have money left to buy supplementary materials. It is worth noting that these important gains in affordability resulting solely from improved and more rigorous bidding and evaluation procedures have been achieved while maintaining textbook extents, improving manufacturing standards and durability and increasing the use of 4-colour presentation. (Bontoux 2002)

In recent years there has been a trend back to sole-source supply policies and even to the reconsideration of the reestablishment of state textbook provision systems in some countries, despite the evidence of widespread and expensive failure in the past. Thus Malawi will continue with monopolistic state primary textbook provision via the Malawi Institute of Education (MIE) with the active support of the donor community. Zimbabwe has adopted recently a single monopolistic textbook policy, also donor supported. Tanzania may be on the verge of reintroducing sole-source textbook supply from the private sector and perhaps of recreating a new state textbook provision system.[8] In Kenya the government is considering a proposal from the Kenya Institute of Education to form itself into an educational publishing parastatal. The DPs have recently supported sole-source textbook supply from the private sector in Ethiopia and at secondary level in Uganda.

Sole-source supply is often justified on the basis of lower costs, which also demonstrates a lack of understanding of the basic facts of textbook pricing (see "the Growth in Learner-Centered and Outcomes-Based Curricula" section, below). Any move towards the reintroduction of monopolistic textbooks and state-dominated textbook provision systems suggests that the almost universal statist system failures of the past have either been forgotten (problems with institutional memory) or have not been recognized or understood by either governments or the donor community.

Centralized versus Decentralized Funding and Selection

The introduction of systems of competing, alternative textbooks raised the critical issue of the point of selection. In general, the tendency in anglophone countries in the past decade has been to shift towards the empowerment of individual schools to make their own selection decisions, although this is not a universal practice. In Ghana, for example, the textbook evaluation process selects five titles at primary for each subject and grade, but it is the responsibility of the

MOE to allocate a single title to each district. Thus, although there are competing alternative titles, each district has a monopoly textbook and schools are not involved in any way in the selection process. The thinking behind this approach is that schools do not have the skills to make title selection decisions. However, practical experience suggests that in most countries schools do have the ability to make selection decisions although training and some practice is usually required. The introduction of school-based selection and ordering in Rwanda in 2010 resulted in 98.6 percent of schools submitting textbook and supplementary materials orders on time, although there was quite a high level of budget over-and under-runs in the first year. However, budgeting problems decreased significantly in the 2nd Cycle of school-based selection and ordering and decreased further in the 3rd Cycle, which clearly indicates that schools became familiar with the process of selection within the limitations of individual school budgets. School-based selection does not remove corruption and there are well-documented examples of schools demanding payments from publishers for selecting their titles and of district education offices exercising corrupt influence over school selection decisions.

Decentralized textbook selection also requires some form of decentralized financing and three options are generally available as follows:

a) Cash transfers by MOEs directly into school bank accounts based on per capita funding formulae (Kenya).
b) The use of Local Purchase Orders (LPOs) cashable through local booksellers, whose value is calculated based on per capita funding formulae (Machakos—one of the Kenyan pilot districts).
c) School order forms using book lists with nationally agreed prices and a school purchasing budget based on per capita funding formulae. The school submits its orders to the MOE, which consolidates the orders and orders in bulk from the publishers. Distribution can be either organized by the MOE (Uganda) or can be the responsibility of the publishers (Rwanda). In this variant the school has selection responsibility and a per capita purchasing budget but has no access to cash, which remains under the direct control of the MOE. Thus decentralized selection is effectively combined with centralized bulk buying to achieve best prices while encouraging school ownership of the process through school-based decision making on the titles and the quantities to be selected.

As a general rule the cash transfer system is administratively the easiest but is more open to corruption and abuse unless it is adequately supervised. The school order form system is administratively the most complex and time and labor consuming but is the best for achieving financial control. LPOs are only a viable option if there is a well-established local retail bookshop network. There is no reason why any country should not use a combination of the above systems. It should be noted that where decentralization involves cash transfers at primary level there will be a large increase in the need for school auditing services. In Kenya, prior to the introduction of cash transfers to support decentralized, school-based textbook financing there were 200 district auditors available to audit approximately 4,000 secondary schools so that each auditor had an average audit workload of 20 schools per year. This was manageable. However, when the system of free primary textbooks funded by cash transfers to school bank accounts was launched in 2003–04 a further 20,000 primary schools were required to manage cash, but there was no increase in the number of district auditors, meaning that individual district auditors were now responsible for an unmanageable average of 120 school audits per year. Under the circumstances it was probably inevitable that the system would be subject to fund diversion and misappropriation, which could have been avoided with the provision of adequate accounts and audit supervision. In 2014 it has been reported that school financial auditing in Kenya is on the point of collapse and that adequate supervision of school use of funds is no longer possible with a consequent increase in fund diversion and maladministration. This is an issue of great concern to the publishers who see their market funding seriously diminished by a lack of financial control over allocated funding.

Enrollment Growth

In the past two decades there has been very significant school enrollment growth in almost all SSA countries as a direct result of the policies adopted at Jomtien and Dakar in support of the attainment of Universal Primary Education (UPE). Increased primary school numbers have increased the system costs of textbooks and other TLM provision; and the increase in the numbers of primary school leavers has inevitably increased the demand for access to secondary school places, which has led to expensive enrollment increases and thus TLM costs in this subsector as well. In many SSA countries governments do not have the finance to build or supply the numbers of new secondary schools required to meet demand or to expand existing secondary schools. Thus, there has been a renewal of interest in the creation of environments that will encourage the private sector to invest and a consideration of the provision of free or subsidized textbooks and TLMs to private schools as well as to public schools. In some countries such as Uganda, a distinction has been drawn between "not-for-profit" private schools, usually funded by religious bodies or local community groups, and commercial private schools where profit is the main motive. In many countries the ownership of profit-driven private schools is often in the hands of education professionals working for the state system, which can create significant conflicts of interest. The growth in privately owned schools has also created a market for the free textbooks supplied to state schools and this in turn has increased theft and illegal sales by head teachers and teachers of the free textbooks into the private school market. There are numerous examples throughout SSA of these activities.

Enrollment growth has increased the potential profits from TLM publishing and has stimulated and supported the growth of locally owned private sector publishers. Where local booksellers and printers have access to school markets these sectors have also benefitted. The growth in privately owned secondary schools has supported both local publishing and local bookselling. The increase in the number of secondary school enrollments has, in some cases, encouraged local publishing in market sectors where previously the market size was too small and unreliable for local publishers to risk investment in new title development. Thus local publishing is now active in junior secondary textbook publishing in an increasing number of countries and this trend is beginning to replace the direct import of secondary school books from British and French publishers. With continued enrollment growth it can be expected that local publishing will move into many senior secondary textbook sectors in time. This shift in publishing locations from Europe to Africa tends to have price benefits for national TLM systems because local and regional publishing tends to operate on lower overhead percentages than imported books.

Comparisons between Anglophone and Francophone Approaches

Approaches to textbook provision in anglophone and francophone SSA countries have been quite different; and government and donor policies towards textbook provision have also differed considerably, even within the same agency. Thus World Bank textbook policies and strategies are often quite different in the francophone and anglophone countries in SSA. As a result the trends in textbook provision policy described above have been most actively pursued in anglophone countries. The speed of change in francophone and lusophone SSA countries generally has been slower; and the involvement, and thus the growth, of the private sector has been more constrained. The issue of copyright ownership of textbooks has largely disappeared as a bone of contention in anglophone countries but is still a subject of discussion and discord between MOEs and private-sector publishers in francophone Africa.

The major areas of difference are summarized in table 2.1, below.

The Growth in Learner-Centered and Outcomes-Based Curricula

In the past decade there has been a noticeable increase in SSA countries in the number of national curricula that stress learner-centered approaches and the development of competencies and higher-order thinking skills. These curricula have often been quite strongly influenced by European and U.S. system examples. For SSA they pose a number of issues that need to be resolved.

Learner-centered and outcomes-based curricula require textbooks and TLMs that support the teacher in the delivery of these approaches and the development of competencies and skills in the classroom. Unfortunately, many textbooks—probably the majority—published for these curricula do not provide the required support to students and teachers. Among the common textbook faults in addressing learner-centered curricula are the following:

- A continuing strong emphasis in textbooks on the presentation of facts
- A lack of orientation in activities, exercises, experiments towards the specific; classroom conditions of rural and poor schools, which are usually the

Table 2.1 Textbook Provision Systems in Francophone and Anglophone Africa—A Comparison

Issues	Francophone Africa	Anglophone Africa
Enrollment	Increasing, particularly at primary but still generally lower than in anglophone countries, so textbook markets tend to be smaller in size.	Generally high at primary and now growing rapidly at secondary, which creates larger textbook markets of great interest to private sector publishers, booksellers and printers. Market size is one of the factors that has supported the growth of private sector publishers in anglophone Africa.
Curriculum policy	There has been a movement toward regional curricula via CONFEMEN, which has been made possible by common education structures and language of instruction policies throughout francophone countries. Regional curricula have increased potential textbook print runs but have also provided considerable competitive advantages to multi-national publishers operating in all CONFEMEN countries against national publishers usually operating only in their home country.	Regional curricula were a feature of the immediate post-colonial period (for example The Entebbe Math Project and the African Science and Social Science Projects) but they were quite rapidly replaced by unique national curricula as each anglophone country developed its own unique education structure and language policies. Attempts at achieving regional curricula in the 1970s and 1980s failed (for example, the Mano River Union project in Guinea, Liberia, and Sierra Leone) but are again emerging as an issue as a result of the East African Community.
Textbook monopolies	Partially or totally abandoned in larger countries (Cameroon, Côte d'Ivoire, Mali, and Senegal) but still in place in smaller ones.	Now rare; the trend is towards a choice-based textbook system with an emphasis placed on competition and the school as the decision-maker. But there are examples of recent monopoly supply (for example Malawi primary, Zimbabwe, perhaps Tanzania soon, Uganda secondary, and so on) some of which are DP funded.
Publishers	Still strong multinational presence; local publishing small and localized. Little regional publishing by African-owned publishers.	Rapid growth in African-owned national and regional textbook publishing, particularly in West, East and Southern Africa. Multi-national publishers no longer dominate in any anglophone country although they are stronger at secondary level; but this is changing as more local publishers move into secondary textbook publishing as secondary markets expand and more DP and government funding is made available for secondary textbooks. Many national publishers maintain good contacts with multinational publishers to access authorship, editorial and production expertise as and when required.
Free primary textbooks	There is a shift toward free primary textbook provision but the pace and extent of changes have been slower than in anglophone Africa.	This has been achieved as policy in most countries but with ongoing affordability and sustainability problems.
Parent purchase of textbooks	Main element of provision in many countries.	Rare at primary but still common at secondary.
Textbook ownership	Parents and/or schools for primary but mostly parent purchase and ownership at secondary.	Schools at primary but parent purchase still common at secondary, although this is changing in some countries e.g., Rwanda.

table continues next page

Table 2.1 Textbook Provision Systems in Francophone and Anglophone Africa—A Comparison *(continued)*

Issues	Francophone Africa	Anglophone Africa
Production standards and durability	Poor, if produced by Pedagogic Institutes. Good durable standards when produced by multi-national and some local publishers.	Durability, long book life and maximum annualized cost amortization are almost universal policies and most anglophone countries operate on the basis of good durable physical production specifications. Regular testing of conformity to production specifications is recommended but even where it is national policy it is often neglected in practice.
Government control of textbook authorship, editing and copyrights	Widespread with consequent copyright disputes	Rare. Authorship and publishing are now dominantly private sector activities and copyrights are usually maintained by the private sector as a result. This has not led to publisher control of textbook reprints and pricing, which was a common MOE fear in the past.
Relationship between local publishers and publishers from developed countries	Generally not as positive as in most Anglophone countries	Generally good working relationships with multinational companies operating as members of local publishers' associations and working cooperatively with local publishers via local branches and subsidiaries.
State distribution	Not uncommon, but not as widespread as it used to be (absent in Mali, in the DRC, from DEOs onwards). District distribution to schools is still a problem in most countries because districts frequently lack budgets, facilities, transport, systems, management and staff motivation.	Still largely state organized although now common for publishers to distribute to districts and for schools to collect from districts. There is bookseller distribution in Tanzania, Kenya and Malawi secondary and publisher distribution to schools in Rwanda. District distribution to schools is still a problem in most countries because districts frequently lack budgets, facilities, transport, systems, management and staff motivation.
National manufacturing	Not usual when private sector publishers are involved.	Publishers are generally free to choose their own printer, whatever the nationality, in order to deliver good prices and required quality manufacturing. Most Kenyan textbooks are manufactured in Kenya but in Nigeria and Ghana where there are reasonable production facilities most publishers still prefer to manufacture internationally for price, quality, reliability and capacity reasons.
Recipients of government/donor funding	Usually producers (publishers, printers).	Increasingly consumers via school per capita funding for textbook procurements.
General orientation for textbook policies	Mix of interventionism and laissez-faire.	Increasingly market-based.
Procurement	Still dominantly first past the post publishing bids or printing bids if textbooks remain in state ownership but approved lists of competing textbooks are gradually making progress in some countries.	Printing bids are now very rare. First past the post publishing bids are associated with sole source systems (for example Uganda secondary). Increasingly the bids are for approved list status where sophisticated evaluation procedures combining price, presentation, physical and content quality apply. These lists are used as the basis for school-based selection and ordering.

Note: COMFEMEN = Conference of Ministries of Education Using French as a Language of Instruction; DEO = District Education Office; DP = development partner; DRC = Democratic Republic of Congo; MOE = Ministry of Education.

majority—not surprising when most authors are drawn from the more prestigious schools (often elite private schools), and are not necessarily very familiar with prevailing facilities, equipment, resources, and conditions in rural schools[9]
- A lack of balance in providing competency-based activities in different subjects at different grade levels
- A lack of variety in textbook content aimed at providing work for multiability groups
- A lack of strategies for dealing with the common wide variety of contact hours both between and within countries
- Variable coverage of target skills and competencies
- Teachers' guides that do not address adequately the skills and knowledge gaps of many untrained and semitrained teachers[10]
- Lack of formative assessment exercises that help teachers to determine whether their students are making progress on the required skills

It would be easy to blame authors and publishers for these faults, but in many instances the problems start with the curriculum documentation. Publishers in submitting bids for evaluation usually stay very close to the official curriculum because they fear that they might fail in the evaluation if they deviate from it to any significant degree. Thus, if there are faults and flaws in the curriculum these inevitably will be transferred into the textbooks and teachers' guides. Among the common curriculum flaws are the following:

- Too many subjects, many of which do not have trained teachers.
- Overloaded content which often cannot be satisfactorily completed in a school year and certainly not in those schools where contact hours are well below the stated norm.
- A lack of clarity in the skills and competencies required by the curriculum so that publishers either have to make up their own definitions or ignore or de-emphasize them in the textbooks. In several cases higher-order thinking skills are required but are nowhere specified or defined in curriculum documents.[11]
- The lack of a method of testing for skills and competences. In this situation many teachers revert to the old but true adage that if it isn't tested it won't be taught.
- A lack of guidance on the teaching and learning methodologies that MOEs wish to develop in national classrooms. Once again the lack of guidance is widely ascribed to a lack of clarity within curriculum development organizations and within MOEs on how the outcomes-based curricula should be taught and delivered.
- A refusal to recognize that there are wide school differences in almost all SSA countries in teacher training, quality, motivation, contact hours, facilities, equipment, and resources that should be reflected in curriculum documents and that these differences will always impact on outcomes.

It is probable that a majority of teachers in a majority of schools have no clear idea how to teach the new curricula and how to achieve the new curriculum objectives and thus continue to teach in the old ways with a continued focus on factual recall. This situation continues because examinations have lagged behind curriculum development[12] and usually have not developed to the point where many of the learning objectives in the new curricula can be effectively assessed.

A Summary of Key Issues

- Primary and secondary enrollments have continued to increase in most SSA countries in the past two decades. As a result TLM provision systems are more expensive to maintain and the importance of sensible cost control measures in all links of the textbook chain is now a priority.
- Increased enrollment has increased the attractiveness of publishing for schools because of greater market size. It has also, in some countries, attracted publishers into market sectors where they were previously not interested in participating. Thus, locally specific publishing for junior secondary textbooks, rather than the importation of international texts, has now become possible in many countries as a direct result of junior secondary enrollment growth.
- The shift in many countries from state TLM provision systems to renewed private sector market access from the late 1980s onwards has encouraged a rapid growth in African-owned textbook publishing companies, and in anglophone Africa it is no longer common for multinational publishing companies to dominate. In francophone countries there has been a less pronounced growth in local publishing and multinationals are still influential.
- Private sector market access has tended—not universally—to be based on the establishment of approved booklists of alternative competing titles. These vary in their effectiveness according to the rigor of the evaluation processes.
- Although competitive private sector involvement in publishing has provided the potential for better production and presentational quality and reduced prices, these will only be achieved and sustained if good management and monitoring processes have been established within MOEs. Thus, price reductions will only be achieved and maintained if price is a key factor in textbook evaluation and approval and if price increases while materials are on approved lists are subject to specific and measurable criteria. Similarly, minimum production specifications as a condition of approval need to be tested both at advance copy stage and randomly in the field to ensure that publishers are aware that their contracted standards must be maintained in practice. Where production specifications are not tested regularly there are plenty of examples of substandard textbooks being supplied to schools and this leads to reduced textbook life and suboptimal cost amortization. Effective state and private sector distribution also needs to be monitored to ensure effective and equitable distribution. The monitoring and reporting systems are not complex but they need reliable budget allocations. Responses from school surveys in

11 countries (see appendix A) suggests that monitoring of supply to schools is a weakness in many countries.
- Approved textbook lists have been the foundation for decentralized school-based financing, selection, and ordering systems.
- Decentralization also requires the creation of specialized management, monitoring, and supervision systems operated by trained staff and supported by regular and reliable budget allocations.
- Textbook provision practices between francophone and anglophone systems have not followed similar paths in the past. Although there are signs of convergence in some aspects of practice there is not yet a common approach. Indeed common approaches may be difficult to achieve because of different traditions and expectations.
- New curricula based on learner-centered approaches and the development of skills and competences are increasingly common in SSA countries but are often not well delivered in practice.

Notes

1. In Tanzania there was even a state paper mill, largely funded by SIDA.
2. As an example of the range of bookseller expertise available, one enterprising bookselling entrepreneur in Kenya operates a camel-back textbook sales and distribution service aimed at nomadic and remote areas of northern Kenya. Some states in Nigeria and much of South Africa also have managed to maintain strong local retail networks for textbooks, but in most SSA countries bookselling outside the main urban areas remains weak.
3. The World Bank–funded Uganda Education III project of the early 1980s was an emergency project that purchased existing textbooks off the shelf largely from U.K. based multi-national publishers to supply the textbook losses incurred through the civil war. This project was not concerned with using the private sector to publish for specific local curricula.
4. The indigenization decree was rescinded in 2008 and foreign companies are now once again permitted to own 100 percent of the equity of Nigerian-based publishing companies, including educational publishing houses.
5. Longman—now Pearson—quickly reestablished itself as a Kenyan company although in 2012 it was closing down its Kenyan business once again because of the decline in the Kenyan textbook market caused by inadequate funding, which itself resulted from the withdrawal of development partner support for textbook provision after a high profile corruption scandal revealed that government textbook funding was being diverted away from schools and into individual bank accounts.
6. One of the reasons for the more rapid development of local publishing in anglophone Africa was the tendency of British publishers to establish local branches, subsidiaries, and local companies employing local staff as editors and managers who were trained in publishing and management skills and thus were capable of starting their own businesses. For example, Oxford University Press, Longman, and Macmillan had opened local companies in South Africa in the first decade of the 20th century; Longman opened a Kenyan branch in 1950 and OUP in 1954. In contrast French publishers

opened local branches and subsidiaries less frequently and much later and tended to operate from Paris-based offices.

7. For example, the current Namibian book list contains approximately 4,000 titles.

8. In 2011 the Attorney General is reported to have ruled that the unilateral selection of two titles per subject and grade as the approved titles from the previously evaluated approved textbook list was in breach of government procurement regulations because further evaluations to select the two titles had not taken place. At the time of writing the proposal to move to the two-title system is therefore in abeyance.

9. A highly experienced and well-regarded science author of more than 20 years' experience in writing science textbooks for SSA was astounded when taken to a rural primary school to discover that there was no science lab and that the total science equipment was a few, mostly broken, test tubes and flasks. He had been writing science textbooks on the assumption that adequate facilities and equipment were as widely available in rural schools as they were in the elite urban schools with which he was familiar.

10. A leading publisher of textbooks for SSA commented that teachers' guides were required by bid documents but were very rarely a significant feature of evaluation and thus were only rarely given the attention that they deserved. The same publisher reported that in her experience very few teachers ever used the teachers' guides in lesson preparation. This view was confirmed by a recent workshop of Advisory Teachers in Namibia (see "Patterns of TLM Usage in the Classroom" section in chapter 11).

11. The inability to clearly define required skills and competences in curriculum documents is often ascribed to the curriculum developers themselves being unsure about what the skills are and how they should be achieved. This is not surprising when a majority of curriculum developers probably have not been required to teach and deliver these skills themselves.

12. An alternative view is that curriculum development has taken place without sufficient attention to the problems of assessing new skills and competences.

References

Bontoux, V. 2002. *Comparing Prices and Physical Quality between Cycle 6 and Cycle 8 Primary Textbooks*. International Book Development, London, United Kingdom, for the Uganda MOES and the World Bank.

———. 2008. *Mission Report on Namibia Textbook Reform Component*. Windhoek: Millennium Challenge Corporation for Ministry of Education.

CHAPTER 3

Current Textbook (and Other Teaching and Learning Materials) Availability, Costs, and Financing in Sub-Saharan Africa

Textbook Unit Costs at Primary and Secondary Levels in 11 Sub-Saharan African Countries

Textbook unit costs appear to vary considerably from country to country and by educational level. Thus senior secondary textbooks are generally more expensive than junior secondary textbooks and junior secondary textbooks are more expensive than primary textbooks, although the total annual costs of primary are usually much higher than secondary because of the much larger enrollments compared to secondary enrollments. However some new primary textbooks printed in four colors may have higher unit costs than elderly secondary textbooks printed in one color

The factors that determine the *system* costs of provision are

- School enrollments;
- The number of required (compulsory) textbook titles (this is determined by the national curriculum design);
- The textbook content specifications, which impact on textbook extents;
- Other teaching and learning materials (TLM) specified requirements (for example, reading books, atlases, dictionaries);
- The unit costs of textbooks and other TLMs (often conveniently expressed as an "average" unit cost);
- The target classroom life (this is determined by the physical production specifications, which determine durability);
- The target textbook–pupil ratios (TPRs) and;
- Loss and damage rates.

The per student annual amortized cost of provision is therefore expressed by the following simple formula:

$$\text{Amortized cost of one textbook set}^1 = \frac{\text{Target number of textbooks} \times \text{average unit cost}}{\text{Target textbook life}}$$

Tables 3.1 through 3.4, provide sample calculations derived from country surveys and these demonstrate clearly the national differences in the costs of basic textbook provision at lower primary, upper primary, lower secondary, and upper secondary.

In table 3.1 the most obvious national contrasts lie in the average unit textbook cost, where Namibia has average unit textbook costs of US$7.50 at primary and US$15.00 at secondary compared to Burundi where average unit textbook cost at both primary and secondary is just US$1.00, although the two costs are not directly comparable because they comprise different cost components (see table 3.1, below).

For example, in Burundi the low unit textbook costs are achieved by only factoring in raw materials and printing costs and neglecting to include all other costs such as warehousing, copyright licensing fees, editorial and management overheads, and storage and distribution costs. In addition the titles are quite short in extent (mostly under 100 pages and therefore typically using cheaper saddle-stitched bindings) and small in format. Printing is only in one or two colors, although the textbooks have physical production specifications suitable for a four-year classroom life.[2] There is a single unified national language of instruction (LoI) in Burundi (Kinyarundi), which prevents the fractionalization of print runs and the associated increases in unit costs. Burundi is a small compact country and distribution costs are not high, but the costs of distribution are not included in

Table 3.1 Textbook Costs for Grade 1[a]

Country	No. of required textbooks	Average unit textbook cost (US$)	Cost of textbook set (US$)	Assumed classroom life (years)	Target TPR	Annualized amortized cost of a textbook set (US$)
Benin	6	2.70	16.20	n.a.	1:1	n.a.
Burundi	9	1.00	9.00	2–3	1:1	3.00–4.50
Côte d'Ivoire	3	3.00	9.00	1	1:1	9.00
Kenya	8	3.80	30.60	4	1:1	7.65
Madagascar	8	0.75	6.00	2	1:1	3.00
Mali	3	4.50	13,60	2–3	1:1	4.53
Namibia	3	7.50	22.50	5	1:2	2.25
Rwanda	4	2.50	10.00	4	1:1	2.50
Chad	2	5.00	10.00	1	1:1	10.00
Median	5.5	3.75	14.25	3	1:1.5	6.125

Source: Author's survey.
Note: n.a. = no data available; TPR = textbook–pupil ratio.
a. The unit costs quoted in tables 3.1–3.4 are almost certainly not comparable in the sense that the cost components included in the individual costs vary from country to country. Some will include full distribution costs (e.g., Rwanda and Kenya) others won't. Some will be based on raw materials and manufacturing only (e.g., Burundi) while others will include all of the costs of publication (e.g., Kenya and Rwanda).

Table 3.2 Textbook Costs for Grade 6

Country	No. of required textbooks	Average unit textbook cost (US$)	Cost of textbook set (US$)	Assumed classroom life (years)	Target TPR	Annualized amortized cost of a textbook set (US$)
Benin	6	2.60	15.60	n.a.	1:1	n.a.
Burundi	10	1.00	10.00	3	1:1	3.33
Côte d'Ivoire	7	4.00	28.00	2	1:1	14.00
Kenya	7	4.20	29.40	4	1:1	7.35
Madagascar	8	0.75	6.00	2	1:1	3.00
Mali	4	5.50	22.00	4	1:1	5.50
Namibia	7	7.50	52.50	5	1:2	5.25
Rwanda	5	3.50	17.50	5	1:1	3.50
Chad	5	6.00	30.00	1	1.3	10.00
Median	7	3.75	29.25	3	1:2	8.50

Note: n.a. = no data available; TPR = textbook–pupil ratio.

Table 3.3 Textbook Costs for Grade 8

Country	No. of required textbooks	Average unit textbook cost (US$)	Cost of textbook set (US$)	Assumed classroom life (years)	Target TPR	Annualized amortized cost of a textbook set (US$)
Benin	7	5.9	41.30	n.a.	1:1	n.a.
Burundi	15	1.0	15.00	4	1:1	3.75
Côte d'Ivoire	8	9.50	76.00	3	1:3	8.40
Kenya	9	4.60	41.40	4	1:1	10.35
Madagascar	7	n.a.	n.a.	n.a.	n.a.	n.a.
Mali	9	10.00	90.00	5	n.a.	18.00
Namibia	8	15.00	120.00	5	1:2	12.00
Rwanda	8	6.00	48.00	5	1:1	9.60
Chad	5	n.a.	n.a.	1	3:5[a]	n.a.
Median	10	8.00	67.50	3	1:1.7	10.875

Note: n.a. = no data available; TPR = textbook–pupil ratio.
a. Chad has a 1:1 ratio for language of instruction, 1:3 for math and 1:5 for other subjects.

textbook prices. The textbooks were originated by Hachette in the 1980s and they have been licensed by the Burundi Ministry of Education (MOE) and are currently printed in India and other international printing centers. They are thus out of date in their content, educational approach, the level of French language (way too high), and the layout; but all the costs of origination have been covered long ago and manufacturing thus only includes the costs of reprinting. The textbooks are monopolistic so that available print runs are not split. In order to achieve comparable unit costs with other surveyed countries the costs of licensing, storage, distribution, and MOE management overheads would also need to be added to the raw manufacturing costs provided here. As an estimate this could increase unit costs by a factor of three, to US$3.00 per title, which would increase the cost of a textbook set to US$27.00. When amortized over three years on the basis of a 1:1 TPR the amortized annual cost of primary textbook provision would increase to

Table 3.4 Textbook Costs for Grade 11

Country	No. of required textbooks	Average unit textbook cost (US$)	Cost of textbook set (US$)	Assumed classroom life	Target TPR	Annualized amortized cost of a textbook set (US$)
Benin	8	4.30	34.40	n.a.	1:1	n.a.
Burundi	16	1.00	16.00	5	1:1	3.20
Côte d'Ivoire	6	13.95	83.70	5	1:5	3.00
Kenya	8	5.00	40.00	4	1:1	10.00
Madagascar	7	n.a.	n.a.	n.a.	n.a.	n.a.
Mali	10	11.50	115.00	5	n.a.	23.00
Namibia	8	15.00	120.00	5	1:2	12.00
Rwanda	8	15.00	120.00	5	1:1	24.00
Chad	7	n.a.	n.a.	n.a.	3:5[a]	n.a.
Median	11	8.00	68.00	4.5 years	1:3	13.50

Note: n.a. = no data available; TPR = textbook–pupil ratio.
a. Chad has a 1:1 ratio for language of instruction, 1:3 for math and 1:5 for other subjects.

US$9.00 per student per year, which is considerably more expensive than Kenya or Rwanda where the textbooks are of significantly higher content quality.

Namibia represents an opposite case. In the past the evaluation processes for textbook approval were not rigorous (no submission was ever rejected) and price was not a factor in the evaluation process. Thus publishers set whatever prices they wanted on a unilateral basis. The system supported competing alternative textbooks despite the very small market size. The textbooks were produced up to developed country standards including expensive four-color production, although total student enrollment was small (around 400,000 primary and secondary students in total) and the print runs were further fractionalized by the use of up to 13 local LoIs, although most textbooks were rarely published in more than seven languages. The terrain and distances can be difficult and distribution is expensive as a result (textbook prices include distribution costs) and government funding is typically released late, leading to last-minute (and therefore more expensive) printing and distribution costs. Slow payment leads to expensive bank borrowing charges.

Kenya and Rwanda have very similar textbook specifications (although print runs tend to be longer in Kenya) and both countries require commercial distribution direct to individual schools. Kenyan publishers publish many of the approved textbooks for both countries. And yet the average unit textbook cost in Kenya at Grade 1 is US$3.80 whereas the average Grade 1 unit cost in Rwanda is US$2.50—a cost differential of almost 50 percent. Why the difference? In Rwanda publishers deliver direct to schools without going through a bookseller middleman with significantly lower distribution costs as a result. In Kenya textbooks are supplied via retail booksellers so that a full retail bookseller discount has to be included in the cost structure. This difference in distribution approach probably accounts for 10 to 15 percent of the cost differential. In Rwanda, publishers are paid by the Ministry of Finance on submission of their Completed Delivery Notes (CDNs) so that there is no risk of nonpayment. In Kenya booksellers are paid by schools and publishers are paid by booksellers. Many Kenyan schools have accumulated debts and the diversion of textbook per capita funding for other purposes is common, leading to much higher risks of late or nonpayment, which has to be taken into account in the calculation of costs. In addition, the Ministry of Finance in Rwanda originally paid publishers in three stage payments (20 percent on signature of contract, 60 percent on delivery of advance copies and shipping documents and 20 percent on presentation of CDNs) so that publishers had considerable support in financing raw materials and manufacturing costs.[3] In Kenya, the total costs are only paid by booksellers to publishers after confirmed delivery and even then schools may continue to delay payment so that the financing costs are much higher for publishers in Kenya than in Rwanda.

The examples provided above demonstrate the considerable difficulties involved in achieving sensible direct cost comparisons between countries without a great deal of local knowledge about the individual components of national textbook costs and an understanding of textbook pricing formulae. They also demonstrate that very similar manufacturing specifications may result in very different cost profiles resulting from other, nonmanufacturing factors. The long-held development partner (DP) view—also the view of many MOEs—that unit textbook costs and TLM system costs are dominantly determined by raw materials and manufacturing costs is clearly incorrect.

Table 3.1 also demonstrates that, although Namibia has the highest Grade 1 textbook unit costs, it has the lowest projected annual amortized Grade 1 costs because it opts for a TPR of 2:1 (rather than the more typical and frequently optimistic 1:1 of the other surveyed countries) and specifies a five-year classroom life, although it is doubtful if this extended book life often will be achieved. It has only recently been specified as a policy (2010). A 2010 Textbook Procurement Baseline Study stated that

> one quarter of the Key Informants at the school level indicated that textbooks generally lasted for more than three years, but less than five years; while another quarter felt that textbooks generally last for more than four years but less than five years. One sixth of the respondents indicated that textbooks generally lasted for more than five years. Only five percent of the respondents felt that textbooks lasted for less than one year. This could be explained by poor technical specifications, due to a lack of vetting… when it comes to obtaining Approved Booklist status. The Baseline Study found that more than two-thirds of the Focus Groups at school level were not happy with the durability of textbooks. They felt that the binding of most textbooks was inferior and that covers of textbooks were not strong enough. Key Informants acknowledged that learners tend not to handle textbooks well, but also emphasized that some textbooks did not last because of poor binding and inferior materials used for textbook covers. (GOPA Consultants 2010)

The impact of curriculum design on textbook system costs is clearly seen in the considerable variations in the numbers of required textbooks in Grade 1, varying from nine required subject textbooks in Burundi down to just two textbooks in Chad, which nevertheless has the highest annual amortized costs because of highly specified textbooks with high unit costs, a 1:1 TPR and a one-year classroom book life assumption. These significant differences are perpetuated through other grade levels with Grade 6 curriculum design requiring 10 textbooks in Burundi but only four in Mali; in Grade 8 Burundi specifies 15 textbooks whereas Chad specifies only five; and in Grade 11 Burundi's 16-textbook requirement contrasts with Côte d'Ivoire's six-textbook specification.

Other significant differences in national policies that affect the costs of provision are in the assumed classroom life, which in Grade 1 is five years in Namibia and four years in Kenya and Rwanda but only one year in Côte d'Ivoire and Chad, so that cost amortization is not a possibility in these two countries. Some textbook unit costs (Kenya, Malawi secondary, Namibia, and Rwanda) include the costs of distribution to schools, whereas other countries do not include the costs of distribution. Although the target TPR are consistently specified as 1:1 these ratios are rarely achieved in practice. However, in upper grades, in order to reduce the TLM system costs, some countries, such as Côte d'Ivoire and Namibia specify TPRs ranging from 2:1 to 5:1.

The result of these different national policy approaches is that the annual amortized per student cost of provision at Grade 1 varies from US$2.25 per student per year in Namibia up to US$9.00 per student per year in Côte d'Ivoire and US$10.00 per year in Chad—a difference in per student annual financing costs of more than 400 percent. Table 3.5, below, provides the average, maximum, and minimum unit textbook costs for Grades 1, 6, 8, and 11 based on the nine countries that have returned survey questionnaires.

It is important to note that unit textbook costs, while important, are not the determining factor in the annual amortized costs of textbook provision. Thus, in Grade 11 Namibia has the most expensive average unit textbook cost but does not have the highest system provision costs because of a modest number of required textbooks, a long target classroom book life, and a 1:2 TPR. The annual amortized costs of Grade 1 textbook provision in Kenya are approximately three times higher than in Rwanda because the curriculum design requires eight textbooks per student in Kenya but only four textbooks per student in Rwanda and the unit cost of textbooks is higher in Kenya than in Rwanda (see above).

Table 3.5 demonstrates that Namibia consistently has the most expensive textbooks in terms of unit costs, but table 3.6 shows that it is not the country with the highest annual amortized textbook costs per student because of policy decisions that limit the number of textbooks specified by the curriculum, long book life targets, and reduced TPRs. A comparison between tables 3.5 and 3.6

Table 3.5 Median, Maximum, and Minimum Unit Textbook Costs

Country	Median unit cost	Maximum unit cost	Minimum unit cost
Grade 1	3.75	7.50 (Namibia)	0.75 (Madagascar)
Grade 6	3.75	7.50 (Namibia)	0.75 (Madagascar)
Grade 8	8.00	15.00 (Namibia)	1.00 (Burundi)
Grade 11	8.00	15.00 (Namibia & Rwanda)	1.00 (Burundi)

Table 3.6 Average Annual Amortized Maximum and Minimum Costs of Provision

Country	Median cost	Maximum annual amortized cost (US$)	Minimum annual amortized cost (US$)
Grade 1	6.13	10.00 (Chad)	2.25 (Namibia)
Grade 6	8.50	14.00 (Côte d'Ivoire)	3.00 (Madagascar)
Grade 8	10.88	18.00 (Mali)	3.75 (Burundi)
Grade 11	13.50	24.00 (Rwanda)	3.00 (Côte d'Ivoire)

Table 3.7 Median Amortized Costs per Student of TLM Provision

Country	Textbooks	Dictionaries	Atlases	Readers	Total
Grade 1	6.13	0.26	0.11	3.29	9.79
Grade 6	8.50	0.30	0.30	2.90	12.00
Grade 8	10.88	0.67	0.91	5.90	18.36
Grade 11	13.50	1.30	1.20	n.a.	16.00

Note: n.a. = no data available; TLM = teaching and learning materials.

strongly suggests that TLM policy reforms aimed to achieve affordable, sustainable, and effective TLM provision should focus more on annual amortized system costs per student rather than on unit textbook costs. Similarly, the dominant DP and government focus on raw materials and manufacturing costs is a clear dead end in terms of reform policies because it is based on a lack of understanding of the system cost components.

Details of atlas, dictionary, and reader costs are provided in appendix A. However, it is noticeable that only the three anglophone countries specify atlases and dictionaries as required TLMs, but the annual amortized cost per student is low because long classroom book life is specified and the supply ratios per student are quite high, varying between 1:5 and 1:10. In order to maintain costs at an acceptable level the policy in these three countries is to ensure small class sets of atlases and dictionaries that can serve as reference materials and as the focus of small group work. Readers are specified by seven out of the nine surveyed countries—usually at the ratio of one or two readers per enrolled student. But some countries do not have policies concerning production specifications and thus realistic book life expectations. None of the countries surveyed specifies the provision of reading books at upper secondary level.

Based on the data provided by the surveyed countries, table 3.7 provides the median annual amortized costs of textbook, atlas, dictionary, and reader provision for Grades 1, 6, 8, and 11 for the surveyed countries that provided questionnaire returns. Bearing in mind the comments above on the problems associated with pricing and supply, it is likely that these average costs could be significantly reduced with better planning and more realistic policies.

From the above analysis it is suggested that average annual amortized costs per student of textbook provision should rarely be higher than US$6 for primary or US$10 at secondary level except where enrollments are very small or are fractionalized by multiple LoIs. These costs would include all costs of supply including distribution to individual schools but would also require sensible curriculum decisions and supply assumptions. In many cases annual amortized costs per student could be even lower if the right policy decisions are in place.

Because of the importance of achieving effective literacy and a lifelong reading habit, investments in the provision of reading books to all grades should be a much higher priority.

Sources of Textbooks for Primary and Secondary Levels

Table 3.8, below, provides details of the sources of authorship, publishing, manufacturing, and raw materials in the surveyed countries. This demonstrates the progress made in the last few years in the development of local authorship and publishing capacity with most countries now having at least some capacity to author and publish locally at least some of their required textbooks, teachers' guides, and readers, particularly at primary level. Regional sources of authorship and publishing tend to be limited to Eastern Africa, where Kenyan and Ugandan publishers have progressed to publishing outside their own borders, and to Southern Africa, where South Africa provides some publishing for neighboring countries. Regional publishing has developed less in anglophone West Africa but has developed in francophone Africa as a result of Conference of Ministers of Education Using French as a Language of Instruction (CONFEMEN) regional curricula. The most common pattern outside the regional publishing centers mentioned above tends to be a combination of local and international sources although in anglophone Africa international multinationals are not as prominent now as they were ten or even five years ago.

There is more local manufacturing now than in the past although the capacity, reliability, and cost of some of the local manufacturing sources are probably still not on a par with international sources; but the growth of local publishing through local companies that do not have a knowledge of offshore manufacturing sources has tended to support local or at least regional manufacturing. Raw materials are still sourced dominantly from overseas although often via local or regional middlemen rather than direct from the mills. This is so even in countries where good local printing facilities exist (for example, Nigeria) and is a result of higher prices and perceived lower quality, uncertain capacity, and lack of reliable delivery.[4]

Sources of Textbook Financing for Primary and Secondary Levels

There are five basic modalities for providing textbook funding. These are

- Free government supply to schools;
- School purchasing or ordering with government funding;
- Parent purchase;
- Textbook rental fees paid by parents; and
- Government provision of limited free safety net supplies with parents responsible for additional supplies.

Table 3.8 Sources of Authorship, Publishing, Manufacturing, and Raw Materials for Grades 1, 6, 8, and 11

Country	Authorship/publishing			Manufacturing			Raw materials		
	Local	Regional	International	Local	Regional	International	Local	Regional	International
Benin	All grades	Secondary	Secondary	All grades	Secondary	Secondary	n.a.	n.a.	All grades
Burundi	All grades	n.a.	All grades	n.a.	n.a.	All grades	n.a.	n.a.	All grades
Côte d'Ivoire	All grades	n.a.	All grades	Primary	n.a.	All grades	n.a.	n.a.	All grades
Kenya	All grades	n.a.	Secondary	All grades	n.a.	n.a.	n.a.	n.a.	All grades
Madagascar	Primary & Junior Secondary	Upper Primary & Secondary	Secondary	All grades	n.a.	All grades	n.a.	n.a.	All grades
Mali	All grades	n.a.	n.a.	All grades	n.a.	n.a.	n.a.	n.a.	All grades
Namibia	All grades	Upper Primary & Secondary	n.a.	n.a.	Upper Primary & Secondary	n.a.	n.a.	All grades	All grades
Nigeria	All grades		Upper Secondary	Some Primary		Primary/Secondary	n.a.	n.a.	All grades
Rwanda	Primary & Junior Secondary	All grades	All grades		All grades	All grades	n.a.	n.a.	All grades
Sierra Leone		Al grades	All grades	n.a.	n.a.	All grades	n.a.	n.a.	All grades
Chad	Secondary		All grades	n.a.	n.a.	All grades	n.a.	n.a.	All grades

Note: n.a. = not applicable.

Table 3.9, below, provides a summary of the different types of funding used by the surveyed countries at different grade levels. There is no example of parent-funded textbook rental fees among the 11 surveyed countries.[5] In lower and upper primary, seven out of 11 countries have free textbooks provided by governments, in two countries governments provide per capita purchasing power budgets to schools for school ordering, and in the remaining two countries the government provides limited safety net supplies of textbooks and parents are encouraged to purchase additional copies. At secondary level, seven out of 11 countries reported some level of parent purchase for textbooks.

Table 3.10, below, provides national responses on the reliability and adequacy of government-funded textbook budgets. Only five out of 11 countries consider that funding for textbooks is adequate, regular, and predictable; six countries characterized government funding as inadequate, unreliable, and unpredictable. Only four out of 11 countries reported that funding for readers was adequate, regular, and predictable. However, there is widespread agreement that funding for school and classroom libraries and other supplementary TLMs is completely inadequate.

Types of Supply

Table 3.11, below, provides data on the different types of supply operational in the surveyed countries. At primary level, five out of the 11 surveyed countries operated monopolistic textbook supply systems with one compulsory textbook on offer per subject and grade level. Five countries operated limited competition systems where schools were free to select from MOE-approved lists of competing textbooks financed by school-based per capita purchasing power budgets. One country operated free and open competition with no approved lists.

At secondary level the number of monopolistic systems had declined to three and there was an increase in the number of countries operating open competition

Table 3.9 Types of Textbook Funding

Country	Grade 1	Grade 6	Grade 8	Grade 11
Benin	S	S	P	P
Burundi	S	S	S	S
Côte d'Ivoire	F	F	P	P
Kenya	C	C	C P	C P
Madagascar	F	F	P	P
Mali	F	F	F	F
Namibia	F	F	F	F
Nigeria	F	F	F/P/C	F/P/C
Rwanda	C	C	C	C
Sierra Leone	F	F	F/P	F/P
Chad	F	F	P	P

Note: F = Free government supply to schools; C = purchased by schools with government funding; P = parent purchase; R = textbook rental fee paid by parents; S = government provides limited free safety net supplies.

Table 3.10 Adequacy, Regularity, and Predictability of Government TLM Budgets

Country	Textbooks			Readers			Libraries			Other TLM		
	Adequate	Regular	Predictable	Adequate	Regular	Predictable	Adequate	Regular	Predictable	Adequate	Regular	Predictable
Benin	No	Yes	Yes	No	Yes	Yes	No	No	No	No	No	No
Burundi	No	No	No	No	No	No	No	No	No	No	No	No
Côte d'Ivoire	Yes	No	No	Yes	No	No	No	No	No	No	No	No
Kenya	No	No	No	No	No	No	No	No	No	No	No	No
Madagascar	No	No	No	No	No	No	No	No	No	No	No	No
Mali	No	No	Yes	No	No	Yes	No	No	Yes	No	No	Yes
Namibia	Yes	No	No	Yes	No	No	No	No	No	No	No	No
Nigeria[a]	Yes	Yes	Yes	No	No	No	No	No	No	No	No	No
Rwanda	Yes	Yes	Yes	Yes	Yes	Yes	No	No	No	No	No	No
Sierra Leone[b]	Yes	Yes	n.a.	Yes	No	No	No	No	No	No	No	No
Chad	No	Yes	Yes	No	Yes	Yes	No	Yes	Yes	No	Yes	Yes

Source: Author's survey.
Note: n.a. = no data available; TLM = teaching and learning materials.
a. Textbook policies vary from state to state in Nigeria thus a range of policies and funding systems can apply.
b. Some countries are heavily dependent on donor funding for TLM supplies. Thus regularity and predictability of funding can be difficult to judge.

Table 3.11 Types of Textbook Supply

Country	Grade 1	Grade 6	Grade 8	Grade 11
Benin	M	M	OC	OC
Burundi	M	M	M	M
Côte d'Ivoire	LC	LC	LC	LC
Kenya	LC	LC	LC	LC
Madagascar	M	M	n.a.	n.a.
Mali	OC	OC	OC	OC
Namibia	LC	LC	LC	LC
Nigeria	M/LC/OC	M/LC/OC	M/LC/OC	M/LC/OC
Rwanda	LC	LC	LC	LC
Sierra Leone	M	M	M	M
Chad	M	M	M	M

Note: n.a. = no data available; M = Monopoly textbook supply; LC = limited competition, usually based on school choice from an MOE list of approved textbooks; OC = Open Competition where schools can choose from any available textbook.

presumably because these countries could not afford to support secondary textbook provision and therefore opted out of any form of system control—including control over quality of content and production standards and control over prices.

Textbook Availability

Eight out of nine surveyed countries reported that there were substantial differences between urban, rural, and remote textbook availability. These differences are the result of inadequate financing and inefficient distribution. Table 3.12 provides a summary of estimated TPRs in the nine surveyed countries. These data, although only averages, confirm significantly different levels of textbook supply between urban, rural, and remote schools in most of the surveyed countries. It should be noted that individual textbook availability surveys in some countries reveal much worse ratios than those listed in table 3.9, above. Thus, from 1997 up to 2006 the Government of Rwanda and different development partners provided very substantial funding to ensure the provision of textbooks to Rwandan primary schools. There was an assumption both in the Rwandan Ministry of Education (MINEDUC) and among development partners that this funding had resulted in adequate levels of textbook provision (1:2 ratios) to all primary schools, although it was recognized that there were ongoing problems in the financing and provision of textbooks and teachers' guides to secondary schools.

However, a research study based on urban, rural, and remote schools in 20 out of 30 districts conducted at the request of MINEDUC in late 2007 (Umubeyi and Bontoux 2007) found that textbook availability in surveyed primary schools, despite the high levels of funding, was very poor indeed, universally inequitable, and very far away from the ratios assumed by government and DPs. Table 3.13, below, illustrates the real average TPRs discovered in the surveyed schools.

Table 3.12 Estimated Primary TPRs in Urban, Rural, and Remote Locations

Country	Urban	Rural	Remote
Benin	1:10	1:10	1:10
Burundi	2:3	1:3	1:10
Côte d'Ivoire	1:1	1:1	n.a.
Kenya	1:2	1:3	1:5
Madagascar	n.a.	n.a.	n.a.
Mali	n.a.	n.a.	n.a.
Namibia	1:5	1:10	1:15
Rwanda	1:3	1:3	1:3
Chad	n.a.	n.a.	n.a.

Note: n.a. = no data available; TPR = textbook–pupil ratio.

Table 3.13 Primary Textbook Availability in Rwanda, 2007

	TPR (1 textbook per ... pupils)					
	P1	P2	P3	P4	P5	P6
English	42	59	21	34	16	18
French	20	15	25	n.a.	n.a.	n.a.[a]
Kinyarwanda	143	103	83	55	74	45
STE	265	46	50	15	13	5
Math	180	141	135	112	117	69
Social Studies	123	93	81	51	47	20

Source: Umubeyi and Bontoux (2007).
Note: n.a. = no data available; P = primary grade. TPR = textbook–pupil ratio.
a. French language textbooks had been evaluated and selected but had not been distributed to schools at the time of the survey.

These widespread shortages of textbooks in Rwandan primary schools occurred despite major efforts to achieve adequate levels of provision by MINEDUC and the development partners. The study concluded that there was no possibility of reaching the target 1:1 ratio of textbooks to primary school students in the near future.

The survey revealed a combination of causes for the shortages:

- Poor planning based on lack of good information about schools, enrollments, school TLM inventories, and school needs
- Poor TLM system management
- Funds-rather than needs-based procurement resulting from a lack of any clear idea of how much funding was required to achieve and maintain government supply targets
- Inefficient storage, distribution, and delivery through districts to schools
- Lack of motivation at central and district level to get TLMs to schools

- High levels of loss and damage of TLMs in schools
- Ineffective monitoring of stocks, inventories, management, and maintenance by government
- Ineffective communication with and information to schools

The scale of the gap between MINEDUC and DP expectations and school realities was so great that government and DPs put in hand a major program of TLM system reform which has been maintained so far up to 2013.

Another example of TPR surveying in Namibia (Bontoux 2008) provides the following more revealing snapshot of textbook availability in the classrooms than is usually possible when only average estimated figures are used:

> According to the number of textbooks procured and distributed over the past years the overall student/textbook ratio in Namibian schools should stand at about 1 textbook per 1 or 2 students on average. However, the field research revealed major deviations from this theoretical standard and the table below indicates that there are widespread current shortages of textbooks in Namibian primary schools, despite the major efforts of [the Government of the Republic of Namibia] and their development partners to address and resolve this issue over the past few years:
>
> Actual Observed Student/Textbook Ratios in 13 Surveyed Primary Schools (2008)

Subjects/textbooks	Grades						
	1	2	3	4	5	6	7
English	2	2	1	2	5	6	4
Local language	2	16	2	4		3	2
Math	62	1	1	2	2	10	1
Natural science				2	7	3	4
Agriculture					3	11	4
Environmental science	3	1	1	2			
Social studies				3	9	7	22

- 13 primary schools were surveyed; none had any central records system in place. So these figures have to be taken with some caution, since the average levels are usually computed from 3 to 6 schools, the ones whose teachers could actually remember the ratios.
- Most of the ratios in the table above would have been better had some schools not lacked all textbooks in some subjects (there was no subject or grade level without serious textbook shortages in any of the surveyed schools, which suggests that distribution inequity is probably a significant problem). Furthermore, it is likely that schools whose teachers could not remember how many books they had per level per subject had actually very little, if any at all. These schools are considered as neutral mathematical factors in the computing of the average whereas they would probably have shifted the balance towards worse ratios. This amounts to giving them, to say the least, the benefit of the doubt.

According to the survey results, core textbooks often achieve ratios of between 1:1 and 1:4. But inequities in the distribution system leave whole streams in some schools without any textbooks at all, which is the explanation for the average ratios revealed by the table. It is also clear that most Namibian teachers have become accustomed to teaching without textbooks, despite the very substantial investments made in textbook procurement and supply over the past few years. (Bontoux 2008)

The GOPA Baseline Study (GOPA Consultants 2010) sent researchers to physically count the number of books in a representative sample of 150 schools (10 percent of the country's total). It concluded:

> Except for grades 10–12, the (findings) indicate that the average number of learners sharing a textbook in a subject in a particular grade ranged between 0.9 and 2.3, counting all textbooks, that is, including those redundant books which should no longer be used. While these values are better than what is commonly perceived, it must be kept in mind that these are average values. Some schools will have more books than they require, while in other schools many learners are sharing textbooks.
>
> Counting only approved books, the average ratios between learners and books indicated that average supply of approved books is not adequate for providing an approved textbook to each learner in Grades 1 through 9. The situation is better in grades 10 and 12, the grades in which learners sit for the public examinations.

Poor availability is probably not caused by high prices because textbooks are supplied free to schools and students, although the high prices create an expensive TLM supply system and stretch available financing budgets. It is rather the distribution system that causes the problem.

A Summary of Key Issues

- Textbook manufacturing cost or even textbook retail prices are not the main determining factors in the system costs of textbook provision. Other factors that need to be taken into consideration include the number of required compulsory textbook titles, the target classroom book life, annual average levels of loss and damage, and the target TPR. It is the combination of these factors that determines the costs of system provision.
- National curriculum development has a profound impact on the national costs of textbook provision by determining the number of required textbook titles; and yet the cost implications of curriculum design are almost never taken into account in determining textbook provision policies.
- Readers are mostly included in TLM provision policies but are often not specified in ways that make them easy to cost; nor are they regularly funded or supplied.
- Atlases, dictionaries, and other forms of TLM, including teachers' aids, are rarely specified as part of the Minimum Teaching and Learning Materials Profile.

- There are large differentials between countries in textbook prices, provision policies and thus in the annual amortized per student costs of provision. It seems clear that the basic facts concerning the costing of textbook provision systems are not known to a majority of countries or to a majority of development partners and that most textbook provision systems are created without adequate professional advice.
- Primary textbooks are dominantly funded by the state even though budgets are widely considered to be inadequate, irregular, and unpredictable.
- In most cases neither governments nor DPs have accurate information on how much funding is required annually to achieve and maintain TLM provision targets.
- Secondary textbooks are more widely subject to parental contributions even though a majority of parents probably cannot afford the costs of the specified textbooks and this has a clear impact on the quality of education that can be achieved.
- Some textbook evaluation and approval systems do not include price as a factor in evaluation. Nor do they specify and test for minimum physical production standards, which are critical in determining long book life and thus maximum system cost amortization. Textbook evaluation and approval systems are in need of upgrading in many countries so that proper control can be exercised over system input costs.
- There has been an improvement in national authorship and publishing capacity and in local manufacturing, although it is likely that it is still often inferior in quality, capacity, reliability, and cost in comparison with international printing centers.

Notes

1. Cost of one textbook set = No of required titles × average unit textbook cost.
2. According to the findings of Umubeyi and Bontoux (2007) "The annual attrition rate hovers between 10 and 20%, chiefly because of wear and tear, but also due to theft." Textbook distribution is so haphazard that schools that do get books just tend to store them or use them very sparsely. So their life expectancy should not be that bad (three to four years).
3. This will be changed from 2014 when 100 percent of invoiced costs will be paid only on presentation of CDNs, thus significantly increasing publishers' financing costs and eventually costs to the MOE.
4. An informed Nigerian publishing source estimates that 70 percent of Nigerian textbook production is outsourced to international printing locations.
5. Lesotho historically operated a successful textbook rental scheme for primary school textbooks from 1982 up to 2005 and has developed a successful rental scheme for junior secondary textbooks since 2005.

References

Bontoux, V. 2008. *Mission Report on Namibia Textbook Reform Component*. Windhoek: Millennium Challenge Corporation (MCC) for Ministry of Education.

GOPA Consultants. 2010. *Namibia Textbook Procurement Baseline Study*. Homburg, Germany: GOPA.

Umubeyi, M., and V. Bontoux. 2007. *Research Study into Primary Textbook Availability in Rwanda*. Windsor, United Kingdom: IE Partners, funded by DFID on behalf of MINEDUC.

PART 2

A Review of the Components of the Textbook Chain

CHAPTER 4

Literacy, Curricula, Teaching and Learning Materials, Requirements, and System Costs

The Crisis of Literacy and Numeracy in Sub-Saharan Africa

This section covers literacy and numeracy achievement in Sub-Saharan Africa (SSA) in the language of instruction (LOI) (that is, not necessarily in English or French).

At a regional conference on Education for All for Sub-Saharan Africa, held in Johannesburg in December 1999, it was concluded that what was provided was

> poor and the curricula often irrelevant to the needs of the learners and of social, cultural and economic development ... education planning and management capacity ... remain largely underdeveloped ... only a small proportion of children are reaching the minimum required competencies and our education systems are not performing to the standards we expect of them. (UNESCO 2000, 26–28)

Six years later the 2005 Education for All (EFA) Global Monitoring Report (UNESCO 2004) reported that

> the quality of education systems is failing children in many parts of the world and could prevent many countries from achieving EFA by the target date of 2015. More children are going to school than ever before, but many drop out before grade 5 of primary school or graduate from primary school without even achieving a minimum set of cognitive skills.

Since 1992 UNESCO has attempted to monitor learning outcomes through measuring pupil performance in many countries, more than half of them in Africa. The vehicle for this measurement exercise has been the Monitoring Learning Achievement program (MLA) carried out in conjunction with United Nations Children's Fund (UNICEF). MLA measures performance in three areas: numeracy, literacy, and life skills (the latter consisting of health, civics and environment, science and technology). MLA was designed to test against a lower and a higher benchmark: MML (Minimum Mastery Learning) and DML

(Desired Mastery Learning). MML was defined as achieving at least 50 percent correct scores, the latter as achieving at least 70 percent correct scores. The Jomtien conference agreed that an acceptable target should be 80 percent of pupils achieving the MML for all three areas.[1]

African countries have performed very poorly in the MLA surveys, and SSA countries have performed particularly poorly (see table 4.1, below). Around one half of all pupils in participating SSA countries failed to achieve the MML.[2] The results of the National Assessment of Primary Education (NAPE) tests in Uganda, conducted by the Ugandan National Examinations Board (UNEB 2003) were particularly revealing:

> The NAPE 2003 report rated 34.3% of children in P3 as "proficient in language"; however approximately 40.9% remained "inadequate." The 2003 report on standards in P3 and P6 came to the conclusion that 67.6% of children in P6 were "inadequate" in performance and only 20% could be described as "proficient" (National Assessment of Progress in Education 2003). By the time the same children reach P7 the actual PLE pass rate is 80%. There may seem to be a contradiction between the low achievement rates recorded in Primary 6 and the high pass rates achieved a year later in the Primary Leaving Exam. In fact, this differential is related more to what is being tested and how the grades are aggregated, rather than any significant improvement in basic skills between P6 and P7. Firstly the PLE examinations test factual knowledge, whereas the NAPE assessment tests are measuring competencies and skills. Secondly the PLE results include an element of norm referencing, thus ensuring a reasonable percentage pass whatever the overall standards.... This does not take into account the percentage of students that fail to complete seven years of primary education. Of the 2,159,850 students who entered P1 in 1997 only 22.5%, (i.e., less than a quarter) were still in school when that cohort entered Primary 7 (Uganda MoES 2003). However, if only 20% of P6 students are proficient in language and only 20% of the P1 cohort survives to P7 then it is easily calculated that only around 4% of the Primary 1 cohort achieve language proficiency by the end of P6.... While there are a wide variety of reasons for this drop-out rate, the failure to learn to read and write to an adequate standard within the first two or three years of primary schooling is probably a very important reason.... A child who cannot read or write in any language after three years of schooling is unlikely to be highly motivated to continue with school and poorer parents are unlikely to feel that the costs of education are worth the results. (Read and Hicks 2004)

The lack of progress in resolving literacy problems is illustrated also by a succession of literacy research studies in Ghana undertaken in the decade from 2001 to 2010. In 2001 it was noted that education in Ghana was confronted with the massive problem of poor quality as attested by *abysmal national criterion-referenced test scores* from 1992 through 1996 (N'tchougan-Sonou 2001). In 2003, Kraft commented that

> There can be no question that the fundamental problem still facing Ghanaian schools ... remains basic literacy skills in English or Ghanaian languages.

Lipson and Wixson (2004) noted that

> There is a crisis of reading achievement in public schools in Ghana. Reading achievement levels as measured by the Criterion Referenced Tests (CRT 2000) indicate that fewer than 10% of school children in P6 are able to read with grade level mastery.

In 2008 a National Education Assessment (NEA) concluded that only 16.4 percent of P3 students and only 23.6 percent of P6 students in Ghana were proficient in English.

Kellaghan and Greaney compared international data and data from national public examinations unfavorably:

> Data from public examinations and national assessments may reveal considerable discrepancies. Concern has been expressed in Senegal over inconsistencies between students' scores on PASEC tests and teachers' promotional practices. Some students who did relatively well on PASEC were not promoted, while others who did relatively poorly were.... There would also appear to be differences between the judgments made on the basis of performance on public examinations ... and judgments based on performance in national assessments. In Lesotho, where four out of five pupils passed the primary certificate examination, less than one in six scored at the minimum level of mastery in a national assessment of literacy. In Malawi, close to four out of five pupils passed the primary certificate examination, but only one in five achieved minimum mastery in a national assessment. (Kellaghan and Greaney 2003)

Similar literacy and numeracy results are also evident in francophone SSA countries.

EFA country reports provide a useful survey of progress on learning achievement in most SSA countries. Table 4.2 provides a comparison of pupil's average achievement scores in a sample of SSA countries, which does not indicate the wide differentials between countries revealed in Table 4.1. The 2005 EFA Global Report (UNESCO 2004) got behind the poor levels of literacy and

Table 4.1 Percentage of Grade 4 Pupils Who Attained the Minimum (MML) and Desirable (DML) Levels of Mastery Learning

Country	Combined		Literacy		Numeracy		Life skills	
	MML	DML	MML	DML	MML	DML	MML	DML
Botswana	57.8	8.7	46.2	6.0	55.4	5.4	71.8	14.9
Madagascar	66.1	11.7	56.9	20.6	34.4	5.6	97.3	60.3
Malawi	54.9	3.0	15.3	1.4	30.7	1.4	95.4	69.4
Mali	54.4	7.3	50.4	13.1	37.9	6.2	69.8	23.7
Mauntius	70.3	24.1	77.6	35.4	70.3	26.4	71.6	32.4
Niger	25.6	2.0	39.3	3.6	15.3	5.7	44.9	7.0
Senegal	31.2	2.0	45.6	6.7	22.9	3.0	36.3	7.0
Uganda	54.4	14.4	64.3	23.3	41.9	10.2	78.8	51.1
Zambia	31.6	5.6	37.8	7.3	19.9	4.4	49.0	26.1

Source: Chinapah 2000. Used with permission from UNESCO.

Table 4.2 Estimated Average Score of Pupils' Achievement in a Sample of African Countries

Country	MLA equivalent level of achivement	Country	MLA equivalent level of achivement
South Africa	49.6	Mauritius	64.1
Botswana	51.7	Namibia	48.1
Burkina faso	52.7	Niger	40.8
Cameroom	60.0	Uganda	58.0
Côte d'Ivoire	51.3	Senegal	42.5
Gambia	40.4	Togo	52.1
Guinea	51.6	Zanzibar	41.7
Kenya	68.8	Zambia	43.3
Madagascar	58.4	Zimbabwe	57.7
Malawi	48.5		
Mali	50.8	**Average**	**51.6**

Source: Mingat 2000.[3] Used with permission from the Association for the Development of Education in Africa.
Note: MLA = Monitoring Learning Achievement.

numeracy and attempted to draw conclusions by comparing the results with other factors and inputs. For example, the Report made telling comparisons between survival rates in primary school and minimum mastery levels. It shows that, while net enrollment ratios (NERs) can be quite high, only a small proportion of school leavers have achieved minimum mastery levels as defined by their own national governments. Thus, for example, in Malawi, where about 90 percent of children attended primary school in the mid-1990s, only about 30 percent stayed in school to Grade 5, and as few as seven percent achieved the minimum acceptable reading standards in Grade 6. The fact that the NER in Malawi at the time was close to 70 percent seems rather irrelevant to whether the average child was benefiting in a minimally acceptable way from attending primary school. Although Malawi is something of an extreme case, on average for the countries shown, fewer than one-third of children achieved minimum mastery levels in Grades 4 to 6, although the average NER for the countries concerned was 65 percent.

Attempts to relate performance levels to input levels are necessarily limited. International surveys and research cannot easily take account of the *quality* of the inputs and processes—in particular, curriculum relevance and suitability, the impact of content overloading, textbook and other teaching and learning materials (TLM) quality, availability and usage, teacher quality, training, attendance and actual contact hours, the availability of basic facilities such as power and adequate storage, and the distances that students may have to travel to reach school, and so on, which vary very widely throughout the continent and within individual countries. School attendance is also often seasonal with much lower levels of attendance in the rainy season, particularly in hilly rural areas. Whatever the causal factors there is widespread agreement that literacy and subsequent learning achievement in many schools in many SSA countries is unacceptably low and reflects badly on the significant investments in primary education throughout the subcontinent. This is an issue of growing priority for many governments and donors.

Constraints on Improved Literacy and Numeracy Performance in SSA

Any discussion of the poor literacy levels in primary schools in SSA must look at the approaches to the teaching of reading. While this is a controversial area in developed countries as well as developing countries (see for example the ongoing acrimonious debate in developed countries between phonics supporters and whole language supporters), there is growing evidence that the teaching of reading in many SSA countries has been neglected. O'Sullivan (2003) comments that at an international level there is a trend towards an eclectic approach to teaching reading in which the teacher uses whatever strategies are most effective in the development of reading skills. O'Sullivan also notes the importance of oral work as the basis for literacy, especially in second language (L2) contexts. Oral fluency provides the basis for recognizing words whether in a sight reading approach or a phonic-based approach. However, throughout SSA the concept of the oral approach in early primary tends to mean rote learning, where the text is no more than a stimulus for recall. One of the leading researchers on teaching reading in developing countries, Eddie Williams, in 1993 commented on the dominant approach to teaching reading in SSA as encouraging rote reading or "barking at print", a method in which the teacher reads each sentence of a text and the pupils repeat it a number of times.

As the baseline for her own research in Namibia, O'Sullivan tested 204 pupils and found that 88 percent were unable to read a text taken from one year below their grade. They were however far better at reading the text from the current reading book, and in fact "read" to the researcher without even looking at the text. O'Sullivan also found that among teachers *no attention was paid to the presentation of meaning and checking understanding.*

One of the causes for poor approaches to teaching reading is that teachers in lower grades often have little or no training in teaching literacy (as opposed to teaching language). In Malawi the pre-service teacher training program that included literacy training was replaced by the Malawi Integrated In-Service Teacher Education Programme (MIITEP) as a short duration crash course in upgrading practicing unqualified teachers while in Zimbabwe the Infant Teacher Training Programme for Grades 1 to 3 was suspended completely from 1980 to 1988. Even where teachers have followed a pre-service training program, there may be no component on teaching reading and writing (for example, in Uganda, the teaching of reading skills to pre-service teachers in training appears to have been omitted from the teacher training syllabus by accident when the Grade 1 Teacher Training Certificate was abolished in the early 1990s. It appears, as a result, that no qualified primary teachers received specific training in teaching literacy in Uganda for at least 15 years. The Uganda Primary Curriculum Review (2004) commented that

> a large part of the (literacy) problem was that reading, writing, listening and speaking were not allocated sufficient time ... and that literacy and numeracy teaching skills in lower primary grades were seriously inadequate. Because students failed to develop early literacy they performed poorly in all curriculum subjects and failure to perform led directly to loss of interest by both parents and students with consequent high drop-out rates. (Read and Hicks 2004)

Benavot and Gad (2004) reviewed studies of actual teacher–pupil contact time carried out in Africa and in other developing countries, and found that on average some 20 percent of scheduled contact time was lost through teacher absenteeism. A Kenya study reported that "in one region of Kenya, teachers were absent from school 28 percent of the time, and absent from class (but in school) a further 12 percent of the time" (Glewwe, Kremer, and Moulin 1999). The Uganda Primary Curriculum Review also commented on the issues of teacher absenteeism and reduced teacher-student contact hours.

> Teacher absenteeism and the doubling-up of classes to create additional free time for teachers were the most obvious causes of large class sizes in many schools. Contact hours in many schools were much lower than the contact hours assumed by the curriculum designers. Up to one third of official contact hours might be lost in many schools. Reduced contact hours have an obvious impact on the ability of schools to deliver curriculum objectives. (Read and Hicks 2004)

In a study of 120 schools in rural Ghana, it was reported that, on average, teachers attended schools four days a week, implying that 5.5 instructional hours were lost each week. When researchers visited sampled Ghanaian schools, almost one-fifth (19.4 percent) of the teachers were absent (EARC 2005). The Educational Assessment and Research Center (EARC) study in Ghana found that, in addition to the 20 percent of primary teachers who were absent on the survey day, another 29 percent were late in arriving at school. The report estimated that, as a result of teacher absenteeism and tardiness, actual pupil-teacher interaction time was only 70 percent of the time specified by the curriculum. By 2010 a World Bank report suggested that contact hours were even worse than this.

> Together, teacher absenteeism, poor ToT and the short duration of the school year can result in the loss of as much as 50–60 percent of teaching time, clearly making this a key constraint to learning. (AFTED 2010)

The main reasons for this level of absenteeism were given as (a) lack of supervision; (b) sickness or medical care; (c) collection of salary at a bank located at a distance; (d) frequent funeral attendances; (e) long travel distances to school; (f) religious practices (for instance, Friday prayers among Muslim teachers); (g) schools lacking facilities, especially sanitation, toilets, and potable water; (h) schools located far from lorry or bus stations and healthcare facilities; (i) rural teachers supplementing their income by farming; and (j) teachers being underpaid or paid late thus forcing them to take on additional jobs to make ends meet. In addition there were frequent breaks in the normal school day when teachers were separated from students; and that down time spent disciplining students, collecting homework, and so on further reduced contact hours.

In 2013 a World Bank report on Uganda (Wane and Martin 2013) commented:

> More than 1 out of 4 (27%) of teachers in public schools were not at work. Of those who were in school, about 1 in 3 (30%) were not teaching. The result is 40% of public school classrooms with no teacher teaching. By extrapolation, the average public Primary 4 student in the North received only 50 actual days of teaching time during the school year, about 90 days fewer than her Kampala counterpart.

The wide variations in teacher–pupil contact hours illustrated above have an obvious impact on textbook design and effectiveness. Most publishers will be required to design and develop their textbooks in accordance with the national curriculum specifications and on the assumption of the official specification of contact hours in which the curriculum objectives have to be delivered. But in reality the real number of contact hours in many schools—perhaps even the majority of schools—may be 30 to 50 percent or more fewer than those assumed by the curriculum and incorporated into the basic textbook design. In the Uganda example quoted above students in the North were receiving only approximately 30 percent of the contact hours to achieve the same curriculum objectives as students in Kampala. In this situation the textbooks are potentially fatally flawed from the outset as vehicles for the achievement of required curriculum objectives. The curriculum, as provided by the textbook, either cannot be delivered in the reduced contact hours available in many schools, or has been rushed through by teachers to such an extent that a high proportion of students will have been unable to keep up and understand. This situation is made far worse when the additional difficulties of L2 LoI policies, rural schools with poor facilities and equipment, and higher levels of untrained teachers are taken into account. In almost every SSA country there are clear differences in the actual contact hours between good urban schools and under resourced rural schools and yet national curricula generally take no notice of these differences. Textbooks are written and designed to fulfil curriculum objectives on the assumption that every school will have the full expected contact hours—but for a majority of students attending a majority of schools this probably does not happen. There are alternative approaches to the provision of teaching and learning materials, which could ameliorate this situation, but to date few, if any, countries have sought to explore these alternatives.

Curriculum Design and System Costs and Effectiveness

The previous sections provided a review of the research evidence and some of the common constraints on the achievement of early literacy and enhanced student performance in SSA. The inability to achieve early literacy for a majority of primary school entrants in many SSA countries leads to high levels of dropouts and also has an impact on the quality of education achieved in higher primary grades and in secondary education. For primary curriculum designers and those responsible for developing TLM provision policies, particularly for primary schools, the following factors need to be taken into full account in the process of curriculum design:

- A high proportion of primary teachers are semitrained or untrained.
- Many primary teachers have not been trained to teach reading and writing.
- There are usually considerable differentials in both the numbers and quality of teachers between urban, rural, and remote schools.
- Many primary curricula do not provide sufficient time allocations for listening, speaking, reading, and writing in the early primary grades.
- Many teachers may not be proficient in the required LoI.
- In many countries there are too many subjects specified by the curriculum often delivered by teachers who have never been trained to teach these subjects.
- Teaching styles in many SSA classrooms discourage active pupil participation in lessons except for repetition as the basis for rote learning. The importance of active speaking and active listening as foundations to the achievement of literacy are neglected. Extreme student passivity is common in many SSA classrooms.
- Actual classroom contact hours in many schools are significantly less—sometimes grossly less—than the assumptions on which curricula content is based.
- Most primary schools are seriously short of attractive, stimulating reading materials at the right level and in the right language for fledgling and new readers.
- Many primary school teachers no longer know how to use TLMs, and even when supplies to schools are good the TLMs often are not used in class but are locked in stores.
- Most curricula are more concerned with language than with literacy.
- Where students are studying in an L2 there are additional practical barriers to literacy and upgraded student performance.

The prevalence of primary curricula with multiple subjects and overloaded content specifications not only reduces the time in early grades when students should be focusing primarily on the acquisition of literacy and numeracy via the practice of their listening, speaking, reading, and writing skills; but it also significantly increases the costs of providing TLMs to support curricula, which are demonstrated to be widely noneffective, hence the unacceptably low levels of functional literacy and numeracy in a majority of SSA countries. There is a clear and urgent need for the development of curricula, TLMs, and teaching and learning strategies, which reflect more accurately the current school realities and are more supportive of often untrained lower primary teachers working in substandard learning environments. More realistic approaches have to start with more realistic curriculum designs. There *are* examples of best practice in African primary schools where significant achievements can take place in very hostile circumstances. The Uganda Reading Pilot Project (Buchan, Hicks, and Read 2006) achieved remarkable early literacy results using alternative low-cost teaching approaches and materials.

There are also problems in the ability of teachers and students to achieve curriculum specifications in secondary education in SSA. These can be summarized as follows:

- Overloaded curriculum content
- Often too many subjects
- Lack of well-trained teachers, particularly in rural secondary schools, and common shortages of trained English language, math, and science teachers
- Teaching styles (and examinations) focused on the acquisition of facts rather than the development of skills and concepts
- The high cost of textbooks and other TLMs needed to support secondary education
- Lack of effective school libraries that would encourage students to develop the habit of reading around their subjects and thus develop research skills and the reading habit
- Lack of effective student and teacher Internet access as a basic research tool
- Lack of science facilities and equipment, which inhibits student experimentation and in many cases reduces science experiments to demonstrations by the teacher or, in the worst cases, to memorization of experiments described in textbooks.

Inadequate curriculum design is mirrored by a common inability to publicize and inform teachers about curriculum content and curriculum objectives. As an example, a recent World Bank report on Uganda (Wane and Martin 2013) concluded that

> Less than 1 in 5 (19%) of public school teachers showed mastery of the curriculum they teach.

The situation described in Uganda is common among teachers—particularly in rural and remote schools—in many other SSA countries

An example of the impact of increased curriculum subjects is provided by Tanzania (Read 2010). In 2007 the number of required textbooks in the primary curriculum was increased from six to nine,[4] which should have required a comparable and proportionate increase in the textbook grant allocated to schools. The introduction of the new primary curriculum in 2007 was accompanied by a Ministry embargo on the use of all old curriculum books. Thus, accumulated old curriculum textbook stocks were discarded but no increased financial allocation to cover the significant additional cost of restocking was provided by the Government of Tanzania (GOT).[5] This is widely reported to have seriously reduced usable textbook stocks in schools (Kimaro 2010).

The estimated national average primary textbook–pupil ratio (TPR) in Tanzania in 2000 was 1:8 averaged over all primary school subjects (World Bank 2005). By 2004, with the funding provided by the World Bank's Primary Education Development Project (PEDP), it was estimated that the national average TPR had improved to 1:4 and government and development partner (DP) targets aimed for 1:1 by 2006. This was not achieved, and since 2007 TPR have deteriorated rapidly because there has been insufficient budget allocation to cover the increased textbook costs caused by the increase in the number of required curriculum subjects. The decision to increase the number of primary subjects and the number of required textbooks and teachers' guides was taken with no consideration of the financial implications of the decision and the knock-on effect on student learning and achievement. This is not an isolated case. Few SSA countries have made the fundamental links between curriculum design, associated costs, and learning achievement.

Table 4.3, below, provides details of the Primary School Leaving Examination (PSLE) pass rates in Tanzania from 2000 up to 2009. These results show exceptional progress in student performance via PSLE pass rates from 2000 up to 2006 when TPRs were improving as a result of adequate textbook purchase grants provided to schools. The decision to increase the number of primary curriculum subjects by 50 percent and then to embargo the use of old curriculum textbooks, thus making redundant all of the accumulated textbook stocks in schools without any compensatory increase in textbook capitation grants, resulted in a significant decrease in textbook availability in schools from 2007 onwards. The impact of these decisions is illustrated in table 4.3, below.

A study in Zanzibar in 2007 commented on the locally developed primary curriculum as follows:

> The weaknesses of current curricula are seen to be (a) overloaded content requirements at all levels; (b) absence of appropriate achievement targets; (c) curriculum regularly not completed in many schools because of double shifting or operational interruptions; (d) curriculum reform is not supported by teacher preparation or textbook development; (e) secondary education curricula do not build on the skills and knowledge of the primary curriculum; (f) there is inadequate provision in the curriculum for non-academic students. (Read and Ibale 2007)

Zanzibar had very low literacy scores in MLA and South and East African Constortium for Monitoring Educational Quality (SACMEQ) assessments. It also

Table 4.3 PSLE Pass Rates, 2000–09

Year	PSLE pass rate (%)
2000	22.0
2001	25.0
2002	n.a.
2003	40.0
2004	48.0
2005	n.a.
2006	70.5
2007	54.2
2008	n.a.
2009	49.0

Note: n.a. = no data available; PSLE = Primary School Leaving Examination.

had no annual government budget line for textbooks or other TLM procurement and was entirely dependent on occasional government funding releases and DP financial support via textbook projects for its textbook supplies. And yet it specified five textbooks for P1 to P3 and eight textbooks for P4 to P7. Thus, textbook provision, driven by the curriculum design, was unaffordable in Zanzibar without DP support; no attention had been paid by either government or DPs to cost-reduction strategies that would enable curriculum objectives to be achieved and sustained.

The proliferation of curriculum subjects, each frequently requiring an accompanying textbook (and increasingly a teachers' guide as well) is not the only system-related cost escalator. The over specification of content requirements reported in Zanzibar is also mirrored in many other national curricula and leads to longer textbooks. This has a double set of consequences. First, the longer textbooks cost more and thus increase the system costs; second, teachers feel under pressure to complete the textbooks during the school year. Secondary school students tend to be acutely aware of their examinations and the need to complete the specified curriculum in good time, which adds to the pressure on teachers. In situations where the actual contact hours may be considerably less than the assumed contact hours, the teaching and learning pace required to complete an overloaded curriculum specification in reduced hours usually means that many students are simply left behind by the pace of curriculum delivery and fail to understand. In addition there is no time for individual student support, for student-centered activities, and for the development of problem-solving and other higher-order skills, which are increasingly specified in SSA curricula (but not often assessed or delivered).

In Lesotho, textbook rental fees and the Textbook Revolving Fund (TRF) were required to cover the costs of just 29 basic textbooks for all primary grades in 1986; by 1999 the TRF rental fees were required to support 59 textbooks to meet increased subject requirements and enhanced curriculum objectives. This represented an increase of 103 percent in the number of textbooks specified by the curriculum designers in just 13 years. This increase brought the TRF under enormous financial pressure, but the fundamental strength of the scheme and the long history of parent and church support enabled it to survive. At the secondary level frequent changes in curriculum requirements in Lesotho caused such significant textbook redundancies that a majority of secondary schools abandoned purchasing textbooks for loan to students and reverted instead to parent purchase because the schools could not afford the financial losses resulting from the constant curriculum changes and the resulting changes in the approved textbook lists (Sehlabi 2000). As a result, textbook availability in secondary school classrooms decreased dramatically and textbook ownership was reserved for the richer families only.

Increased curriculum subject requirements are sometimes simply not feasible in schools. The 2000 Uganda primary curriculum specified nine subjects for upper primary. DPs agreed to fund textbooks for only four subjects, but the additional five subjects were retained despite the fact that there was no funding to provide teacher training, textbooks, and teachers' guides for these new subjects. Kiswahili was made a compulsory subject, but there were insufficient Kiswahili teachers available; 90 percent of schools simply ignored the requirement to teach the subject. A new subject—Integrated Production Skills—was also not taught by 40 percent of primary schools because there were no teachers trained to teach the subject and most schools could not afford the specified raw materials (Read and Hicks 2004; Sehlabi 2000). This was also true of primary agriculture, which had been conceived by the curriculum designers as a practical subject but was taught almost entirely as a theoretical subject because of the lack of any budget allocation to provide the specified tools and raw materials. The 2006 thematic curriculum in Uganda reduced the lower primary subject requirements to just literacy and math so that schools could concentrate on achieving rapid literacy and numeracy. All other required subject content was taught via the literacy and maths themes.

In Malawi[6] the 1992 curriculum developed by the Malawi Institute of Education (MIE) with World Bank project funding specified four subjects and textbooks for Standards 1 to 4, six subjects and textbooks for Standards 5 and 6, and eight subjects and textbooks for Standards 7 and 8—a total of 44 textbooks plus accompanying teachers' guides. By 1999 the MOE was proposing to increase the primary curriculum requirement to eight subjects and textbooks per grade—a total of 64 textbooks plus teachers' guides. This was an increase in the textbook requirement of 45 percent at a time when education budgets were coming under great strain because of spiralling primary and secondary enrollments caused by the introduction of free primary education. Between 1994 and 1995 primary enrollments increased by 53 percent from 1.9 million to 2.9 million. The decision to expand the TLM requirements specified by the curriculum and thus to significantly increase the costs of TLM provision was taken at a time when the MOE was having great difficulty in meeting any of its financial commitments to education and was increasingly dependent upon DP support. But the curriculum decision was taken with no consideration of either the educational or cost implications. By 1994 World Bank support for textbooks had ceased and the MOE, faced with the prospect of no external funding for primary textbooks, signed an agreement with two commercial publishers to provide commercial editions of just three of the textbooks for sale to parents (thus reneging on the promise of free primary education). However, one year later, in 1995, the MOE signed another agreement with the Canadian International Development Agency (CIDA) to reprint for free distribution all of the MIE-developed textbooks. The two commercial publishers were left with large quantities of unsold and unsellable stock on their hands, and for many years after there were ongoing threats of legal action and complex negotiations between the publishers, the MOE, and the Canadian International Development Agency (CIDA) in attempts to resolve the problems.

In South Sudan the development of a national textbook and TLM policy and progress on curriculum review and redesign and LoI policies were developed separately with little or no interlinking between the three policy areas and no attempt to specify the cost implications of these decisions. The Department for International Development (DFID) Annual Review of the textbook component in South Sudan commented as follows:

A much closer link needs to be created between curriculum and language of instruction policies on one hand and the development of a national TLM policy on the other. The financial implications of policy decisions need to be clearly established in order to fully inform and support policy decisions for both [the Government of South Sudan] and development partners and the full range of cost reduction strategies needs to be considered as part of TLM policy formation. (Jones and Sayer 2013)

Some francophone countries, frequently supported by DP-funded projects, are now specifying much lower TLM profiles. Thus, Côte d'Ivoire provides free of charge three textbooks per child for junior primary, and five textbooks to senior primary students funded by the World Bank's *Projet d'Appui au Secteur Éducation Formation* (PASEF). In Burkina Faso each primary student has been provided since 2006 with three free textbooks (French, math and "observation"), which represent a requirement of around 2.5 million copies per year. The Democratic Republic of Congo was provided with 14 million textbooks during the first two years of the World Bank–funded PARSE *(Projet d'Appui au Redressement du Secteur de l'Education)*, which was scheduled to run from 2008 to 2013. The textbooks comprised one French language teaching (FLT) and one math textbook for P1 and P2 students only. All other textbooks have to be bought by parents. In Senegal primary textbooks are officially free and are provided by the state (two books per child in P1 and P2, three in P3 and P4, four in P5 and P6). In the Republic of the Congo a 2009 Programme d'Analyse des Systèmes Éducatifs de la CONFEMEN (PASEC) study estimated that only 25 percent of primary students had an FLT textbook and only four percent had a math textbook. Table 4.4 provides data on textbook possession in Cameroon in 2007 (PASEC 2007) where all textbooks were parentally funded. It is striking that parents were more willing to purchase textbooks in senior primary than in junior primary where the early achievement of literacy is essential for later progress through the education system.

From the early 1960s onwards the number of primary curriculum subjects has tended to increase[7] in many countries and there have been examples of 11-and even 12-subject primary curricula. All subjects were generally required to have their own textbook (even though many of the subjects could have been delivered via a good teachers' guide only) and horizontal scoping and sequencing was often poor or even nonexistent. Thus syllabus content for any subject often took little account of what was being taught in other subjects so that there was often much duplication and repetition. Because the gap between real and theoretical contact hours was rarely, if ever, addressed in curriculum design, most textbooks

Table 4.4 Textbook Ownership in Cameroon, 2007

	Francophone part		*Anglophone part*	
	P2 (%)	P5 (%)	P2 (%)	P5 (%)
FLT	34	72	30	82
Math	25	56	22	85

Source: Ministry of Education annual statistics.
Note: FLT = French language teaching; P = primary grade.

contained far too much content for many schools, which made syllabuses and learning outcomes difficult to deliver and the textbooks more expensive than they should have been.

Finally, the new subjects often required knowledge and skills that existing teachers did not possess and pre-service and in-service training often lag years behind the launch of new curricula and new subjects so that in many cases the new subject knowledge and skills are not taught or are taught and learned badly. Thus, the Economic Development Poverty Reduction Strategy in Rwanda (EDPRS2) commented that

> Teachers are generally unfamiliar with teaching methods that support the acquisition of catalytic skills by students. The great majority of teachers are familiar only with teacher-centred, highly didactic approaches to teaching and learning, with a high level of student passivity observed in school classrooms. (Government of Rwanda 2013)

In these circumstances it is perhaps somewhat unfair to allocate blame to textbooks for failing to change classroom pedagogies and student learning outcomes when there are far more fundamental factors at work in the form of unrealistic curriculum expectations and a lack of effective teacher training and support.

The Minimum Profile of Required TLMs and Associated Cost Implications

Desired curriculum objectives and student learning outcomes are rarely achievable with textbooks and teachers' guides alone. At the very least there is a requirement for some supplementary reading materials to attract students into reading, to stimulate reading skills, and to support the development of lifelong reading habits. In order to achieve an affordable profile of the materials required for effective curriculum delivery all new curricula should create their own Minimum Learning Materials Profiles (MLMPs) as the basis for a calculation of the TLM cost implications of the curriculum design.

The MLMP is an agreed minimum list of the TLMs needed by students and teachers in order for all students to achieve the learning objectives of the curriculum. Typically the MLMP should be qualified with supply guidelines (for example, one per student; five per class; one per teacher), assumed life expectancy, and assumed loss and damage rates. The MLMP is also usually specified by grade level and by subject. If the curriculum is to be effective in increasing student achievement it must have an MLMP that is affordable to government (including DP contributions) or to parents and it must be sustainable.

The basic menu of print materials from which the MLMP can be constructed is provided below:

- Textbooks and teachers' guides
- Reference books (for example, dictionaries, atlases, encyclopedias)
- Readers and fiction—stories, drama, poetry, anthologies, and so on
- Picture books and big books (for young learners)
- Nonfiction curriculum support topic books

- Games, work cards, and activity books
- Consumable workbooks (but very expensive to deliver)
- Teachers' didactic aids (for example, flash cards and vocabulary cards, abacus, and so on)
- Maps and wall charts
- Posters
- Poster card, marker pens, A4 paper
- Science equipment
- Science consumables

Countries with substantial investments in operational equipment in classrooms could provide also a menu of e-materials for the MLMP.

The provision of TLMs needs to take into account the *real* teaching and learning environment in the typical school classroom: for example, classroom space; classroom and school storage facilities; security; weatherproofing; the type, quantity, condition, and usage of furniture (desks, chairs, numbers of pupils per desk or bench, and so on); realistic contact hours; teacher capacity, background, training, and attitudes (motivation, commitment, and so on); and available equipment in operational condition (for example, cassette recorders, DVD players, TVs, PCs, and so on).

Curriculum developers, materials developers, and policy makers need to have a clear school/classroom/teacher/student/parent profile in mind when establishing the MLMP, and this requires an understanding of the conditions under which the objectives and outcomes of the curriculum have to be achieved and a good knowledge of the pros and cons of different types of TLMs and what they can reasonably be expected to deliver.

In Uganda in 2006 an MLMP was developed for the new thematic primary curriculum by a group comprising curriculum developers from the National Curriculum Development Centre (NCDC) and teachers drawn from all regions of the country. After debate the group decided that teacher support materials should be given top priority in lower primary classes and these were specified as follows:

- Simple and easy to use teachers' guide with *detailed* daily lesson plans
- A teachers' resource book with traditional rhymes, singing games, word games and ideas for low- or no-cost student activities—provided in nine local languages
- An anthology of stories to read to children—at least one story per school day
- Large size, large print wall charts specially designed to illustrate key curriculum themes in order to encourage student discussion, speaking, and listening as the basis for vocabulary enhancement
- Sheets of poster card and marker pens so that teachers could make their own posters and "big books"
- Alphabet cards, flash cards, vocabulary cards, and number cards

Student materials were also specified by the group as follows:

- No textbooks for P1–3
- Picture books

- Decoding books
- Big books
- Simple readers—both graded readers and readers for free reading
- Durable, reusable work cards

The Uganda MLMP provided direct support to literacy and numeracy and provided even unqualified teachers with easy-to-follow instructions. By avoiding textbooks in nine local languages for the first three grades, costs were significantly reduced so that emphasis could be placed on providing students with interesting, attractive, and stimulating reading books (Read and Enyutu 2005).

In Rwanda in 2008 a MLMP workshop was organized to develop a primary MLMP. Table 4.5, below, indicates the costs of supplying a P1 class of 70 with the textbooks specified by the curriculum. Table 4.6 provides a costing for an alternative approach to TLM provision for P1.

The total cost of provision for the MLMP in table 4.5 is US$1,065. The total cost of provision for the alternative MLMP in table 4.6 is US$620.50. When amortized over a four-year period the basic cost comparisons are US$366.25 (US$5.23 per student per year) and US$155.125 (US$2.22 per student per year). These changes to the MLMP profile provided basic textbooks for three subjects at a 1:1 TPR, teachers' guides for all subjects, increased teacher support, and a good collection of reading books for a classroom library. The alternative profile was

Table 4.5 Costs of Basic Textbook Provision for P1, 2008

Item	Rate	Quantity	Assumed life (years)	Unit cost (US$)	Total cost (US$)	Annualized cost (US$)
Textbooks	1/student	6 x 70	4	2.50	1,050.00	262.50
Teachers' guides	1/class	6 x 1	4	2.50	15.00	3.75
Total cost	n.a.	n.a.	n.a.	n.a.	1,065.00	366.25
Costs per student	n.a.	n.a.	n.a.	n.a.	n.a.	5.23

Source: Author's calculations based on current costs and Ministry of Education targets.
Note: n.a. = no data available; P1 = primary grade 1.

Table 4.6 Costs of Alternative Approach to TLM Provision for P1, 2008

Item	Rate	Quantity	Assumed life (years)	Unit cost (US$)	Total cost (US$)	Annualized cost (US$)
Textbooks	1/student	3 x 70	4	2.50	525.00	131.25
Teachers' guides	1/class	6 x 1	4	2.50	15.00	3.75
Class teachers' guide	1/class	6/1	4	3.00	18.00	4.50
Story anthology	1/class	1	4	5.00	5.00	1.25
Teachers resource book	1/class	1	4	5.00	5.00	1.25
Reading books	1/class	70	4	0.75	52.50	13.125
Total cost	n.a.	n.a.	n.a.	n.a.	620.50	155.125
Costs per student	n.a.	n.a.	n.a.	n.a.	n.a.	2.22

Source: Author's calculations based on current costs and Ministry of Education targets.
Note: n.a. = no data available; P1 = primary grade 1; TLM = teaching and learning materials.

provided at a reduced cost per student per year of 59 percent. Further cost reductions could be achieved by applying basic cost reduction methods (see below).

There is a significant waste of time and money in providing textbooks to every student based on "high-end" contact hours if a majority of students go to schools that operate at "low-end" contact hours. In this situation it makes more sense to design textbooks on a 1:1 basis to provide coverage of the "core" curriculum and to provide extension materials and expanded teachers' guides for those schools and students who have the contact hours or the motivation to attempt the total curriculum. This approach supports the prioritization of early literacy and the creation of simple classroom or school libraries (where extension or remedial material can be located) and by doing so supports the pedagogic shift to student-centered learning, which is specified in many new curriculum documents, but in practice is not often delivered.

LoI Policies and Cost Implications

It is generally recognized that children will perform better and learn faster if early education is conducted in a familiar language, although considerable care is needed in developing an effective and practical policy for the selection and use of local languages (Ward, Penny, and Read 2007). If reading in the local language is badly taught by teachers with little formal training in either the local language itself or in the teaching of reading and literacy, or if it is not well supported by appropriate teaching and learning materials, it could undermine progress towards basic literacy, the development of learning in other subjects, and the later acquisition of literacy in an international language and thus effective access to education in upper primary grades and in secondary school. Many countries in SSA often have many potential LoIs and thus the selection of a local language to use as the LoI in lower primary grades has a number of implications, which need to be taken into account in the development of a local language policy for education. These include:

- Financial implications—the use of too many local languages would increase origination costs and thus the average unit costs of textbook provision. They could also fractionalize print runs for essential learning materials, which would also increase unit costs and increase the costs of provision. Too many languages operating in small numbers could also be a disincentive to potential publishers of educational materials in local languages. There is a risk that smaller language groups would be less well served than larger language groups. The cost implications would be greater if other primary curriculum subjects such as math, social studies, science, and agriculture also required textbooks in multiple local languages.
- Staffing and training implications—instruction in local languages also requires teachers who are trained to use the local language as an LoI. Teachers using local languages must be confident in their ability to read and write the language accurately. This has implications for course options and staffing requirements in Primary Teacher Training Colleges (PTCs). Too many LoIs will increase the costs and the complexity of teacher training and could have

obvious implications for the posting, selection, and promotion of teaching staff between districts and even subdistricts.
- Political implications—it is clear that the selection of a local language as the LoI is not just a pedagogic issue but also may have cultural and political implications, particularly where there are a number of rival and competing language possibilities.[8]

Different local languages operate at different levels of development. Some languages may be relatively widespread and developed with an established orthography; a flourishing supportive literature of newspapers, magazines, fiction, children's books, poetry and drama, radio and TV stations; and a cadre of trained language speakers and authors. Other languages may have no established orthography, little or no supportive literature (or even print of any kind), no trained language teachers, and no established authorship capability.

There is also an obvious difference in the early childhood exposure to written languages, particularly between urban and rural areas. Thus, in urban areas all children are constantly exposed to written language in the form of shop and street signs, product packaging, advertisements, newspapers, magazines, TV, cinema, bookshops and libraries, and so on. In many rural areas none of the above exists and there is little or even no cultural conditioning and exposure to written language as the foundation for the basic decoding of letters and words into sounds and meaning. Many rural children arrive at school for the first time from home environments that are almost entirely oral and thus with little or no print awareness. In this situation the absence of *any* supporting literature in school for a language selected as an LoI could have a very damaging impact on the early acquisition of literacy.

Primary teachers throughout SSA have often commented that classes in lower primary grades were the most difficult teaching assignments because of the lack of trained and experienced reading specialists, the absence of suitable instructional materials or reading books and the scarcity of trained teachers with specific local language knowledge.[9] Also, in many schools, teachers allocated to lower primary classes are often the least qualified and may not even be very fluent in the local LoI.[10] Education policies have tended to stress the importance of upper primary over lower primary in the allocation of the most qualified and experienced teachers. Even where lower primary teachers are fluent in the spoken language they often lack confidence in reading and writing the local language, even when it is their own mother tongue. Although parents and community groups are often supportive of the use of local languages in primary schools there is usually a significant percentage who consider that the use of a local language as the LoI in primary might delay and therefore hinder their children in the acquisition of English or French. Literacy in English or French, even with parents who strongly support the use of local languages, is generally more valued by the community than literacy in local languages. Community groups almost always want to be consulted about the choice of language to be used in their school and there are many examples of local communities refusing to accept district local language policies. There is often widespread concern among many of the smaller local language groups that a rival language might be imposed. In this situation, most communities would rather use a Main Area Language (MAL) or English as the LoI than a rival local language. For all of these reasons, clear guidelines from MOEs on local language selection should always be a high priority.

Chatry-Komarek (2003) defines the causes of high levels of illiteracy in the primary sector as poor language policies, deficient teacher training, a lack of educational materials (in the language of reading acquisition), the absence of a literate environment, dramatically reduced teacher–pupil contact hours, and overcrowded classrooms. The same author comments that the use of a familiar language in the classroom does not guarantee fluent reading. Children also need appropriate learning activities and motivating reading materials (Chatry-Komarek 2003).

In order to reemphasize the need for minimum local language criteria in order to achieve literacy it is recommended that all local languages to be used as the LoI should meet minimum standards for the successful achievement of basic literacy and numeracy. The key recommendations are that any language used as an LoI should be able to meet the minimum criteria specified below:

- An established and approved orthography, if possible supported by an academically respectable dictionary or word book
- An established literature suitable for young learners in P1–4
- Evidence that there is the capacity to provide good quality local language training to primary teachers in the proposed LoI(s) such as via local language modules in a local PTC
- Undertakings that the district will provide schools with the necessary reading support materials for both students and teachers to underpin the early achievement of literacy
- Local community languages and dialects, spoken only in limited areas, which do not meet the minimum criteria can be used as the oral medium of communication and support in lower primary grades but literacy should always be taught in a language that meets the minimum criteria specified above
- The LoI used as the language of assessment and evaluation in appropriate grades

Regional Curricula

The advent of regional curricula (for example, the Conference of Ministries of Education Using French as a Language of Instruction [CONFEMEN] in francophone Africa) has potentially greatly expanded market size and potential print runs, which should have reduced unit costs to some extent. This would have been particularly beneficial for local languages common to several countries (for example, Hausa in Nigeria and Niger) but only if they were used as LoIs, which is not common on a national scale in francophone Africa. It was expected that the development of regional curricula and thus regional markets would encourage the growth of locally owned regional publishers but progress in this direction has been slow and the dominant publishers for regional textbooks—often in country-specific local variants—continue to be the French metropolitan publishers. The basic problem is the small size and lack of capitalization of most of the locally owned francophone publishers and the barriers to, and high cost of, access to investment finance to develop publishing contacts and expertise outside the home base.

The actual take-up of CONFEMEN curricula in francophone Africa is quite difficult to determine. A review of the minutes of the numerous symposia, colloquia, and retreats with a curriculum or secondary education theme posted on the CONFEMEN website emphasizes the need for curricula to be as close as possible to national cultures and backgrounds. In a curriculum focused meeting in Brazzaville in July 2010 it was agreed that *any curricular reform must be based on each country's or society's philosophy, culture, national vision, and mission*. At the same meeting Philippe Jonnaert from the Université du Québec à Montréal, warned the participants against *reproducing an imported or mechanically reproduced curriculum pattern*. In another meeting in Bujumbura in 2010, Mbaye Ndoumbé Guèye, former Planning Director at Senegal's MOE, recommended that the curricular reform be *steered by national governments with the support of experts, the mobilization of relevant resources, teacher training, and the setting up of design and piloting devices*. These meetings demonstrated little concern with the regional harmonization of national curricula. But francophone Africa's MOE officials always refer to the CONFEMEN curricula when approving secondary textbooks. However, in another curriculum seminar in 2008, one of the recommendations was to *reduce distortions between the official curricula and the curricula that are actually implemented*, which suggests that approved textbooks may not necessarily be well adjusted to national variants of the regional curriculum. In most SSA countries the implementation of the curriculum is usually undertaken via the textbooks in use. Thus there is perhaps a hint that textbook evaluation, selection, and approval processes may need a little more rigor.

The situation in anglophone countries is different. Locally owned publishers are much more developed in most of anglophone SSA and, at least in East Africa, have already taken advantage of competitive bidding opportunities and well-designed and objective evaluation and approval methodologies to win business on their merits in neighboring countries and thus to create significant regional export markets. Ugandan publishers compete successfully for approved list status in Kenya, and Kenyan publishers do the same in Uganda. Both Ugandan and Kenyan publishers are active also in Rwanda and in South Sudan; and MK, a Ugandan publisher, has recently (2011) won a major Ethiopian secondary textbook contract against stiff international competition. South African publishers have not yet made any significant impact in textbook markets outside BOLESWA[11] countries and Namibia and there is little regional business among the anglophone countries of West Africa. Throughout most of anglophone SSA, multinational publishing companies no longer dominate the educational markets at primary level and are less significant than previously at secondary level as more curricula are demanding locally originated and published materials.

The high point of anglophone regional curricula in SSA came in the 1960s and 1970s with programs like Entebbe Maths and the African Science and Social Science projects. Thereafter, national curricula and education structures diverged (for example, 7+2+2 in Uganda, 8+2+2 in Tanzania, 6+3+3 in Kenya) and national educational publishing developed strongly as soon as state publishing collapsed and provided market access and market opportunities. Nevertheless the East African Community (EAC) is giving priority to harmonizing regional curricula, and the publishing industries are well placed to compete for regional business as and when the opportunities emerge.

A Summary of Key Issues

This review has demonstrated that the educational realities of SSA schools frequently are not well represented in the assumptions of the curriculum developers, which in turn means that many of the approved textbooks that conform to national curricula are also not necessarily well adjusted to local learning realities. Schools and classrooms are often closed or unusable due to political conflicts, natural calamities, or harsh climatic conditions. Many schools suffer from poor infrastructures; lack of facilities, equipment, and furniture; high noise levels; overcrowded conditions; double-shift policies; and teacher absenteeism. Rural schools frequently have difficulties in filling teaching posts and sustaining teacher commitment once they have been posted there. A high proportion of teachers are underqualified, and many reception class primary teachers have little idea how to teach literacy and numeracy effectively. Highly didactic teaching styles with an emphasis on strict discipline and rote learning frequently result in extremely passive and even robotic student attitudes and militate against the successful introduction of new curricula that specify student-centered learning pedagogies and the development of new skills and competencies, which are unfamiliar and even alarming to a majority of teachers.[12] In both quantitative and qualitative terms, the actual contact time received by many SSA students is reduced appreciably owing to the complex pressures faced by the education systems. Significant proportions of teachers (and head teachers) go absent or arrive at school late every day. Many teachers are present in school but absent from their classrooms. Considerable classroom time is set aside for nonlearning tasks, while pedagogical methods rarely stray from conventional teacher-centered approaches (Millot and Lane 2002). Reported examples suggest that actual contact hours in many schools are often at least 30 percent below official contact hours, but in some schools in some countries the difference could be as high as 50 to 60 percent.

The Uganda Primary Curriculum Review concluded that reform of the primary curriculum, by itself, would be insufficient to achieve high levels of basic literacy and numeracy by the end of primary education. Urgent but closely integrated reforms were also required in local language policy, learning materials provision, management and use, pre-service and in-service teacher training, primary school supervision and mentoring, and assessment. Nevertheless, the primary curriculum review team did conclude that there were significant flaws in the then-current primary curriculum[13] and that a failure to provide both sufficient time and adequate syllabus concentration on the achievement of early literacy and numeracy in lower primary grades was by far the most fundamental problem that needed to be addressed. Failure to achieve basic literacy and numeracy in any language in lower primary grades inevitably has a devastating impact on educational quality and student performance (and therefore student and parent interest and motivation) in all other subjects. Failure to achieve early literacy was clearly the issue of greatest concern to teachers, parents, and the wider community that emerged from the research. It was also perceived to be one of the major causes of dropouts and poor performance at higher grades.

The key issues for curriculum design and TLM provision emerging from this review are as follows:

- A clear link needs to be established in every country between curriculum and syllabus design, practical school realities, and the cost implications. If a curriculum cannot be afforded on a sustainable basis then the associated learning objectives cannot be widely delivered. If the curriculum does not take account of school realities in both urban and rural areas then it is unlikely that levels of learning will improve. Frequent changes in curriculum content and the overspecification of subjects and subject content are costly and contribute greatly to unaffordable TLM system costs and therefore to the achievement of sustainability. All curriculum design should be subjected to a reality check and cost analysis.
- Close links must exist between curriculum and LoI policies on one hand and the development of a national textbook and TLM policy on the other. The financial implications of curriculum and LoI policy decisions need to be clearly established in order to fully inform and support policy decisions for both government and DPs, and the full range of cost-reduction strategies needs to be considered as part of a unified policy formation.
- There should be a realistic approach to curriculum design and subject content specifications that takes into account actual as opposed to assumed contact hours and current classroom realities. This should be reflected also in textbook content specifications that currently are too often based on the teacher qualifications, facilities, and resources existing at the best schools rather than in average, and the substandard schools. Textbooks and teachers' guides should contain a range of activities and exercises, which are accessible for the best, the average, and the substandard schools and students; and content should take into account a range of ability levels.
- There should be fewer curriculum subjects at both primary and secondary levels with reduced content extents that take into account realistic student and teacher time on task wherever possible
- More effort needs to be made to ensure that all teachers are familiar with curriculum content and objectives.

- There is an absolute requirement for more active participation by students in their own learning and a movement away from highly didactic teacher-centered methodologies, which often encourage extreme student passivity. At primary level a start should be made on creating packages of textbooks, teachers' guides, and other TLMs that encourage or require speaking, listening, reading, and writing practice by all students as the most fundamental basis for early literacy and numeracy.
- Better, more-detailed, larger-print, and lie-flat teachers' guides containing detailed daily lesson plans based on a more accurate assessment of primary teachers' capacities and needs are essential. Undertrained and underqualified teachers need all the help that they can get if standards are to be improved.
- The more content that can be removed from the textbook (supplied often at target TPRs of 1:1 up to 1:3) and placed in a teachers' guide (supplied at a ratio of one per class) the cheaper the system costs will be, although it should be recognized that if teachers don't or can't or won't use a teachers' guide then it's better for the students to have access to the content in the textbook.
- In lower primary grades there is a very urgent need for the recognition by curriculum designers, authors, publishers, inspectors, and teachers that teaching a language is not the same as teaching literacy.
- Language policies in lower primary, and particularly those policies concerned with local languages, should meet the basic criteria for providing a basis for literacy.
- Clear decisions by curriculum designers on the *minimum* profile of teaching and learning materials required to deliver the curriculum objectives and learning outcomes should be the basis for all TLM provision policies.
- In lower primary grades there is an urgent need to prioritize the provision of attractive and stimulating reading books in appropriate local languages.
- Finally, it is important that there should be regular and accurate assessments of the full and on-going cost implications of curriculum design and TLM provision strategies against available finance and an understanding of the need to maintain minimum expenditures over time in order to achieve and sustain the required minimum levels of provision.

Notes

1. http://www.hsrcpublishers.co.za/user_uploads/tblPDF/2073_00_With_Africa_for_Africa.pdf A short analysis of the MLA results is also produced by Vinayagum Chinapah, the recognised authority on MLA results in Africa; see http://www.adeanet.org/biennial2003/papers/2Ac_MLA_ENG_final.pdf. For other examples of MLA question types, see http://www.literacyonline.org/explorer/un_act.html.

2. It should be noted that by grade 4 very large numbers of pupils have already dropped out of primary education in most African countries and that failure to achieve early literacy is widely regarded as a major cause of student dropouts. When this has been taken into account, the failure to achieve literacy in primary schools in Sub-Saharan Africa is almost certainly far higher than the data suggests.

3. http://www.adeanet.org/biennial2003/papers/3C_Mingat_ENG.pdf.

4. English, Historia, Kiswahili, Sayansi, Jiografia, Historia, Sanaa na Michezo, Sayansi Kinu, Sayansi Kilimo, and Siasa.
5. The capitation grant levels were calculated to be sufficient to maintain and improve target TPRs. The need for complete restocking went far beyond maintenance and should thus have attracted significant additional funding if previously achieved textbook levels were to be reestablished.
6. This case study has been developed from information extracted from Nyerendra (2001).
7. There have been exceptions. Kenya's 2003 curriculum reduced primary subjects from nine down to six, and Uganda's thematic curriculum reduced the previous 6-subject curriculum in lower primary to no subjects at all by using themes so that teaching and student learning could be concentrated on literacy and numeracy. Required subject knowledge was delivered within the themes. In Tanzania the World Bank–funded 2000 curriculum reduced the number of primary curriculum subjects to six, but these were increased back to nine by the TIE and MOE in 2006.
8. In Uganda, the decision to break Tororo District into three smaller districts along local language lines is an example of this issue.
9. Effective teaching of literacy in a local language requires that teachers should not only be able to speak the selected language of instruction but should also be able to read it and write it with a degree of accuracy and confidence. Evidence collected from field work in Uganda suggests that for many local languages in Uganda these basic skills are quite rare, largely because few teachers have ever been formally taught in their own language. As a result there is a widespread tendency to assume that the use of the local language in lower primary is for purposes of verbal communication only and that the language of literacy remains English.
10. There is no guarantee that lower primary teachers will be proficient in the local language used as the LoI. For example, in one Ugandan school where Kiswahili was being used as the LoI, the two teachers who were most fluent in Kiswahili (with Grade V diplomas and formal language qualifications) were teaching in P6 and P7 where the LoI was English. One of the P1 teachers, with a basic Grade III teacher qualification, was not even a fluent Kiswahili speaker and was obviously struggling with the problems of teaching reading, writing, listening, and speaking in a language with which she was not very familiar. The Deputy Head Teacher thought that her language problems were not significant because she was only teaching P1 students.
11. BOLESWA = Botswana, Lesotho, and Swaziland.
12. The Uganda Primary Curriculum Review reported that in 80 hours of classroom observation there were only three examples recorded of students asking a question of their teacher on their own initiative.
13. The Road Map does not provide the detailed evidence and conclusions on the problems of the current primary curriculum, but these are available in detail in the Primary Curriculum Review Report (Read and Hicks 2004).

References

AFTED. 2010. *Education in Ghana: Improving Equity, Efficiency and Accountability of Education Service Delivery*. A World Bank Study, report 597555-GH. Washington, DC: World Bank.

Benavot, A., and L. Gad. 2004. "Actual Instructional Time in African Primary Schools: Factors that Reduce School Quality in Developing Countries." *Prospects* 34 (September 3): 291–310.

Buchan, A., R. Hicks, and T. Read. 2006. *Final Report on the Uganda Reading Pilot Project*. Kampala: USAID for the MOES.

Chatry-Komarek, M. 2003. *Literacy at Stake*. Windhoek: Gamsberg Macmillan.

Chinapah, V. 2003. *Monitoring Learning Achievement (MLA) in Africa*. Association for the Development of Education in Africa (ADEA) Biennial Meeting in Mauritius.

EARC (Educational Assessment and Research Centre). 2005. *A Look at Learning in Ghana: The Final Evaluation of USAID/Ghana's Quality Improvement in Primary Schools Program*. The Mitchell Group and the Educational Assessment and Research Centre, Accra, Ghana, October 2005.

Government of Rwanda. 2013. *Second Economic Development Poverty Reduction Strategy (EDPRS2)*.

Glewwe, P., M. Kremer, and S. Moulin. 1999. *Many Children Left Behind? Textbooks and Test Scores in Kenya*. Cambridge, MA: National Bureau of Economic Research.

Jones, B., and N. Sayer. 2013. *Annual Review of the South Sudan Textbook Project*. Juba: DFID.

Kellaghan, T., and V. Greaney. 2003. *Monitoring Performance: Assessment and Examinations in Africa*. Paris: Association for the Development of Education in Africa.

Kimaro, Y. 2010. *Daily News*. Dar es Salaam, January 5.

Kraft, R. 2003. *Primary Education in Ghana: A Report to USAID*. Kampala: USAID Ghana.

Lipson, M., and K. Wixson. 2004. *Evaluation of BTL and ASTEP Programs in the NE and Volta Regions of Ghana*. Kampala: International Reading Association for USAID Ghana and MOES.

Millot, B., and J. Lane. 2002. "The Efficient Use of Time in Education." *Education Economics* 10 (2): 209–28.

N'tchougan-Sonou, C. H. 2000. *Values Learned through Formal Education*. A Comparative Study of Anglophone and Francophone Ewes in Ghana and Togo.

Mingat, A. 2000. *Analytical and Factual Elements for a Quality Policy for Primary Education in Sub-Saharan Africa in the Context of Education for All*. Association for the Development of Education in Africa (ADEA).

National Assessment of Progress in Education. 2003. *Achievements of Primary Pupils. Draft Report*, 41.

Nyerendra, G. 2001. "Malawi Case Study." In *Upgrading Book Distribution in Africa*, edited by T. Read, C. Denning, and A. Buchan, 55–85. Paris: Association for the Development of Education in Africa.

O'Sullivan, M. 2003. "The Development of Effective Strategies to Teach Reading among Unqualified Primary Teachers in a Developing Country Context." *International Journal of Early Years Education* 11 (2): 129–40.

PASEC. 2007. Programme for the Assessment of Education Systems, UNESCO.

Read, T. 2010. *The Future of Our Children's Education*. Windsor, United Kingdom International Education Partners.

Read, T., and S. Enyutu. 2005. *Uganda Primary Curriculum Reform Road Map*. Kampala: Royal Netherlands Embassy for MOES.

Read, T., and R. Hicks. 2004. *Uganda Primary Curriculum Review*. Kampala: Royal Netherlands Embassy for MOES.

Read, T., and A. Ibale. 2007. *Zanzibar Textbook Policy and Financing Study*. A World Bank Study. Washington, DC: World Bank for MOEVT.

Sehlabi, C. 2000. "The Financing of Textbook Provision in Lesotho." In *Financing Textbooks and Teacher Training Materials*, edited by A. J. Cruz. Paris: Association for the Development of Education in Africa.

Uganda MOES (Ministry of Education and Sports). 2003. *Planning Department Statistics*. Kampala: MOES.

UNEB (Ugandan National Examinations Board). 2003. *Draft Report, Achievements of Primary Pupils: National Assessment of Progress in Education*. Kampala: UNEB.

UNESCO (United Nations Education, Scientific, and Cultural Organizations). 2000. *Report on the EFA Meeting in Johannesburg*.

———. 2004. *Education for All: The Quality Imperative; EFA Global Monitoring Report 2005*. Paris: UNESCO.

Wane, W., and G. H. Martin. 2013. *Education and Health Services in Uganda: Data for Results and Accountability*. A World Bank Study. Washington, DC: World Bank and African Economic Research Consortium.

Ward, M., A. Penny, and T. Read. 2007. *Education Reform in Uganda—1997 to 2004: Reflections on Policy, Partnership, Strategy and Implementation*. London: DFID.

Williams, E. 2007. "Extensive Reading in Malawi: Inadequate Implementation or Inappropriate Innovation." *Journal of Research in Reading* 30 (1): 59–79.

World Bank. 2005. *PEDP Implementation Completion Report*. Washington, DC: World Bank.

CHAPTER 5

Teaching and Learning Materials Financing

Issues in Teaching and Learning Materials Financing

Sub-Saharan African countries have increased their real expenditure on education by more than 6% each year over the past decade, yet despite these investments, many countries in the region are still a long way from providing every child with a good quality primary education. Between 2000 and 2008, the number of children in primary schooling increased by 48%—from 87 million to 129 million. Enrollment in pre-primary, secondary and tertiary education has also grown by more than 60% during the same period.... On average, education accounts for more than 18% of all public spending in Sub-Saharan Africa compared to 15% in other regions. Overall, the region devotes 5% of its gross domestic product (GDP) to education, which is the second highest regional proportion after North America and Europe at 5.3%. Yet despite these investments, many countries in the region are still a long way from providing every child with a good quality primary education and levels of achievement, particularly in the early achievement of literacy and numeracy are unacceptably low. The most recent data show that in one-third of the countries, half of all children do not complete primary education. Thirty-two million children of primary school age are still out of school in the region. The report forecasts that this number will rise as the population of 5 to 14 year-olds is expected to grow by more than 34% over the next 20 years. Given the recent economic crises, most African governments will have to make strategic decisions on how to best serve their growing populations of students and how to make the best use of the scarce resources available. (UNESCO Institute for Statistics 2011)

For many countries and development partners (DPs) the most desirable scenario would enable all required teaching and learning materials (TLMs) to be provided in sufficient quantity, free of charge, and at a frequency sufficient to maintain adequate stocks in good condition. In reality this objective has proved difficult to realize and the majority of Sub-Saharan African (SSA) countries using their own resources have failed to maintain the investment in basic TLM supplies required to satisfactorily underpin the educational process (Da Cruz et al. 1998). Donor interventions have generally been aimed at emergency interventions, supporting government financing, or increasing the capacity of local publishing but the cause of the interventions is always the same: the partial or complete failure of the existing TLM supply systems (O'Connor 1999). The most common cause of these failures has been the inability to provide the financing required to maintain TLM provision. This section reviews a variety of financing patterns in different countries in order to identify the most common causes.

Affordability, Sustainability, and Predictability

Financing systems for TLMs should be

- Affordable;
- Sustainable; and
- Predictable.

Affordability requires

- Clear and consistent policies on funding (Who will pay?);
- A clear understanding (based on market research) of what government and parents can realistically and consistently be expected to contribute;
- A realistic curriculum and syllabus design, which has been costed so that year-on-year funding implications are clearly understood and accepted and are within the affordability parameters defined by market research;
- A minimum profile of TLMs needed to deliver the curriculum, which is also within agreed affordability limits; and
- The application of cost-reduction strategies if so required.

Sustainability implies

- Reliable year-on-year funding always up to projected budget requirements;
- High rates of collection if parents are expected to contribute (for example, via annual rental fees);
- The consistent achievement of assumed book life targets (so that textbooks and materials do not wear out before replacements arrive such as in Somalia); and
- The consistent achievement of low levels of loss and damage (thus efficient distribution, good school storage, effective system management, good school management, care and conservation, which in turn requires adequate training and effective supervision).

Predictability requires

- Consistent policies that have been carefully researched, well designed, and implemented without major changes over time so that Ministry of Education (MOE) officials, teachers, students, and parents all understand how the system works;

- Full and regular consultation with all major players in the system, particularly if significant changes are planned or envisaged;
- Good lead times for any required inputs (for example, new textbooks for a new curriculum) or significant system changes; and
- A distribution system that is accurate, reliable, and (preferably) based on school-level decision making and management.

Underfinancing

Most SSA countries have underfinanced even basic TLM provision. In some cases the underfinancing is irregular or temporary; in other cases it is consistent and almost permanent. For example, in 2005 a European Union (EU) report (PricewaterhouseCoopers 2005) on textbooks in Zambia concluded that

> The policies of the Ministry of Education are being frustrated through apparent lack of commitment to the MoE's declared policies on implementing the decentralization of textbook procurement. Within the.... MoE, there is limited appreciation of the benefits of textbook decentralization, how the processes mesh together or of the negative impact that delays in getting the new textbooks into schools will have on teaching of the new curriculum. Fund releases to the programme under the Grade 1 cycle have been less than requirements and indications are that the same situation will prevail for the Grade 2 and 5 cycle.

In 2009 a second EU-funded report (Bontoux and Musonda 2009) on the same subject in Zambia reported that

> various MoE monitorings were showing that most of the findings of the 2005 report were still valid, but that none of its recommendations had been applied.

Many other examples in SSA could be provided of TLM underfinancing. In Zambia the two consultancy reports, researched and written by two different organizations, both agreed that there was consistent underfunding combined with a lack of control over the input costs of the TLMs procured. But over four years no action had been taken to rectify the problems.

The underfinancing of textbook provision not only covers the underprovision of government financial allocations to TLMs but can extend also to controls on parental contributions, which in turn has ensured in some cases that even parental funding was insufficient to cover the costs of adequate textbook and TLM provision, even when parents were prepared to pay. A number of case studies to illustrate different under financing scenarios are provided below.

Malawi Secondary Textbooks—1976–99[1]

In 1976 the MOE established a compulsory annual textbook fee as a component of general school fees for all students enrolled in Conventional Secondary Schools (CSSs). The value of this contribution was equivalent to around US$5 per student per year, and when combined with direct additional annual government textbook grants it provided the basis for a satisfactory level of textbook access for all secondary students for all subjects at all grade levels. Over the next 23 years inflation and devaluation took their toll on the local currency but the Government of Malawi (GOM) refused to allow any increase in the annual textbook fee. By 1999 the value of the textbook fee had deteriorated to the equivalent of US$0.0125 per student per year. At the same time there had been a spectacular increase in secondary enrollments as the impact of Universal Primary Education (UPE) in Malawi increased the pressure for secondary school places. In the eight-year period from 1979 to 1987 CSS enrollment increased by over 240 percent from 29,326 to 70,858. In the same period the enrollment in Distance Education Centers (DECs)[2] rose from 19,596 to 108,846—a growth of 555 percent in eight years. The overall increase in secondary enrollments for the period was 367 percent. The enrollment growth rate created enormous pressure on government secondary education budgets and from the early 1990s onwards GOM secondary education budgets declined sharply. By 1998 neither CSSs nor Community Day Secondary Schools (CDSSs) had many textbooks and teachers' guides for any subject at any level. In 1999/2000 Malawi's secondary schools achieved the lowest ever Malawi Secondary Certificate of Education (MSCE) pass rate with CDSSs achieving only a three percent pass rate. In 1998 in response to the critical shortage of textbooks the World Bank's Secondary Education Project (SEP) procured one-off textbook supplies for CSSs, and the Danish International Development Agency (DANIDA) undertook to support and reform textbook supplies to CDSSs. In 2000, as a result of donor pressure, the annual secondary textbook fee was reestablished at the equivalent of US$4.25 per student per year and DANIDA provided matching funding for the textbook fees collected by the schools. DANIDA's matching funding concept was extended to CSSs in 2000. The closure of the Danish diplomatic presence in Malawi in 2002 resulted in the termination of Danish support to education, but the impact of the DANIDA intervention was so significant that 85 percent of students were continuing to pay the upgraded textbook fee four years after all donor support for secondary textbooks had ceased, which was a clear indication that most parents were prepared to pay a realistic fee for reliable access to core secondary textbooks.

In July 2014 the Ministry of Education, Science, and Technology (MOEST) in Malawi decided to revert once again to the textbook rental scheme and revolving fund originally established with the support of DANIDA in 1999/2000. The Introduction to the MOEST's 2014 *Textbook Revolving Fund Handbook* commented on the reasons for this decision to reintroduce a previous scheme as follows:

> The introduction of the Textbook Revolving Fund (in 1999) marked a significant departure in financing Teaching and Learning Materials (TLMs) in secondary education. While textbook shortages, severe delays and inadequate matching of resources to school requirements were ubiquitous under the previous system of centralized procurement, the TRF significantly improved the availability and timing of textbook supply in secondary schools through school-based procurement. This undeniable success-story for MOEST in improving textbook availability has been

undermined in recent years by two separate factors. Firstly, while the initial TRF amount raised by secondary schools was MK180 in 2000, a failure to annually adjust this figure for inflation meant that until recently, the TRF, at MK250, had lost almost all of its purchasing power. Secondly, MOEST's support for school-based procurement also lowered over time. In the original 1999 TRF guidelines it was noted that "Malawian booksellers are small, under-financed and have very little practical experience of school supply and need time to develop the necessary skills and management capacity." As such, two parallel systems kept operating alongside one another, "direct supply through nationally approved textbook retailers" and "centralized supply." However, in recent years, MOEST stopped all financial contributions to the matching fund and reverted almost entirely back to central procurement, thus slowly undermining the well-functioning system of school-based procurement. Moving to the present day, MOEST finds itself in very similar positions as during the initiation of the TRF. It has just completed its Secondary School Curriculum Assessment and Review (SSCAR) and the steady and timely supply of textbooks and supplementary reading materials is again a vital concern. This thus provides a perfect time to reinvigorate and strengthen its system of school-based procurement for secondary education, in line with the second Education Sector Implementation Plan (ESIP II). As such, MOEST has decided to dedicate all funding for textbooks and reading materials to the system of direct supply through nationally approved textbook retailers, while ensuring adequate student contributions by raising the TRF to MK3,500 (adjusted annually for inflation). This decision will significantly improve the availability and timing of textbook supply, while also strengthening a decentralized system with greater choice for all secondary schools. (MOEST 2014)

This is an example of ministry and DP inability to learn lessons from previous experience. The causes of the failure to maintain adequate textbook supplies to secondary schools in 2014 were exactly the same as those that applied in 2000. The political reluctance to increase textbook fees to maintain purchasing power parity with inflation and currency devaluation has been noted in a number of SSA countries, for example in the unrealistic textbook rental charges established by governments in the Gambia and Guinea, the reluctance to approve textbook rental fee increases to maintain parity with inflation in Lesotho, and the refusal to increase textbook capitation grants to schools in Tanzania. In all cases the refusal by governments to allow inflationary price increases for political reasons resulted in the collapse or near collapse of the schemes.

Guinea—1958–2000[3]
After independence the state assumed responsibility for textbook development and provision and established primary education in French plus eight local languages. Unfortunately the costs of the textbook provision system were beyond the capacity of the Government of Guinea (GOG) and for those schools using national languages no books at all were provided. Annual per pupil textbook allocations declined to the equivalent value of US$0.20. In 1985 the national language policy was abandoned and DPs intervened to finance textbook provision via

the off-the-shelf procurement of imported textbooks in French. Seventeen locally written and published textbooks were planned, but by 1990 only three were ready for production and these were funded by Belgian Technical Cooperation (BTC) and printed in Belgium. The MOE organized a government controlled distribution and sale in which textbooks were delivered to districts and collected by head teachers who then sold them to students. Unfortunately record keeping and revenue collections from head teachers were poorly managed and the sales income was never made available to the MOE to fund future textbook supplies.

The United States Agency for International Development (USAID) reported in 1998 that no GOG financial contributions to textbook supplies had been made between 1991 and 1998. Distribution remained a major problem. From 1994 to 1996 distribution was contracted to two local companies on the basis of a 37 percent discount[4] and this system seemed to work well. However, in 1997 the MOE terminated the distribution agreement and launched a textbook rental scheme at short notice managed by local committees. From 1998 onwards textbooks were delivered to MOE warehouses where they were collected by private contractors who delivered them to urban schools and subdistrict centers (*sous-préfectures*) from where they were collected by schools. Textbook Management Committees (TMCs) were set up in every school and were responsible for scheme administration and management, the collection of rental fees, and their transfer into a central fund established to finance replacement copies. The annual rental fee was set at the equivalent of US$0.60 for a set of seven textbooks. Lost books had to be paid for and failure to return the loan books at the end of the school year resulted in suspension or even expulsion from school. From the outset the scheme ran into many problems. There was uncertainty on which titles were included in the scheme, confusion over the quantities to be delivered to each school (a mismatch between supplies and enrollment and high levels of stock loss in distribution), and the price of replacement copies, and so on. Some parents were so fearful that they would be charged the full price for any lost or damaged books or that their children would be excluded from school if loan books were not returned that they confiscated the textbooks so that they could be returned in full and undamaged at the end of the school year. Collections of rental fees from many of the schools proved to be a problem and the GOG was so anxious to maintain rental costs at low levels[5] that the central fund could not accumulate enough money to buy adequate replacement stocks.

From 1985 to 2000 a variety of different DPs provided funding for many millions of textbooks in Guinea. The main DPs were the World Bank, the African Development Bank (AfDB), *Agence Internationale de la Francophonie* (AIF), the European Community (EC), *Coopération Française* (CF), and USAID. The multiplicity of DPs obviously presented problems of coordination, particularly because different DPs held different policy positions. Thus AIF and CF favored book sales to parents as the financing mechanism and the only way to ensure sustainability and long book life (parents and students only care for textbooks that they have paid for); the World Bank and USAID favored free distribution to ensure genuinely national provision; nongovernmental organizations (NGOs) tended to favor the rental fee approach in association with parent teacher associations (PTAs).

But during this long period of DP support for textbook supplies there was no evidence of a serious attempt to create an affordable profile of TLMs or to move towards sustainable systems. Underpinning all of the above were two overarching issues.

- The fear that when DPs had tired of funding, Guinean students would have no textbooks.
- The poor performance of the distribution system that negated most of the investment in book development, production and procurement. A USAID study in 1998 estimated that 67 percent of textbooks were lost in distribution and poor management at HQ, district, and school levels.

French was reinstalled as the language of instruction (LoI) for all levels of the school system from 1985 and national languages were subjects in the curriculum. However, the GOG continued to want national languages to play a more significant role in education and the national culture. The Language Academy had been renamed the Institute of Applied Linguistic Research (*Institut de Recherche Linguistique Appliquée*), whilst the former Pedagogic Institute was now the *Institut National de Recherche et d'Action Pédagogiques* (INRAP). INRAP was in charge of developing and producing primary and secondary textbooks. However, research conducted by The Conference of Ministries of Education Using French as a Language of Instruction (CONFEMEN) in 2005 showed that only 50 percent of the textbooks present in schools actually came from INRAP (Pôle de Dakar 2005).

According to the 2005 CONFEMEN survey, primary students should have had French language teaching (FLT) textbooks in the ratio of 1:2 and math textbooks at 1:3. However, there were large disparities. Thus 19 percent of students in schools had no access to an FLT textbook and only 21 percent were in schools with better than one FLT book for two learners. A 2006 *Programme d'Analyse des Systèmes Éducatifs de la CONFEMEN* (PASEC) study (*Secrétariat Technique Permanent de la CONFEMEN* 2006) reported that 58 percent of *Cours Preparatoire* 2 (P2) students had no FLT textbooks at all and 62 percent had no math textbooks. In 2005, USAID[6] provided enough books to "officially" reach a 1:1 ratio in P1 and P2—even though subsequent monitoring proved that these books hadn't left the boxes they were delivered in.

Textbooks are now collected by schools at the local *Direction Communale de l'Education* (DCE), or Local Education Authority: head teachers go to the DCE warehouse and take the school's textbook allocation. Parents are required to pay a GF500 contribution (US$0.07) for a primary textbook set and GF1,000 (US$0.14) for a secondary set. Primary head teachers quoted in a 2008 International Institute for Educational Planning (IIEP) report (Baldé et al. 2008) think that this charge is now irrelevant, since textbooks haven't been renewed since 2002 (1998 for secondary) and are now officially considered as damaged or sometimes even lost. The "textbook fee" collection rate is almost 100 percent, even though schools seldom get deliveries of new textbooks. Head teachers talk about "one book per five or six students." The GF500 of the textbook fee is included within a GF10,000 (US$1.40) annual school fee. Grassroots teachers complain that in spite of this contribution, teachers and parents have no say about the number and the contents of the textbooks they are being provided with.

To *maintain the 1:3 textbook–pupil ratio (TPR) reached in primary in 2007*, the 2008–15 *Programme Sectoriel de l'Education* (PSE) funded by the *Fonds Commun*, Guinea's Education Sector Wide Approach (SWAp) will devote US$15.5million to buy one textbook per student per year.

The Guinea case study illustrates the following:

- The total dependence of the GOG on DP funding for the TLM provision system
- That after 25 years of multiple DP involvement in textbook financing there still isn't an effective, reliable, and sustainable system of TLM provision
- The lack of any GOG or DP effort to seriously address affordability or sustainability issues
- The numerous changes in GOG textbook provision policy
- The maintenance of very high physical textbook production specifications based on French metropolitan standards and French pricing levels, which obviously had an impact on affordability and sustainability
- The failure to come to grips with the recurrent and devastating distribution losses
- The ongoing inability to manage effectively the textbook provision system
- The unrealistic textbook fees and lack of transparency over the destination and use of parental contributions for textbook supplies

Tanzania—1988–2010

In 1988 the World Bank funded a Tanzanian Book Sector Study as part of a series of national studies in a number of African countries, aimed at providing the raw material for the 1991 African Ministers of Education Conference, where the conference theme was sustainable textbook provision (Buchan et al. 1991; Read 2010). The Tanzanian study reported that textbook availability was very variable, even in adjacent schools, and with considerable geographical differences in supply. A Kiswahili book in the central zone was available at a ratio of 1:2 but in the coastal zone at only 1:10. A math book in the southern highlands was available at 1:2 but in the Lake zone at 1:700. In inaccessible areas books were often nonexistent. There was evidence that urban supply was much better than rural supply. Textbooks were funded through District Offices, which often lacked purchase funds, and fund diversion to nontextbook uses was common.

In 1988 the primary school curriculum required eleven textbooks per student per grade, which was a considerable burden on government finances. The book sector study estimated the average national level of primary textbook provision as one book per 13 students across all core subjects and primary grade levels.

Substandard production specifications affected readability through poor quality text paper. Textbooks were mostly one color and were not considered to be attractive and stimulating to either students or teachers. Lack of cover finish, low-grade cover card, and unsewn bindings reduced estimated book life to less than two years, which affected textbook availability and the recurrent costs of textbook provision.

Primary textbooks represented about 90 percent of publishing turnover in Tanzania, but for many years only parastatal publishers were permitted to publish for this market. Despite their dominance of the core primary textbook market, parastatal publishers suffered from increasing financial problems caused by inadequate levels of Government of Tanzania (GOT) textbook financing, which resulted in decreased textbook and supplementary materials sales, cash flow problems, shortages of working capital, shortages of raw materials, and rapidly increasing debts. These financial problems led inevitably to a further drop in textbook provision and publishing standards. There was an acute shortage of books in all secondary schools, both government and private. In secondary schools textbook provision comprised, at best, sets of very old textbooks, lovingly maintained by the schools and rebound on more than one occasion, providing sometimes one book per student but more often one book per two or three students. In many rural secondary schools there were no textbooks at all.

By 1988, after almost 20 years of state textbook provision, textbook availability in schools was insufficient to support curriculum objectives. From 1981 to 1991 it was not unusual for a child to go through primary school without access to a textbook in any subject (Read et al. 1988; Saiwad 2001).

The Swedish International Development Agency (SIDA)–funded Pilot Project for Publishing in the 1990s followed by the World Bank–funded Primary Education Development Project (PEDP) created a framework for reform by returning to private sector publishing and reforming the curriculum to make it more affordable. In 2001 the PEDP established a capitation grant for primary schools of T Sh10,000 per head per year, of which T Sh4,000 was allocated for school textbooks. Up to 2004 the textbook component of the capitation grant was paid to District offices for procurement on behalf of schools. From 2004 onwards the textbook component was paid direct into school bank accounts. The textbook component was calculated to provide a ratio of one textbook per three students for each of the six textbooks specified for use in the revised primary curriculum.[7]

In 2000, the average exchange rate for the year was T Sh790 to US$1. Thus the school capitation grant was worth US$12.68 and the textbook component of the grant was worth an effective US$5.06 per student per year. Table 5.1, below, shows the average annual exchange rates from 2000 to 2009.

On the basis of the exchange rates quoted above, the value of the T Sh in 2009 had fallen by 40 percent since 2000. This is important because all raw materials for textbooks were purchased in US$ and more than 80 percent of all textbooks used in Tanzanian schools were printed outside Tanzania and paid for in US$. In 2007 the number of required textbooks in the primary curriculum was increased

Table 5.1 Average Annual US$ Midpoint Exchange Rates, 2000–09

Year	T Sh to 1US$
2000	790
2001	805
2002	1,020
2003	1,050
2004	1,090
2005	1,130
2006	1,170
2007	1,300
2008	1,160
2009	1,300

Source: Tanzania National Bank.

from six to nine.[8] Inflation in raw materials and printing costs between 2000 and 2010 was estimated at between 10 and 15 percent. On this basis the total capitation grant for schools in 2009 should have been at least T Sh21,000 per student if parity with the original 2000 capitation targets was to be maintained. The annual grant for primary textbooks should have increased from T Sh4,000 in 2000 to T Sh9,240[9] by 2009. In reality, the total capitation grant allocations declined, despite continued overall increases in the education budget. The total primary capitation grant reached T Sh13,000 in 2006 but fell to T Sh6,000[10] in 2008–09 with T Sh3,150 allocated to textbooks—around one-third of the value required to reach and maintain the agreed target textbook ratios in the schools. The introduction of the new primary curriculum in 2007 was accompanied by a ministry embargo on the use of all old curriculum books. Thus accumulated textbook stocks were discarded but there was no financial allocation to cover the additional cost of restocking.[11]

Even during the operation of the PEDP there were problems with the regularity and timing of the release of capitation grants, and the PEDP implementation completion report (ICR) notes that there were delays in funding the District Councils and further delays in the release of funds by District Councils to schools. In some cases the Councils did not release all of the funding to schools. Also, the release of funding in four equal quarterly tranches, often released very late, meant that schools always had problems in procuring sufficient textbooks for the beginning of the school year. Other expenditures were considered to be more important than textbooks.

Secondary school capitation grants were first introduced through the Secondary Education Development Project (SEDP). The first grants, set at T Sh25,000 per student per year were released in 2006 and were intended to support improved textbook provision to secondary schools. Unfortunately, the impact of the SEDP was so great that secondary enrollments, which grew by 136 percent from 2004 to 2007, far exceeded even the "high-end" estimates of budget allocations for capitation grants so that the available funding had to be spread more thinly across the actual student enrollment. Thus, in 2006 the capitation released to secondary schools was only T Sh16,900 (68 percent). Qualifying non-government community secondary schools received only T Sh5,700 per student (23 percent). Data on capitation grant allocations after 2006 were not available but the World Bank SEDP Implementation Completion Report[12] noted that if substandard capitation grants continued school supplies of textbooks would be adversely affected, which would contribute to a poorer quality of education.

Between 2004 and 2007 the number of government secondary schools increased from 828 to 2,806. A high proportion of this growth was concentrated in underserved remote and rural areas and in poor urban areas. Thus, the cohort of secondary students who were taking secondary school exams for the first time in 2008 contained a high proportion of students from schools in disadvantaged areas compared to previous exams. Over the same period pupil–teacher ratios (PTRs) in secondary schools had deteriorated from a national average of 30:1 to 37:1, with the worst PTRs in rural and remote areas. As a result secondary examination pass rates suffered a downturn.

The 2009 Primary Expenditure Tracking Survey (PETS) report provided data on the factors that affected exam results. Thus, on PSLE results the PETS commented as follows on the 2008 exam results:

> Spending on non-wage inputs appears to influence school performance measured by PSLE ranking of schools.... [H]owever there are significant variations, first and foremost among rural schools. (Claussen and Assad 2009)

Thus good primary exam results were associated in Tanzania with schools with higher levels of nonwage expenditure (including textbooks). At secondary level the PETS commented as follows:

> The difference in examination performance is significant between government and community schools. While government owned schools have a 90% pass rate on average, community owned schools have an average pass rate of 71%. For Form IV results the same pattern is observed. With an overall average pass rate of 84%, the average for government schools is 96% while community schools have a pass rate of 82%. Urban government schools are performing better as measured by Form II and IV pass rates while rural community schools have lower pass rates. It is in rural community schools that a major share of the expansion in enrollment has taken place during the last years. Pass rates are not correlated with overall P/T ratios. ... Our data suggest that non-wage spending per student is correlated with the performance of a school (measured by pass rates). The more total non-wage spending per student the higher the average O-Level GPA for a school. (Claussen and Assad 2009)

Fund Diversion

This is also common in many countries and is a major contributory factor in underfinancing. Tanzania provides good examples of the various types and levels of fund diversion problems but these are common in many other SSA countries.

In FY 2008 the Tanzanian state budget allocated a total of T Sh544 billion to primary education. T Sh473 billion was actually released for primary education representing 87 percent of the original allocation (Claussen and Assad 2009). Of this figure a further 1.2 percent remained unspent by District Councils and 6.1 percent was diverted by District Councils for noneducation uses. The combined Capitation Grant and Development Grant scheduled for transfer to primary schools was only T Sh6,436 per student (equivalent to US$5.10). However, the amount actually received by the schools was only T Sh6,046 per student (equivalent to US$4.50). This represented a diversion between transfers and actual receipts which was equivalent to T Sh6.2 billion (US$4.9 million) for all of mainland Tanzania. From this figure the PETS reported that T Sh3,150[13] (US$3.34) was recommended for textbook purchase by the schools. At 2008 prices this was equivalent to about half a textbook per student. On the assumption that the allocation was fully utilized by the schools and that there was a basic curriculum requirement for nine textbooks per year for primary schools, a three-year book life, and a target 1:3 TPR, this level of textbook grant provision provided for an actual ratio of 1:12, which was only 25 percent of the GOT's target textbook provision requirement.

The two main grants allocated to schools from the District Councils were the Capitation Grant and the Capital Development Grant. In total these grants constituted 99.8 percent of all grants to schools. The former was intended to support non-wage inputs to schools (including textbooks); the latter provided for school infrastructure improvements. In 2008 the average capitation grant per student received by schools was T Sh4,189 per student (US$3.30), which was approximately 20 percent below the T Sh5,000 used by government in the formula for allocating capitation grants. It should be noted that the T Sh4,189 was only 40 percent of the actual unadjusted 2000 capitation target and less than 20 percent of the capitation grant after adjustment for currency devaluation and other factors. Out of this capitation grant schools had to take their textbook funding. If the original PEDP 40 percent recommendation was used as a baseline, schools had only T Sh1,675 per student for textbooks (US$1.25), or approximately one-fifth of a textbook per student. This level of funding using the same assumptions noted above would have produced a TPR of 1:14.

Schools also faced significant delays in receiving their grants. The October 2009 PETS noted that many schools received the first grant allocation several months into the school year. While schools in Dar es Salaam on average recorded their capitation grant transfers at the beginning of the fiscal year, other schools did not receive their FY2008 capitation grant before the middle of the school year. Late grant payments meant that very few schools outside Dar es Salaam were in a position to buy sets of textbooks at the beginning of the school year.

At the school level the main expenditure categories recorded by the PETS were construction (30 percent) and textbooks and other TLM (29 percent). Other teaching tools and inputs like exercise books, pens/pencils/chalks, and so on constituted another 12 percent of school level expenditure. Desks and other equipment for schools constituted six percent of school level expenditure and administration and other expenses accounted for nine percent. In some cases the administration category covered allowances to teachers performing extra classes. If expenditure on TLMs (including textbooks) averaged 29 percent of the capitation grant, then in 2008 only T Sh1215 per student was available for textbook purchase (US$0.90), which was equivalent to one-seventh of a textbook per student per year, which produced a TPR of 1:20.[14] The PETS noted that average expenditure per student on textbooks and TLMs varied between schools and was worst in rural schools. Four percent spent less than T Sh500 (US$0.37) on textbooks and teaching materials per student and 13 percent of the schools spent less than T Sh1,000 per student (US$0.74). This was in contrast to urban schools in which 94 percent of the schools spent more than T Sh1,000 per student. It is clear that for the 17 percent of schools that spent less than T Sh1000 per student per year, the achievable TPRs were completely inadequate. The Tanzania example provided above demonstrates how funding diversion of allocated textbook grants reduces the possible TPRs from the target of 1:3 to 1:20 or even less. The Tanzania PETS recorded fund diversion at every level of the system. Fund diversion occurs in many SSA countries. Fund diversion does not imply stealing or embezzlement. The term means the diversion of the funding away from its intended purpose to other purposes where higher spending priority is perceived. Diversion, is a symptom of underfunded education systems where ministries, districts, and individual schools are struggling to meet competing claims for available finance. Under these circumstances textbook provision may not be the highest priority at HQ, District, or the level of individual schools. In the PETS survey quoted above 13 percent of the original budget was not released at all but was retained by the central government; a further 6.1 percent was used by District Councils for noneducational purposes and in 17 percent of schools very little of the grant was spent on textbooks. Thus, of the total textbook grant allocated to schools, at least 36.1 percent was diverted away from the procurement of textbooks. Obviously, the maintenance of textbook targets in this situation can only be achieved with rigorous ring-fencing of allocated funding.

Fund Misappropriation and Piracy

The most notable recent example of alleged misappropriation of textbook funds has been the arrest in 2009 of many MOEST officials in Kenya accused of diverting primary textbook grants before they had been transferred to schools. Although full details are yet to emerge, the scale of the misappropriation is reported to be large and to have seriously affected the sales and delivery of textbooks and other TLMs to a majority of primary schools in Kenya.

> The first two years of the free primary textbook scheme went well with DPs working closely with the government and PricewaterhouseCoopers monitoring the transfer of funds and following up the distribution process. The schools were buying books as programmed and publishers reported good sales. The problems started when donors handed over the management of the funds to the government.

Billions of Ksh were reported to be disbursed but schools were not buying textbooks as expected. An audit was carried out after complaints from stakeholders, publishers and DPs. The audit report indicated anomalies in the disbursement of the textbook grants. This led to discontinuation of funding by DPs through the Ministry in 2009. Since then the Government of Kenya (GOK) has had to take on the entire funding burden. This has led to a drop in the funds allocated per child and as a result it has not been possible to achieve the initial target objective of a 1:1 textbook:pupil ratio. With inadequate funding publishers have recorded low sales and have not been able to clear stocks which they had prepared for the programme. In 2011 a total of Kshs550 was allocated per child in primary schools for the purchase of books. The disbursement programme was split into three instalments: 50% in January 2011, 30% in May 2011 and 20% in September 2011. This works out as follows:

- January Kshs275 per child (USD3.20 per child)
- May Kshs165 per child (USD1.92 per child)
- September Kshs110 per child (USD 1.28 per child)

At the end of the first term publishers have reported low sales and slow stock movement.

In March 2011 DFID funded textbook procurement via the Kenya Independent Schools Association (KISA) for non-formal schools in slum areas. A total of Kshs600 million (USD6.98 million) was spent. KISA invited only 7 publishers to supply books and left out publishers with books which had been recommended by the Kenya Institute of Education. The criteria used for textbook selection was not made clear to the publishers. Some of the books bought are not on the recommended textbook list. All the publishers with approved books should have been invited to participate. Enrollment in Secondary Schools doubled from 0.8 million students in 2002 to 1.6 million students in 2010. In 2011 the first group of pupils who benefitted from free primary education joined Form 1. In January 2011 the MOES disbursed Kshs3,857 (USD44.0) per child to public secondary schools. Out of this Kshs1,388 (USD16.0) per child was allocated to tuition. This was to be used as follows:

- Exercise books Kshs277 (USD3.22) per child
- Laboratory Equipment Kshs111 (USD1.29) per child
- Teaching/learning materials Kshs28 (USD0.33) per child
- Chalk Kshs14 (USD0.16) per child
- Reference/library material Kshs874 (10.16) per child
- Internal Examination Kshs84 (USD0.98) per child.

The vote for reference and library materials was supposed to cater for textbooks as well.[15]

In 2014 Kenyan publishers continue to report seriously diminished sales from school textbook grants, the late and unpredictable release of textbook grants, long delays in bookseller payments to publishers, the collapse of school auditing of the use of textbook grants (and other school expenditures), and the associated widespread misuse and diversion of textbook grants by schools.[16]

The stealing of free textbooks from warehouses and the sale of textbooks by school principals to private schools also represents additional misappropriation of funds.

There are regular reports of textbook piracy. Piracy and photocopying divert available funding away from legitimate textbook purchases and focus school expenditures on texts with poor quality reproduction, which is also commonly associated with low-level durability because pirates do not bother with thread-sewn bindings or durable finishing but produce the books in poor-quality glued bindings. The net result is lower pedagogic usefulness through poor-quality presentation and reproduction and early book destruction, which affects cost amortization and thus the recurrent cost of the TLM provision system. The use of local printing facilities can exacerbate this problem because it is easy for local printers to run on additional copies using exactly the same plates, machines, paper, and cover card as the legal editions ordered by the publishers. When this happens it is impossible for anyone to distinguish the pirate editions from the legal original editions. Schools may benefit from this type of piracy because they receive illegal copies that maintain the original presentation and durability standards but at lower costs. More commonly they pay the same price as for the legal edition and all of the profits go to the pirates. The losers are the legitimate publishers and authors.

The most common form of misappropriation in decentralized funding situations is an agreement between an unscrupulous head teacher and a bookseller to invoice textbooks, which are then never supplied. The head teacher and the bookseller split the invoice value between them. Funds are utilized but without benefit to either teachers or students. It is impossible to quantify the extent of piracy, photocopying, and misappropriation but it is considerable.

Textbook Pricing Markups

This is a problem associated with decentralized financing systems where publishers sell through local booksellers or traders. Publishers typically report discounts to booksellers for textbook supplies to schools in SSA of between 20 and 30 percent with occasional discounts of up to 37.5 percent for trusted important wholesalers. Publishers expect that booksellers should be able to cover the costs of supply and make a profit out of this discount. However, publishers have reported cases in many SSA countries where booksellers have marked up the official retail price by 20 to 50 percent in order to increase their profitability. Sometimes the markup may be agreed with a head teacher and the agreed markup is then shared. Once again, it is difficult to quantify the extent of pricing markups but they may be very extensive, particularly in rural and remote areas where most schools will not be able to access competitive sources of supply. Schools often have no access to official price lists or even to the recommended price lists of individual publishers. Booksellers sometimes produce their own price lists which are given to schools. If there is a lack of MOE supervision of commercially supplied approved textbooks then price markups are more likely. Price markups decrease the effective purchasing power of schools with limited textbook procurement budgets and thus undermine the effectiveness and sustainability of textbook provision systems. Because price markups are more likely in rural areas (where booksellers and distributors try to justify the markups as a result of higher transportation costs) they increase rural versus urban inequity in the system.

Supervision and Accountability

The solution to all of the issues listed above lies with effective system monitoring and supervision; and the lack of these, plus ineffective and unprofessional management and the use of untrained staff, are major factors in poor performing TLM provision systems. Chapters 10 and 11, below, provide evidence of the impact of substandard system management and monitoring. In most countries the inspectorate has no idea what has been supplied to schools and thus is not in a position to check on what has been received and whether or not it is still *in situ* and in good condition. When storekeepers and head teachers know that they will never be checked on their TLM inventories and management paperwork, then the temptations for misappropriation are greatly increased. Liberia and Rwanda have recently introduced TLM management databases that can capture every stage in the process from order through to delivery so that HQ departments, district education officers (DEOs), and the inspectorate know what stock schools have been supplied with—and signed for—and when it was supplied. This information, properly used, enables the monitoring of delivered stock against stock in schools and an easy identification of schools with unacceptably high levels of loss and damage. It also identifies stock movements from HQ to districts and to schools and thus pinpoints where stock losses are taking place. Properly applied, these basic systems should be able to control and eliminate the high level of stock loss and misappropriation that is common in many SSA countries. And behind these systems there should be the audit facility. The extract below on school auditing is taken from a 2008 report on secondary school TLM financing in Kenya.

> The MOES School Audit Unit (SAU) is charged with the responsibility of performing audits and inspections of all public educational institutions. This is an internal control exercise intended to provide the MOEST and the public with the assurance that the considerable funds allocated to Free Primary and Free Day Secondary Education (FPE and FDSE) are used for their intended purposes and in compliance with guidelines. The SAU is expected … to report to the MOEST and to the MOF that public educational institutions are operated in compliance with MOEST policies, procedures and regulations.

The Education Act requires that school accounts (both primary and secondary) are certified annually and the SAU is also expected to audit all schools at least once a year.... The SAU is also expected to carry out investigations ... requiring their intervention. Such circumstances may include ... fraud, theft and non-compliance with regulations.

Currently there are around 200 provincial and district school auditors responsible for the certification and audit of more than 18,000 primary schools, 4,000 secondary schools and a range of other special and further education institutions. In addition, both DEOs and DSAs are short of transport and operational expenses that inhibit their ability to visit educational institutions on a regular basis. Rural and remote schools are therefore not visited and inspected as often as schools closer to urban centers.

The MOEST expects that each district auditor should be responsible for 18 school audits per year—a maximum of 3,600 audits per year with current staffing levels - when there are at least 24,000 education institution audits required per year in order to meet the requirements of the Education Act. Clearly the task cannot be achieved with the resources currently available to the SAU. Secondary schools currently report average audit frequencies of between 5 and 10 years. Many primary schools report never having received an audit or an inspection. A number of provinces/districts are instituting "pool" audits conducted at Divisional offices in order to increase the current audit frequency, but "pool" audits are typically a cursory examination of school books without recourse to the physical, on-site checks of stocks, assets and systems, which are necessary for a full and satisfactory audit.

Clearly, the current audit and supervision arrangements for secondary schools are unacceptable in a situation where public primary and secondary schools are likely to be in receipt of over US$1 billion of public funds over the next 4 years as a result of the introduction of FSE and FDSE. (Read and Read 2008)

It is worth noting that the identification of corrupt practices relating to TLM funding in Kenya and the subsequent termination of most donor funding for TLMs via the MOEST occurred just a few months after this report was submitted.

A Summary of Key Issues

The case studies and issues provided above suggest that there is no single universal cause behind the persistent underfinancing of textbook provision in SSA countries. There are, however, some common components. These are the following:

- The pressure on TLM budgets caused by rapid enrollment growth, which is often caused by free textbook provision. Textbook purchase is one of the major expenses that families incur in sending their children to school and there is plenty of evidence to demonstrate that reductions in textbook costs to parents in SSA are directly linked to higher levels of school enrollment. In some countries, the provision of free textbooks and free tuition has led to explosive growth in school enrollments at both primary and secondary levels, often well in excess of the projections.

- The repeated tendency for curriculum designers to increase the number of subjects and to make decisions that completely fail to take into account the cost implications on the system as a whole. New subjects do not just require additional textbooks; they also often require specialist teacher recruitment and additional pre-service and in-service teacher training programs. The decision to embargo the use of existing stocks of old curriculum textbooks in Tanzania was taken with no concern for either cost or for TPRs. The changes appear to have passed without comment from the DPs most involved in creating the conditions for reduced-cost reform in the first place.

- In some countries (for example, Guinea and Malawi from the case studies above) investment in textbook provision has not been a major problem because a variety of donors have provided financial support. But the DP support has rarely addressed affordability and sustainability issues apart from noting that sustainability is an objective. Cost reduction in TLM provision has rarely been addressed systematically in an attempt to create a system that can be maintained by governments. Thus, in many countries, there is concern about what might happen when or if DPs terminate their financial support. In Mozambique, DP support took a basic fund aimed to support the poorest and transformed it into a mechanism for providing all primary textbooks free of charge. The Mozambique case study noted GOM concern that the system developed through DP support could not be sustained without continued external support.

- Manufacturing cost versus textbook cost. This is very widely misunderstood by both MOEs and development partners. In retail sales the manufacturing cost is only approximately one-fifth of the textbook cost, but development partners in particular have tended to see cost reduction in terms of reducing manufacturing costs only.

- Textbook cost versus system cost. In many countries the primary concern in cost reduction has been to focus on reducing the average unit costs of textbooks. While this is an important consideration there is frequently a lack of concern with system costs, and in a majority of countries the system costs are the main problem in sustainability. Ideally, the reduction in average unit textbook costs is only one activity in cost reduction, which should be a part of an overall and wider review of system costs. Unit textbook costs and system costs are treated in more detail in "Underfinancing" section, above.

- The nature and extent of fund diversion, fund misappropriation, piracy, and price markups in undermining allocated TLM funding may be appreciated in general but are rarely reviewed and managed in detail by either MOEs or DPs. Well-designed and regularly performed PETS usually provide the basic information, but there is often a lack of will (or perhaps specialist knowledge) to make the necessary adjustments to improve the situation when major flaws have been identified. In Tanzania the deterioration in the value of the school textbook grants was not recognized even when the PETS provided the information. In Kenya, it was the outcry from publishers, booksellers, and schools that raised the alarm that the textbook grants were not being released as intended. In Malawi the government financing decisions that led to the collapse of secondary TLM provision and the launch of the Textbook Revolving Fund in 1999/2000 were then repeated again in the period up to 2013/2014, which led to the reintroduction of the Textbook Revolving Fund once again. These are issues that governments and the DP community need to monitor constantly in order to ensure workable and effective systems that will consistently achieve agreed TLM targets.

- Finally, it is probable that in most SSA countries the monitoring, inspection, supervision, and financial audit systems are not up to the job of ensuring that all links in the financing and supply chain are operating effectively. It is this lack of properly organized systems, trained staff, and operational budgets that enables the systems to break down. The Kenya example provided above, where the number of auditors was quite insufficient to meet the minimum government legal requirements for institutional audits, is a clear example of the kind of issues that need to be addressed.

Notes

1. This case study has been developed from information extracted from Nyerendra 2001.
2. Although they were called Distance Education Centers (DECs) it was clear by the mid 1990s that very little distance education was taking place. Enrollment pressures had turned them into a type of safety valve in which the enormous parental demand for secondary education could be partially provided with minimum financial inputs from government. The DECs—later renamed Community Day Secondary Schools (CDSSs)—often used existing primary schools to provide after-school lessons in the afternoons and evenings. Primary school teachers were paid extra to teach additional shifts as secondary school teachers. Although tuition fees (including the costs of TLMs) were tightly regulated by government, each school was free to levy its own boarding charges and other incidental fees. As a result there was never enough money to provide adequate sets of TLMs and most CDSSs operated with very seriously deficient supplies.
3. This case study has been developed from information extracted from Sow, Brunswic, and Valérien 2001.
4. This level of discount seems very high. See chapter 7.
5. *Vide* Malawi secondary textbook fees in "Affordability, Sustainability, and Predictability" section, above.
6. This is quoted in the PASEC study.

7. English, Hisabati, Sayansi, Stadi za Kuzi, Kiswahili, and Maarifa ya Jamii.
8. English, Historia, Kiswahili, Sayansi, Jiografia, Sanaa na Michezo, Sayansi Kinu, Sayansi Kilimo, and Siasa.
9. Calculated as T Sh10,000 × 1.4 (for currency devaluation) × 1.5 (to cover the costs of an increased curriculum requirement for textbook titles) × 1.1 (for printing cost inflation).
10. Based on data in the October 2009 PETS Final Draft Report, page four. This figure is not strictly comparable to the 2000 allocations because it also includes the value of the Development Grant. Thus T Sh6,000 is actually a high side figure.
11. The capitation grant levels were calculated to be sufficient to maintain and improve target textbook-student ratios. The need for complete restocking went far beyond maintenance and should thus have attracted significant additional funding if previously achieved textbook levels were to be reestablished.
12. SEDP Implementation Completion Report, June 2008, World Bank, Washington.
13. If this is correct it would represent 52 percent of the capitation grant instead of the original 40 percent recommended for textbook purchase. However, these percentages don't take account of the fact that the T Sh6,046 allocation also included the Development Grant. In reality the actual amounts available to schools for textbook purchase were almost certainly far less than T Sh3,150. Thus the 1:6 ratio is clearly a very optimistic estimate.
14. The calculation is as follows: a full set of textbooks would be US$6 × 9 textbooks = US$54, amortized at 1:3 ratio and book life of three years = US$54/9 = US$6/student per year to achieve a 1:3 ratio for three years. If the actual expenditure is US$0.90 per student per year, the ratio would be 6 × 0.9/9 = 1:20.
15. Personal communication from Kenyan Textbook Publisher—April 2011.
16. From private correspondence with leading Kenyan textbook publishers.

References

Baldé, G., A. Camara, A. Diallo, and C. Ta. 2008. *Ecole et Décentralisation le Cas de la Guinée*. Paris: IIEP.

Bontoux, V., and L. Musonda. 2009. *Review of the System for Decentralized Textbook Procurement and Distribution in Zambia*. Luxembourg: Proman for the EU and the Zambian MOE.

Buchan, A., C. Denning, and T. Read. 1991. *African Book Sector Studies Summary Report*. Windsor, United Kingdom: International Book Development for World Bank African Ministers of Education Conference.

Claussen, J., and M. J. Assad. 2009. *Public Expenditure Tracking Survey for Primary and Secondary Education in Tanzania (Final Draft Report)*. Dar es Salaam, Tanzania: MOEVT.

Da Cruz, A. J., T. A. George, F. Z. Gnahare, F. Z. Kouakou, P. Mendonca, C. Schlabi, M. Simao, and A. Read. 1998. *Financing Textbooks and Teacher Training Materials*. Perspectives in African Book Development Series. Paris: Working Party on Books and Learning Materials, Association for the Development of Education in Africa.

MOEST (Ministry of Education, Science, and Technology, Malawi). 2014. *Textbook Revolving Fund Handbook*. Lilongwe: MOEST.

Nyerendra, G. 2001. "Malawi Case Study." In *Upgrading Book Distribution in Africa*, edited by T. Read, C. Denning, and A. Buchan, 55–85. Paris: ADEA.

O'Connor, B. 1999. "Donor Support for Textbooks in Africa." In *Educational Publishing in a Global Perspective*, edited by S. Sosale. A World Bank Report. Washington, DC: World Bank.

Pôle de Dakar. 2005. *Le système éducatif guinéen: Diagnostic et perspectives pour la politique éducative dans le contexte de contraintes macro-économiques fortes et de réduction de la pauvreté*. Dakar: CONFEMEN for the GOG.

PricewaterhouseCoopers. 2005. *Implementation of Decentralized Textbook Procurement in Zambia*. Brussels: European Union for the Zambia MOE.

Read, A., C. Denning, and A. Buchan. 1988. *Tanzania Book Sector Study*. London: Book Development Council for the World Bank.

Read, T. 2010. *The Future of Our Children's Education: Providing the Best Textbooks for the Next Generation in Tanzania*. Windsor, United Kingdom: International Education Partners, 16–18.

Read, N., and T. Read. 2008. *Free Day Secondary Education in Kenya: Tuition Vote Management Training and Research Report*. Windsor, United Kingdom: International Education Partners for the World Bank and MOEST, Kenya.

Saiwad, A. 2001. "Tanzania Case Study on Distribution Issues." In *Upgrading Book Distribution in Africa*, edited by T. Read, C. Denning, and V. Bontoux V. Paris: ADEA.

Sow, M. A., E. Brunswic, and J. Valérien. 2001. "Guinea Case Study on Distribution Issues." In *Upgrading Book Distribution in Africa*, edited by T. Read, C. Denning, and V. Bontoux. Paris: ADEA.

Secrétariat Technique Permanent de la CONFEMEN (STP). 2006. *La formation des enseignants contractuels: Etude thématique, Guinée, 2006*. Washington, DC: World Bank and CONFEMEN for the Government of Guinea.

UNESCO Institute for Statistics. 2011. *Financing Education in Sub-Saharan Africa: Meeting the Challenges of Expansion, Equity and Quality*. Montreal, QC: UNESCO Institute for Statistics.

World Bank. 2008. *SEDP Implementation Completion Report*. Washington, DC: World Bank.

CHAPTER 6

Authorship and Publishing

The Textbook Publishing Process[1]

The main components and the sequencing of the textbook publishing process are:

- Developing and specifying the textbook concept;
- Costing, pricing, and financial management;
- Identifying authors and commissioning, reviewing, and finalizing the manuscript;
- Editing the manuscript;
- Designing the manuscript using desktop publishing (DTP) software, managing page layouts and proofs, and so on;
- Specifying and commissioning illustrations;
- Preparation for press;
- Identifying, selecting, contracting, and supervising manufacturing;
- Marketing and sales; and
- Warehousing, distribution, and delivery.

Writing and manufacturing are normally external activities. However, there are some publishing organizations in which writing and even printing may be maintained in-house. This is typical of some state or Ministry of Education (MOE) publishing. In these cases it is not uncommon for the roles of curriculum development, textbook writing, and editing to be combined in one individual or group. This is widely regarded as a less effective method of working because it diminishes or removes the creative role of interpreting the curriculum to create an effective textbook and the critical role of the editor in working on and improving the manuscript.

There are also publishers—usually small—who work by outsourcing most of the work of textbook development to outside companies or freelancers including writing, editorial, design, illustrations, print preparation, and manufacturing.

There are two basic approaches to the management of the publishing process. These are

- A *linear approach*, in which each task in the publishing process is handled in sequence—common in many MOE publishing houses; and
- An integrated *teamwork* approach, in which the full range of required skills are applied from conceptualization through the stages of planning, writing, development and production to the finished book.

The three critical components in effective textbook publishing are management, planning, and scheduling. In most textbook publishing organizations there will be more than one title in development at the same time. In large publishing houses multiple titles are normally in development simultaneously. They usually have to be available in time for the beginning of the school year and careful planning and monitoring are essential to ensure that editorial, design, illustration, and production departments are all utilized to best advantage and maximum efficiency. Workflow needs to be scheduled to ensure an even distribution of work across the year in order to avoid the bottlenecks and delays that can occur when several titles require, for example, design and illustrations work at the same time.

Key Characteristics of Commercial Publishing

Successful commercial publishers have to develop systems to promote and encourage good teamwork and the application of specialist skills to a common problem and to develop effective planning, scheduling, and progress monitoring. These are common objectives of all effective textbook publishing management. However, in commercial publishing houses there are characteristics which are not often found in state or MOE publishing. They are the following:

- *Financial management.* This is a very significant component of commercial publishing management and one that is rarely found in MOE publishing departments. Even in state publishing houses it tends often to be more of an accounting function rather than an active management function. Commercial publishing houses operate to make a profit and price is a key component in competitiveness, and achieving market share and a return on capital invested. As a result, commercial publishers tend to be much more cost conscious in their textbook planning and in their financial management and tend also to be far more conscious of the strengths and weaknesses of rival publications. They also need to be conscious of cash flow because they need to handle both the recurrent overhead costs and the publishing expenses relating to authors' fees and royalties, the costs of freelance artists and designers, the purchase of raw materials and the need to pay printers. Thus cash management including bank borrowing, the need for access to foreign exchange as required, maintaining sales income, paying suppliers, maintaining credit control over purchasers, and so on are all substantial components of commercial publishing management, which are rarely found in MOE publishing departments. The pressure to achieve best prices means that commercial publishers are generally more efficient in achieving cost reductions and in achieving best raw materials and printing prices. Few private-sector publishers any longer maintain their own printing plant and are thus free to seek the best quality at the best price. State publishers and MOE publishing departments maintaining their own print houses have to use their facilities to maintain work flow, even when the plant is not suitable for textbooks or is not price competitive.

- A commercial publishing company has a number of *legal requirements* which have to be fulfilled. These include the preparation and finalization of annual accounts (including profit and loss accounts and balance sheets), the requirement for annual audit and the payment of taxes such as corporation tax, value added tax, payroll tax, and so on. Of course, there are major state publishing companies, which operate to all intents and purposes as independent companies and are thus required to provide accounts and to undergo audits, but many state publishing units are not independent but are parts of government and thus have reduced legal obligations.

- In order to manage the financial component of the business, commercial publishing companies have developed *financial management tools* such as the preparation of detailed title-by-title estimates and costings, departmental or divisional forward publishing plans and budgets, financial projections extending three to five years into the future, and management accounts, which enable continuous monitoring of the financial position of the company. Management accounts are usually produced on a monthly basis and are reviewed by every operational department of the company and by the finance department. Few state publishing houses or MOE publishing departments are required to maintain these kinds of management tools.

- *Professional staffing*. Large publishing companies will try to hire high quality professional staff in a number of key specialties. Thus in big educational publishing companies there will be editorial management staff (commissioning editors), copy editors, permissions editors, picture editors, rights managers, designers, illustrators, production staff, sales and marketing, warehousing and distribution, financial management, and so on. In small commercial publishing houses the opportunity for specialization is much less and job descriptions often combine more than one specialism. Small publishing companies often outsource specialist tasks to avoid having to maintain permanent payroll commitments and even large publishing companies have moved towards outsourcing tasks as a means of controlling costs. Authorship is a commonly outsourced task, but editing, design, illustrations, and even production management, warehousing, and distribution can be outsourced as well. Twenty to thirty years ago, many publishing companies maintained their own printing houses, but these have largely been sold off as an efficiency measure because there was always a temptation for a publisher to use its own in-house printing facility in order to maintain work flow even when the in-house facility did not have the right plant or processes or was not the lowest cost supplier. In the other direction, typesetting and page design and layout have tended to be produced in-house rather than to be outsourced as technology development has made this possible. However, whether a commercial publisher is employing professional specialists or multipurpose managers, all commercial publishing is based upon the requirement for the staff to perform to high levels in order to maintain profitability and thus the continued existence and operation of the company. Staffing tends to be more tightly controlled; and the staff are expected to perform to more or less high standards and to have demonstrable professional skills. Failure to perform well tends to result in dismissal and the recruitment of replacements.

- By contrast, the work force in many MOE publishing departments is recruited by posting or internal transfer from other government departments, often without regard to previous experience, relevant professional skills, or aptitudes. Dismissal or reposting to other work as a result of failure to work effectively is generally time consuming and rare. Similarly, staff with valuable experience may be posted away to other unrelated jobs. In one well-known case a senior staff member in a state publishing house was financed by a donor organization to attend a one-year overseas training course in book production management. Within weeks of his return he was posted as the local municipality Director of Parks and Gardens. State publishing houses and MOE publishing departments may have specialist design, illustrations, and production staff but they are rarely subjected to the same requirement to "perform or perish" which is often typical of commercial publishing houses. Many MOE publishing departments have curriculum specialists who are also expected to operate as authors and editors even though they may have little or no previous track record or even expertise in these tasks. In commercial publishing authorship and editorial work are regarded as separate skills and there is a perceived positive benefit in having authorship and editorial inputs performed by different people. Objective quality judgments become much more difficult when the same person is responsible for syllabus design, authorship, and editorial control.

- *Competition*. Commercial publishing houses have to compete to survive. State publishing houses rarely have to compete because they tend to operate as monopolistic publishers. There are some countries where state publishers compete on equal terms with commercial publishers. For example, in Kenya the Jomo Kenyatta Foundation (JKF) and the Kenya Literature Bureau (KLB) are both 100 percent state-owned companies that compete on a level playing field basis with each other and with private sector publishers. They receive no state subsidies and are not given any preferential treatment in the selection of titles or the award of contracts. But this requirement for state-owned publishers to actively compete for market share on equal terms is rare. Lack of competition is associated with lower standards simply because there is no possibility of title replacement.

What Can State Publishing Learn from Commercial Publishing Management?

The following are the most important issues where state publishing or MOE publishing units can improve their publishing output by emulating some aspects of commercial publishing management:

- *Cost Awareness.* Because most commercial publishers are involved in active competition and price is a key factor in the sales and marketing of school textbooks, most commercial publishers are acutely aware of the need to achieve the right balance between content quality, attractiveness, physical durability, and price. In state publishing, which is often monopolistic, there is much less concern with "value for money" and with achieving the best price possible. A recent study in Jordan concluded that unit cost savings on textbooks in the region of 50 percent would be possible if the publishing department in the Directorate of Curriculum and Textbooks applied some of the practices common in commercial publishing. It is probable that most state publishing units or MOE publishing departments do not achieve effective price control over their textbooks, teachers' guides, and other teaching and learning materials (TLM).

- *Market knowledge.* Competition requires private sector publishers to explore every avenue to improve the saleability of their output. Commercial publishers typically examine rival textbooks, look at similar books from other countries, identify and discuss strengths and weaknesses, visit schools to identify school realities and to discuss textbook requirements with schools and teachers, and attempt to identify promising authors with interesting ideas and approaches. State publishers, in monopoly situations, do not have the same incentive to explore other possibilities or to develop genuine market knowledge. It is striking that in many MOE publishing departments, individual curriculum or editorial staff may have sample copies of other textbooks but these tend to be studied individually and are rarely discussed together with other staff members. Few small publishers have well-developed sample textbook libraries that can be used to develop ideas and new or alternative approaches to textbook content and presentation. Too often, the members of a subject curriculum unit who are also expected to be authors and editors are effectively cut off from school realities by bureaucratic barriers and budget constraints on school visiting. Visiting schools to observe and learn and to discuss teaching and learning materials requirements with practicing teachers is rarely perceived to be a major part of the job description.

- *Editorial control.* The need to achieve a good price-quality balance requires commercial publishers to exercise more editorial control over their authors and, in particular, to limit the amount of text. Many state publishers often fail to exercise the same editorial control. This can lead to overlong text and variations in writing styles and presentation (particularly where several members of a writing team are handling different units in the same textbook). When authors are drawn from senior academics in prestigious universities, curriculum subject specialists may often feel too intimidated to direct or control the authors. In many cases authorship is either unpaid or is poorly paid by state publishers or by MOE publishing units and this does not attract the best writers. Commercial publishers who have to pay attractive royalty rates or fees can attract a higher quality of authorship but also can demand more from their authors.

- *Scheduling and planning.* The need to control costs, achieve the right quality, and ensure on-time production and delivery in advance of the beginning of the school year means that most commercial publishers are much more aware of the need for tight planning and scheduling and thus exercise more management control than many state publishers or MOE publishing departments. There is a tendency in many state publishing institutions to allow writing schedules to be missed or manuscript approval deadlines to be constantly extended while corrections are made on the assumption that the lost time can be made up when manuscripts are passed to design and illustrations or to the production department. The inevitable result is overstretched design, illustrations, and production staff rushing to achieve deadlines at the last minute with all of the associated loss of quality, which is inevitable when complex tasks are performed at speed against tight deadlines.

A Brief Review of State Publishing in Sub-Saharan Africa

Up to independence most school textbooks were either exported unchanged from commercial publishers in the United Kingdom or France or, in some anglophone countries, were developed or adapted by local branches of U.K. commercial publishers. In East Africa the colonial government established a state-owned textbook publisher—East African Literature Bureau—but this was not a common development.

After independence there was a rapid growth in state monopolistic textbook publishing in many Sub-Saharan African (SSA) countries, often associated with state-owned printing and distribution companies. In francophone countries monopolistic textbook publishing was associated with national pedagogic institutes. In some countries such as Tanzania, the monopolistic textbook publishing entity developed all of its own textbooks; in other countries (for example Uganda and many francophone countries) the monopolistic textbook publisher subcontracted commercial publishers to develop courses. Comments on the impact of state publishing in Africa (and elsewhere) are provided in "Trends in National Teaching and Learning Materials Provision" section, in chapter 2.

Even in 2014 the primary and secondary school textbook market in many SSA economies still represents more than 90 percent of total national book turnover. If this turnover is reserved only for state companies there is little or nothing left to support all other types of publishing output including the critical children's book publishing sector.

In Tanzania state textbook provision was on the verge of collapse by the late 1980s. The Kenya School Equipment Scheme collapsed in 1988. Although state publishing lingered on in some countries (for example, Ghana) until the early years of the 21st century, by the late 1980s most state textbook provision systems in SSA (and in the former Soviet Union as well) were in trouble. In 2014 most state textbook publishers are no longer operational or have ceased to be involved in textbook publishing. Their main failures were as follows:

- *Poor quality textbooks* in terms of writing, page layout and design, illustrations, and general readability.

- *Inertia.* Having produced a textbook many state publishing companies were rarely motivated or financed to produce corrected reprints, revisions, or new editions. Thus poor quality textbooks were perpetuated year after year.

- *Underfunding.* Many of the state publishers suffered from consistent underfinancing, which prevented them from meeting required textbook publishing programmes, which led in turn to underprovision of textbooks in schools.

- *Poor physical production quality.* This typically meant low-quality paper in terms of grammage, chemical composition, caliper (thickness), opacity, and brightness; inadequate binding processes; poor quality cover materials; a lack of adequate cover finishing (lamination or UV varnishing); and poor use of processes. Thus cover and text paper grain direction were often incorrect, covers were not thread sewn onto the book blocks, and covers were rarely scored and hinged. The net result was low-quality books with low classroom book life expectations, which in turn either decreased textbook availability in schools or increased the recurrent costs of textbooks provision.

- *Irregular, inaccurate, and ineffective book distribution.* Because the state book distribution systems were underfunded and were not paid on evidence of completed delivery, there was no motivation to perform efficiently. Often the books could be stuck in district or subdistrict warehouses with no attempt to deliver them to schools because there was no district transport or funds to rent transport. Many of the district stores were in such poor condition that books suffered serious damage from rain, damp, dust, and vermin. In Guinea, for example, it was reported that over 60 percent of textbook stocks were "lost" regularly during transportation. In Ghana, the national audit office reported in 2004 that 50 percent of districts inspected had no records of textbook supplies to schools.

- *School complaints* about damaged, inaccurate, or late supplies were usually ignored because there was no motivation to do anything about the complaints. Kenyan schools were astonished when they discovered in 2003 that commercial suppliers would correct errors and deliver accurately direct to school premises, because they could not be paid until they could prove successful delivery.

- *Poor financial management*, which meant that available financial resources were poorly used. Fund misappropriation was also a common problem. Unfortunately, state textbook provision was no better served with reliable and adequate funding from government than private sector systems have been since.

Very few of the monopolistic, heavily subsidized state companies have managed to survive into the 21st century. Only the KLB and the JKF have managed to survive as active state-owned textbook publishers because the Kenyan MOE cut off their subsidies and insisted that they survived as competitive state companies operating on a level playing field with commercial companies. Both companies still survive and are operational but they are no longer dominant national textbook publishers. Where a state publisher may have survived (for example, The Ghana Publishing Corporation) it is typically no longer involved in textbook publishing.

The Reemergence of Private Sector Textbook Publishing

Since the demise of state publishing from the 1990s onwards there have been a number of developments that have supported the reemergence of private-sector textbook publishing. These include

- The development of public-private partnerships (PPPs) to replace state textbook provision systems;
- The transition to textbook provision systems utilizing private sector involvement;
- The introduction of competing alternative textbooks to replace monopoly provision;
- The decentralization of textbook selection to individual schools;
- An increase in the quality of textbooks as a result of competition;
- Reduced prices or increased value for money as a result of competitive price pressures and extended book life through the widespread use of minimum production specifications as a condition of approval for sale to schools; and
- The rapid development of local authorship and publishing capacity.

The above policy trends have provided private-sector publishers with renewed access to the core national textbook markets and have generally resulted in a rapid growth in local and regional textbook publishing companies. There are now few SSA countries where the new competitive textbook markets are dominated by multinationals. But centralized bulk purchase by government is cheap and easy for successful private sector publishers, whereas school-based selection from a list of multiple approved textbooks requires substantial investment in national marketing and distribution structures and also implies potential risk. Generally, the newly emergent private sector is prepared to take on the extra costs and the risk, but there are some who hanker for the security and ease of private sector supply to a centralized government procurement office and lobby for this option.

The rapid growth in the emergence of local, nationally owned textbook publishers has been encouraged by national educational publishing indigenization policies, which require that textbook publishers supplying textbooks to state education systems must be at least majority owned by nationals. This has occurred in both Ghana and Nigeria where multinationals were required to sell majority equity to their local partners. In East Africa both Longmans (now Pearson) and Heinemann sold their local Kenyan companies to local interests; although Pearson reopened in Kenya, it then closed down its local offices for a second time. The high court judgement against Macmillan for corrupt practice in South Sudan has led directly to the selling off of Macmillan companies in some SSA countries and the scaling down of Macmillan activities. This has created market opportunities for local publishers and there are now strong locally owned textbook publishing sectors in many SSA countries. In 2001 when the first competitive textbook bids were announced in Uganda, 14 publishers participated of which five were Ugandan owned and five were Kenyan owned (Bontoux and Buchan 2001). In 2009 the Rwanda textbook evaluation and approval bid attracted 15 participants of which three were local Rwandan publishers, four were Kenyan publishers, three were Ugandan companies, four were U.K. multinationals, and one was a French multinational (Buchan and Read 2009).

Progress in local textbook publishing capacity has been slower in francophone Africa, but there are now local textbook publishers in many francophone countries although Paris-based multinationals probably still dominate in most countries.

Local Authorship Capacity

The development of local authorship capacity predated the development of locally owned publishing companies. Multinational publishers in both the United Kingdom and France initially paired local authors in all subjects at all levels with an experienced external author. These authors learned their skills by working closely with experienced authors and rapidly developed their own skills and capacity. In 2011 it is now rare for any textbook intended for use in the SSA not to have local authors.

Cost Implications of Local Textbook Publishing

Chapter 8 analyzes the cost components of textbook pricing in SSA. A comparison of textbook prices for competing textbooks submitted for national textbook evaluations demonstrates that locally owned publishers and the local offices of multinational publishers can compete on prices on equal terms. However, there is a significant price differential between locally published school textbooks and imported textbooks originally conceived, developed, and priced for developed world markets where operational overheads are much higher, profit expectations tend to be greater, production specifications are more sophisticated, and purchasing power is greater. In most of SSA primary textbooks are now locally developed and published, but secondary textbooks still provide direct export possibilities for foreign publishers but at prices that are widely unaffordable for most parents or MOEs. However, as primary enrollments have exploded and created pressure for more secondary places, secondary textbook markets have expanded and there is now growing local publishing specifically for junior secondary markets, which demonstrates conclusively the beneficial differences in pricing between local secondary publishing and direct importing. Generally, local publishing has not yet percolated upwards into senior secondary markets that are still largely dependent upon imported books, but as senior secondary markets grow local publishing at more realistic prices will also develop.

A Summary of Key Issues

- The state textbook publishing experiments of the 1960s to the 1980s did not resolve textbook provision problems, and from the 1990s onwards state publishing structures have been widely terminated and replaced by private sector publishing involvement.
- Most state textbook publishers failed to adapt to market conditions and are no longer active in textbook publishing in 2013.
- Low state textbook prices were achieved by only including printing and raw materials costs and ignoring the costs of staffing, accommodation, operational costs, plant, and even authorship, which were paid by governments as part of the general education budget.
- There is increasing adoption of textbook provision systems based on approved lists of competing textbooks from which schools can select what they want against per capita purchasing budgets.
- The provision of market access to private sector textbook publishers has led to a rapid growth in local publishers and local publishing capacity throughout SSA.
- Multinational publishers are no longer dominant in anglophone SSA although they are probably still dominant in francophone countries.
- Authorship capacity is available in most countries for most subjects at most levels although there is always the possibility of combining experienced international or regional authorship with local authorship teams to build local skills and experience.
- Locally published lower secondary textbooks are significantly cheaper than imported textbooks originally published for developed world markets and thus carrying developed world overheads.[2]

Notes

1. "The Textbook Publishing Process," "Key Characteristics of Commercial Publishing," and "What Can State Publishing Learn from Commercial Publishing Management?" sections have been derived from Read and Smart 2010, and used with permission from Creative Associates International.
2. Some multinational publishers have been successful in developing textbooks specifically for SSA markets at relatively affordable prices. The tropical edition of McKean's Biology, published by Hodder, is a case in point.

References

Bontoux, V., and A. Buchan. 2001. *Uganda Bidding and Evaluation Report*. London, United Kingdom International Book Development for MOES Uganda and DFID.

Buchan, A., and T. Read. 2009. *Rwanda Bidding and Evaluation Report*. Windsor, United Kingdom International Education Partners for NCDC and Belgian Technical Cooperation.

Read, T., and A. Smart. 2010. *An Overview of the Publishing Process*. Vol. 1 of *Handbooks of Educational Publishing Good Practice*. Washington, DC: Creative Associates International for the Oman Ministry of Education. Used with permission.

CHAPTER 7

Manufacturing Issues

Local and Regional Textbook Printing Capacity in Sub-Saharan Africa

Local printing in Sub-Saharan Africa (SSA) has largely failed to achieve genuine international (or even regional) competitiveness in price and quality and equally often hasn't managed to develop capacity in key processes for durability, such as thread-sewn binding or high-quality cover finishing. Printing quality may be adequate but price and process often have been problematic. Where there are only a few local printers with adequate facilities, textbook printing has to be organized *in sequence* (that is printing one book at a time in one—or a limited number—of printers), which requires the early preparation of materials ready for printing and thus increased investments in early prepress and in storage until all the books are ready for distribution at the beginning of the school year. The great advantage of sourcing printing regionally or internationally is the possibility of printing *in parallel* (that is in different printers simultaneously), which greatly reduces the printing lead time thus avoiding the need to tie up investment capital for long periods. However, printing in parallel requires more management skills from the publishing production department. While many governments have been keen to develop their local printing industries and have put pressure on procurement systems to favor local printing (for example in many countries in the Middle East), this is only practical if the local printing industry has

- The processes, raw materials, and skills required for textbook manufacture;
- Sufficient capacity in the key processes (for example, for durability);
- Competitive prices or a government or development partners (DPs) who can afford and are prepared to pay the (frequently) higher costs; and
- Reliable delivery (textbooks have to be ready for the beginning of the school year and reliable on-time delivery is an essential requirement for textbook publishers).

Kenya, Nigeria, and South Africa all have well-developed printing industries capable of high-quality work and with the capacity to meet local needs, but competitive pricing and reliability are still problems. In other SSA countries there may be printers who can provide quality printing but the industry may lack the variety of plant and processes, the capacity, reliability, and price competitiveness required by textbook publishers. The local printing industry shouldn't be developed on the basis of higher costs and inferior quality for the education system.

A good recent example of the issues that need to be addressed in using local printing resources was provided by the *Reconnaissance Study of Textbook Printing Capacity in Ethiopia*, which concluded as follows:

(a) Not one of the Ethiopian printing enterprises surveyed had the technical capacity to complete the quantity of book printing required by the project within the time that an international contractor of the project actually did (see table);
(b) However, four Ethiopian enterprises (Berhane Selam, Branna, Bole, and EMPDA) had the potential to offer services comparable with those of the international printer, provided their equipment was upgraded; and
(c) Of the above four enterprises, two enterprises were either already upgrading their equipment (EMPDA) or planning to do so in the near future (Branna).
(d)

	In comparison with international printers the Ethiopian printer can:		
	Print books in four colors?	Thread sew the printed book pages?	Print covers and bind the books?
Berhane Selam	Yes	No	Yes
Branna	No	Yes	Yes
Bole	No	No	Yes
EMPDA	No	No	Yes

However, the table above indicates that only one printer out of the 9 that had been researched in Addis could print the required quantities in the specified 4 colours (Berhane Selam) and that only one (Branna) could thread sew the signatures, whereas all were able to print covers and draw them on to the book block. (De Guzman 2011)

The study quoted above only considered local capacity to manufacture the required quantities of textbooks. However there are three other characteristics that professional publishers have to take into account in their selection of a printer. These are

- Reliability—can the printer guarantee delivery on schedule?
- Quality—can the printer provide the required quality of manufacturing? and
- Price—is the printer competitive in price?

In discussions with publishers who had surveyed local printing capacity in Ethiopia the following conclusions were drawn:

- Reliable delivery dates for the large printing quantities specified in the bid documents could not be guaranteed by Ethiopian printing.
- Quality printing from some printers was acceptable although there were ongoing questions about consistent binding quality when large quantities were involved. This is a particular issue when so few printers have plant or experience of thread-sewn binding in large quantities.
- Better prices for reliable delivery and quality were available from a number of international printing sources in India and Malaysia, among others.

Thus, publishers were more confident in using international printing sources rather than Ethiopian printing sources until more investment and experience in color printing and thread-sewn binding plant came on stream.

As far as it could be ascertained no studies had been undertaken on print factories in the regions although one international publisher commented that there was a possible printer in Oromiya Region. However, the general consensus was that regional printing was unlikely to be better than printing facilities in Addis, and in some of the more remote regions printing facilities were likely to be unacceptable in quality for the standards required by the Ministry of Education, (MOE). There is of course nothing to stop regions procuring their printing from Addis or from international sources but this would rely on the availability in the regions of experienced production controllers capable of handling competitive printing procurement from different sources and ensuring the required quality levels.

Among the problems faced by Ethiopian printers are the following, which need to be taken into account by the Government of Ethiopia (GOE) in the development of local manufacturing capacity:

- *Raising finance for major investments in plant and raw materials.* Many printers commented that they had to pledge their premises as security for bank loans and that interest rates were expensive.

- *Getting access to foreign exchange for purchasing raw materials in the quantities required by the bids.* Printers can only start to purchase raw materials once the manufacturing contracts have been signed and awarded and the letters of credit have been raised. But the clock starts to tick against the delivery deadline as soon as letters of credit are raised, and raw materials may arrive too late for the printers to meet the deadlines.

- *Getting access to foreign exchange for purchasing plant.*

- *Taxes and duties on text paper, cover card, and other raw materials.* This puts local printers at a disadvantage against foreign printers because there are no duties on the importation of finished books. (Read 2013)

Textbook Specifications

Chapter 8, below, demonstrates the financial advantages of long textbook life over short textbook life, and this is an important issue for all countries where textbook financing is limited. Extended book life also reduces the frequency and costs of distribution, although it simultaneously increases the pressures on school-level storage. In order to achieve long life and maximum cost amortization, governments and DPs should seek the help of a professional printing and production specialist with a deep knowledge of book usage in local conditions. However, the following notes provide broad guidance.

The main purpose of specifying physical production standards is to ensure that every textbook, teachers' guide, or other supplementary material uses raw materials and manufacturing processes that will ensure the minimum target book life in the classroom. In general, four to five years of book life should be achievable with the right specifications, quality manufacturing, and good care and conservation in the classroom. There are well-documented examples of extended book life being regularly achieved if the above conditions are met. The key components in durable book specifications are as follows (Read 2010):

Text Paper

Text paper should have a minimum grammage of 70 grams per square meter (gsm), although 80 gsm would be better. The paper used should be wood free in composition with a machine finish (mf[1]) and should be white for maximum contrast and readability with a good opacity in order to prevent see-through. Whiteness, brightness, and opacity can all be defined in terms understandable to every professional publisher and printer. Clearly, the size of the printed page has to be related to the size of the sheet used to print the book and this is determined by the size of the printing machine. Printers will normally have stocks of paper that fit their own printing machines and publishers will normally use textbook formats that get the most economic use of paper from the selected printer. Failure to relate textbook design and page formats to the available printing machine sizes can lead to excessive paper wastage and thus increased cost.

Cover Card

There are different grades of cover card, and the highest grade should always be specified because maintaining the cover on the textbook is the basic protection to the book block. When the cover is detached from the textbook, the textbook is almost certainly finished in usable terms. The basic specification is a one-sided art card with a minimum weight (grammage) of 240 to 260 gsm. Chipboard is the cheapest grade and is not very durable. Experience has shown that better protection is provided by 280 to 300 gsm, but many African publishers object to the higher specifications on the grounds that these art cards are not easily available in-country and therefore favor international publishers who can more easily access higher grade card. The response to this is quite simply that if every publisher specified the higher standard then higher standard cards would become common because the market will always respond to demand. The card itself should be relatively rigid and should have a caliper (thickness) of at least 30 microns.

Finishing
Ideally the cover card should be "finished" with either a laminate or UV (ultraviolet) varnish which provides some waterproofing protection to the book block. The cover finish would normally be 12 to 15 microns in thickness. The finish also enables covers to be wiped clean with a damp cloth to remove dust and grit, which can damage covers. Lamination provides better water protection for the textbook although UV varnish can be effective if the process is properly performed. Machine varnish and nitrocellulose (NC) varnish are cheaper forms of finishing and provide some protection, but neither add significantly to the strength or durability of the textbook.

Binding
Textbooks up to 96 pages in extent can use saddle-stitched binding (that is a wire stitch through the spine of the textbook and closed against the center pages), which can provide adequate binding if the cover card is strong enough to "hold" the stitch. Above 96 pages all textbooks and teachers' guides should have thread-sewn bindings, gathered into signatures with "drawn-on" covers with four scores and two hinges so that the cover opens against the hinge and not against the spine. Under no circumstances should unsewn bindings be used for textbooks because the life of an unsewn textbook binding can often be measured in weeks, particularly if the process is not well performed. Standard unsewn binding is called "perfect" binding, which is a classic misnomer. Another form of binding that should never be used for school books is "side stabbing" in which a metal staple is inserted from the front cover through the book block to the back cover. This kind of binding leads to "mouse trapping" in which the textbook will not stay open so that students have to press out the "gutters" of the textbook, thereby breaking the binding and effectively ending textbook life.

Other forms of binding are sometimes used, such as "notched" binding—sometimes known as sewing with glue. These bindings are only effective if well performed and even then they are not to be compared in durability with thread-sewn bindings.

Wastage
The standard wastage allowance from a good printer is 1.5 percent per color, that is a four-color book would have a standard wastage allowance of six percent. If wastage exceeds this figure then textbook costs are increased.

Grain Direction
There are other considerations such as text and cover grain direction, which should always be parallel to the spine. Correct grain direction

- Helps the textbook to open more easily;
- Reduces creasing across the page;

- Reduces the tendency of the corners from folding inwards (known as "dog-ears"); and
- Prevents curling.

Color Printing

The debate over four-color, two-color, and one-color printing is now largely academic because in most countries primary school textbooks tend automatically to be printed in four colors, although this does add significantly to cost. Secondary textbooks can be printed in one or two colors, although some textbooks, such as biology and geography can benefit from four-color sections. The real policy issue with color is the level at which the economies of scale are reached. In four-color textbooks modern printing technology can usually generate acceptable economies of scale and prices at between 30 and 50,000 copies. One-color textbooks can achieve cost benefits of scale from only six to 10,000 copies. Four-color textbooks can become very expensive for small countries where print runs are small, such as Botswana, Namibia, and Zanzibar. The specification of local languages of instruction can fractionalize print runs below economic levels and significantly increase unit costs.

Processes

Publishers need to make sure that their selected printer has the plant and the expertise to deliver the required quality. There are plenty of examples of printers delivering substandard varnishing when UV varnishing has been specified or delivering substandard binding. Failure to quality control the processes specified can also lead to substandard textbooks that fail to meet durability and book life requirements. Failure to achieve the required standards and thus short book life will lead to diminishing textbook availability in the classroom and increased cost.

Publishers' Production Knowledge

Many local publishers lack detailed production knowledge and do not employ professionally trained production controllers. They will pass on production specifications to their selected printers but often have no ability to determine whether the printer has actually supplied according to the specifications. As a result many textbook bid submissions for evaluation fail specification tests and are rejected for approval. In the 2009 Rwanda textbook evaluation (Buchan and Read 2009) 45 percent of all submitted titles failed to meet the specified production standards. Even when conditional approval was provided on the understanding that the finished copies supplied to schools would meet specifications or be penalized, 25 percent of the titles still failed to meet specifications. It should be noted that some titles from international publishers also failed[2] to meet specifications because they assumed that their printers would automatically supply according to the specifications. This problem is compounded by the widespread practice of local publishers not having contracts with printers; thus, failure to supply according to specifications can be penalized.

Testing

Durability, long book life, and maximum cost amortization are such critical issues in achieving financially sustainable textbook and other teaching and learning materials (TLM) provision systems that testing for conformity to specifications by MOEs is considered to be essential. Testing has been introduced into a number of countries (for example, Kenya, Malawi, Rwanda, and Uganda) but it has not always been maintained as a regular process. Most countries do not test and therefore run the considerable risk that their textbooks do not meet the required specifications. Even worse, many countries do not specify accurately in order to achieve durability.

Developing local testing capacity is neither difficult nor expensive. The basic testing equipment costs no more than US$5,000 in total, and someone with a production background can learn the basic testing techniques in about a week from a qualified production professional. In the 2009 Rwanda bid evaluation, 14 separate production tests were conducted on each of more than 2,000 submitted samples in a period of three weeks. It is also recommended that testing should not just be confined to advance copies but also should be conducted in the field on delivered copies because there have been cases where titles were supplied for testing in one specification but were supplied to schools in another.

A Summary of Key Issues

- Kenya, Nigeria, and South Africa have well-developed printing industries capable of providing quality printing and with the capacity to meet local textbook needs. However price and reliability can be issues.
- Other SSA countries may have individual printers capable of providing acceptable quality but in most cases capacity, reliability, and price remain uncertain.
- Long textbook life and maximum cost amortization are critical issues in reducing textbook provision costs and achieving affordable and sustainable textbook provision systems.
- Many countries do not provide adequate textbook specifications.
- Many local publishers do not have the expertise to control and assure the required textbook production standards.
- Testing of advance copies and of delivered stock to ensure production quality up to required standards is strongly recommended but testing is rare even though the testing equipment and skills are cheap and easy to acquire.

Notes

1. MF means that the paper has been given a smooth surface by compressing it between hot rollers (calendaring) as it comes off the paper-making machine.
2. One publisher of an internationally used dictionary refused to believe that its stock failed to meet the required specification, but when it checked its own warehouse stock it discovered serious errors in gluing.

References

Buchan, A., and T. Read. 2009. *Rwanda Bidding and Evaluation Report*. Windsor, United Kingdom: International Education Partners for NCDC and Belgian Technical Cooperation.

De Guzman, A. 2011. *A Reconnaissance Study of Textbook Printing Capacity in Ethiopia*. Washington, DC: World Bank.

Read, T. 2010. *The Role and Significance of Teaching and Learning Materials: A Good Practice Paper for DFID Engagement*. London: DFID.

———. 2013. *Ethiopia: The Textbook Component in GEQUIP 1 and GEQUIP 2*. A World Bank Study. Washington, DC: World Bank.

CHAPTER 8

What Should Textbooks Cost?

Cost Components

The main cost components of a textbook are

- Typesetting;
- Design, illustrations, and artwork;
- Other reproduction;
- Raw materials (mostly text paper and cover card but also thread or wire, glue, varnish);
- Manufacturing—printing, binding, and finishing;
- Authors' royalties;
- Ocean freight, clearance, delivery charges (if printed overseas);
- Booksellers discount or other distribution charges; and
- Publisher's administrative, editorial, and marketing overheads and profit.

To avoid confusion it should be noted that the textbook cost components listed above are not the same as the links in the Book Chain (see chapter 4) although some of the cost components are part of the Book Chain.

Tables 8.1 and 8.2 provide the comparative percentage contributions to the retail price of a commercially published textbook made available for retail sale in Sub-Saharan Africa (SSA) in 2011.[1] It is clear from these data that the two largest cost components are the publishers' overheads and profit (27 percent) and the booksellers' discount (25 percent). The booksellers' discount assumes a profit margin for the bookseller. If textbooks are supplied in bulk to a government or development partner (DP) the booksellers' discount is subtracted from the retail price. If the publisher is required to supply direct to schools, the booksellers' profit margin (10 to 15 percent) should be subtracted from the quoted price. Textbooks imported from developed world publishers would normally require a higher publisher overhead because developed world overhead costs are higher. Thus switching from developed world publishing to local publishing would tend to reduce the overhead component of the price. Similarly, speeding up payments to publishers would reduce the publishers' bank borrowings and thus reduce the financing costs, which can be a very considerable part of the overhead if payment is long delayed; and there are plenty of examples of ministries of education (MOEs) or governments delaying payment by two years or more.

In state publishing many of the costs listed in table 8.1, below, seem to disappear. Thus there is no requirement for profit and the publishers' overhead is often not included. This doesn't mean that the publishers' overhead doesn't exist in state publishing; but the overhead is subsumed under other budget heads such as salaries, maintenance, and so on. Similarly, the distribution charge included in the commercial publishers' pricing formula may be reduced or omitted from state publisher pricing because it is covered (frequently inadequately) under district administration budget heads. State publishing may not pay royalties to authors. This is only rarely a genuine saving because under-remunerated authors tend to produce substandard teaching and learning materials (TLMs). The items that are likely to be common to both commercial and state pricing systems are origination costs, raw materials, and manufacturing. Table 8.2, provides a more typical state publishing pricing formula.

State publishing only appears to be cheaper than commercial publishing. The "missing" components have not disappeared; they are just concealed under other MOE or government budget heads. Thus the large variation in unit costs quoted for textbooks in different countries is largely the result of differences in what is included in the quoted costs. This makes direct comparisons between

Table 8.1 Commercial Textbook Price Components

Component	Percent of price
Publishers' overheads & profit[a]	27
Bookseller discount[b]	25
Origination costs (includes typesetting, design, artwork, other reproduction, etc.)	14
Raw materials	12
Manufacturing	10
Royalties (these are the costs of authorship)	7
Ocean freight	4
Bank charges	1

Note: a. This includes marketing, research and editing, staff and administration, financing and credit costs, premises, equipment, and utilities, etc.
b. This only applies if teaching and learning materials (TLMs) are supplied via the retail book trade. If they are supplied to the Ministry of Education (MOE) or the district the distribution cost will be lower for the publisher because the distribution costs will be transferred to the MOE or to the districts.

Table 8.2 State Publishing Textbook Price Components

Component	Percent of price
Origination costs (includes typesetting, design, artwork, other reproduction, and so on)	20
Raw materials	40
Manufacturing	35
Royalties (these are the costs of authorship)	5

unit textbook costs in different countries very dangerous unless full information is available.

One-Year versus Four-Year Book Life—Cost Comparisons

Table 8.3 provides examples of primary and secondary textbooks specified for one-year book life and for four-plus years of book life and the prices quoted for these specifications from a leading textbook printer in Mumbai, India. These are real quoted prices supplied in September 2011. They are not invented prices. The four-year book life has higher-grade text paper and cover card and durable binding styles with UV varnish finishing. The one-year book life specifications opt for lower-quality text and cover card and cheap and nondurable bindings with no lamination or UV varnish finishing. Otherwise the print runs, formats, and use of color are identical between the paired comparisons. The four-year and the one-year specifications are typical of the kind of specifications that a publisher would nominate to a printer to achieve the required book life.

Costings 1 and 2 compare the costs of a four-color 96-page primary textbook. The four-year specification is only 19 percent more expensive in production costs than the one-year specification.

Costings 3 and 4 compare the costs of a one-color 96-page primary textbook. The four-year specification is 29.5 percent more expensive in production costs than the one-year specification.

Costings 5 and 6 compare the costs of a four-color 144-page secondary textbook. The four-year specification is only 23 percent more expensive than the one-year specification.

Costings 7 and 8 compare the costs of a two-color 144-page secondary textbook. The four-year specification is only 26 percent more expensive than the one-year specification.

Table 8.4 presents price comparisons of these costings. These costings demonstrate clearly that a four- to five-year extended book life is significantly cheaper in terms of annual amortized cost than a one-year specification.

Table 8.3 Comparative Prices for One- and Four-Year Textbook Specifications

Item	Title	Size	Cover pages	Text pages	Cover colors	Text colors	Text paper	Cover card	Binding style	Print run	US$ price FOB
1	Primary TB	7.44 × 9.68"	4	96	4	4	62 gsm	180 gsm	Saddle Stitch	75,000	0.464
2	Primary TB	7.44 × 9.68"	4	96	4	4	80 gsm	250 gsm	Saddle Stitch	75,000	0.553
3	Primary TB	7.44 × 9.68"	4	96	1	1	62 gsm	180 gsm	Saddle Stitch	75,000	0.381
4	Primary TB	7.44 × 9.68"	4	96	1	1	80 gsm	250 gsm	Saddle Stitch	75,000	0.540
5	Secondary TB	7.44 × 9.68"	4	144	4	4	62 gsm	180 gsm	Perfect Bound	20,000	0.788
6	Secondary TB	7.44 × 9.68"	4	144	4	4	80 gsm	250 gsm	Section Sewn	20,000	0.969
7	Secondary TB	7.44 × 9.68"	4	144	1	2	62 gsm	180 gsm	Perfect Bound	20,000	0.624
8	Secondary TB	7.44 × 9.68"	4	144	1	2	80 gsm	250 gsm	Section Sewn	20,000	0.780

Note: FOB = freight on board; gsm = grams per square meter; TB = textbook.

Table 8.4 One- and Four-Year Price Comparisons

Comparing items	One-year price	Four-year price	Differential (%)
1 and 2	0.464	0.553	1.19
3 and 4	0.361	0.540	1.30
5 and 6	0.788	0.969	1.23
7 and 8	0.624	0.780	1.26

Reasons for Textbook Cost Variations in Some Approved Book Lists

In Uganda in 2007 there was no national approved textbook list and each individual secondary school made up its own textbook list. These were derived from the stock lists of Kampala booksellers. Very few schools had a clear idea of the full range of available titles and very few were aware of the strengths and weaknesses of any one textbook in relation to the demands of the curriculum or examination. Also, because most secondary schools in Uganda no longer bought books themselves for loan to students but expected parents to purchase the books for each individual student, there was little concern with price in the construction of the book list. Most schools didn't expect parents to buy the full book list or even a significant part of it. Thus for most secondary schools, students, and parents, the school textbook list had become a symbol rather than an expected reality. For secondary schools in remote areas or the down-market private schools there was little expectation that any pupils would buy their own textbooks. As a result some extremely expensive imported books, often with very little local relevance to the curriculum, were included on the school book lists. In one school in Uganda the recommended biology textbook for S5 and S6 was an imported undergraduate biology textbook at a price of almost US$90. But no student in the school had purchased this title and the school hadn't purchased a copy for its own library despite the fact that this was one of the specified textbooks on the school book list.

In Lesotho there was a national approved textbook list from which schools were expected to select their titles for their own individual school book lists. But price was not a factor in the approval process for the national list and some of the textbooks on the official approved list had very expensive prices. Once again, because most schools no longer bought textbooks for loan to students, there was little concern for price in the construction of individual school book lists.

Some book lists are dominated by very old textbooks, which were used by teachers when they were at school. Other lists concentrate on examination textbooks only and ignore textbooks for nonexamination years. In some schools first year students were recommended to buy the examination textbook only. In Uganda, it was not uncommon for a student to be recommended to use the same S4 textbooks throughout the four years of junior secondary as preparation for the Uganda Certificate of Education examination without access to any other books unless provided by the school. It was equally common for book lists to be given only to S1 and S5 students. One school book list recommended

13 different titles for use in senior secondary geography alone and five different titles for use in senior secondary biology. These were not considered to be alternatives. In many countries, in districts away from the capital city or main provincial towns, few schools produce any sort of recommended book lists. The majority of schools in rural and remote areas simply recognized that parent affordability was too limited for most parents to be able to consider buying any textbooks and secondary textbooks in any case were usually not available for purchase outside the capital city.

Kenya probably had the lowest secondary textbook prices of the surveyed countries in 2007, largely because there was a national secondary textbook approval process and a national approved textbook list and price was one of the factors that was given great prominence in the evaluation and approval process. This was also true in Ghana and Togo, although the textbook approval process worked in different ways in each country. In these situations there was a positive incentive for publishers to achieve good prices because low prices achieved higher marks in evaluation schemes and thus contributed to getting on to the approved textbook list. Failure to achieve approved list status can be very serious for the publishers who fail. As a result, private sector publishers, both indigenous and multinational, can sometimes oppose approved textbook lists, which are compiled on a competitive basis in which price is one of the factors in the evaluation process.

In Malawi an approved textbook list was introduced in 1999. The original evaluation and approval criteria combined content, curriculum conformity, presentational quality, durability,[2] and price factors in order to achieve good books at good prices. But Malawi still had only a relatively small secondary enrollment in 1999, particularly at senior secondary level, and the requirement for new books to be developed to meet new local syllabus requirements resulted in increased unit costs.

Another factor that has an influence on the cost of secondary school textbook requirements was the physical production specification. Thus, in Ethiopia until recently, secondary textbooks were specified on 58 gsm newsprint or part mechanical paper with insubstantial covers and saddle-stitched or side-stitched bindings. These specifications produced cheap initial prices but did not provide good book life, particularly in difficult environments, so that textbooks had to be constantly replaced and repurchased—sometimes more than once in a school year. Where physical specifications are established at very low levels in order to achieve cheap prices, a typical pattern tends to emerge in which damaged and destroyed textbooks are not replaced and textbook–pupil ratios (TPRs) deteriorate steadily throughout the school year. In Kenya, Lesotho, and Malawi and in most francophone countries, physical specifications[3] are very much higher than those of Ethiopia. Higher specifications lead to longer book life, which reduces the annual amortized cost of provision. Good production specifications and long book life also create the possibility of secondhand markets, which can have a dramatic impact on the costs of provision to students. In general, higher-level physical production specifications and a longer book life produce much lower annual amortized costs. Some secondary schools with high levels of book care and conservation can achieve very extended book life and thus very low annual costs of provision.[4]

In Uganda, despite the recent development of local secondary school textbook publishing for junior secondary, the majority of the textbooks recommended for senior secondary are still U.K.–published textbooks that have presentational and production standards designed for a U.K. or international market, which could afford much higher prices than the average Ugandan secondary school pupil. This was also true for many other countries in both anglophone and francophone Africa. The basic problem, of course, is that the still relatively small secondary roll numbers in many countries, particularly at senior secondary level, combined with widespread low parental purchasing power and a lack of sustainable government or donor funding for secondary textbooks doesn't add up to a market that will attract investment in new title development for specific countries. Because there is a scarcity of local titles, particularly at senior secondary, that have been conceived and originated in the context of local conditions, local curricula, and local purchasing power, there is little alternative except to recommend imported textbooks. In some cases, where there are particularly popular imported textbooks (for example, McKean's Biology), the overseas publisher may create a special "tropical" edition, which is made available at lower, but still durable, production specifications and at significantly lower prices. But this is still the exception rather than the rule. There are similar examples from French publishers also, and particularly where titles are particularly suitable for transnational curricula.

The 2005 High School subsector study in Zambia complained of the lack of secondary school textbooks written and designed specifically for the Zambian market at prices that were affordable in the Zambian context. However, Zambian secondary school syllabuses had not been significantly changed since the early 1980s and there was little government funding provided to secondary schools for textbook purchase. There was also no tradition of parental textbook purchase and thus the realistic available market was too uncertain to attract publisher interest.

Unpredictable potential sales also militated against lower prices. However, the willingness of publishers to invest in and develop secondary school textbooks to satisfy local market requirements when a viable market is seen to exist is clearly demonstrated in Botswana, Cameroon, Côte d'Ivoire, Ghana, Kenya, Malawi, Nigeria, Tanzania, Togo, and others.

Perhaps the most significant variant in textbook prices is the local distribution profile. In South Sudan (Jones and Sayer 2013) the cost of consolidation and distribution from Mombasa to schools represented 75 percent of the total costs of manufacturing and delivery combined and were three times higher than the total production costs and the costs of delivery to Mombasa from the Republic of Korea, where the manufacturing took place. The distribution costs were high because the difficulties to be overcome in delivering to schools were extreme. South Sudan was a postconflict country with only one tarmac surfaced road in the entire country. During the rainy season a high proportion of roads (over 65 percent) were underwater and unusable. Under these circumstances long book life, which reduces the requirements for frequent deliveries, is an important objective in cost-reduction strategies. More accurate Education Management Information System (EMIS) data in the future will reduce the costs and operational difficulties associated with stock redistribution. The proportion of distribution related costs in South Sudan should be compared with Kenya where a well-established national book trade and a much better internal road network can achieve national distribution costs via the commercial book trade at only 20 to 25 percent of the retail price compared with the 75 percent required in South Sudan. Thus, the national distribution profile has to be analyzed to determine how much funding needs to be allocated to this activity. There is no formula pricing cost that can be applied to every situation.

It should also be noted that losses in distribution and in school book care and management have a significant impact on system costs over time and that the delivery of books that are not well used or even used at all is a significant waste of scarce financial resources. Thus additional investments in school-level training in book care, stock management, and TLM usage and the encouragement of more effective supervision and monitoring are all important components in the creation of a cost-effective and cost-efficient system of TLM provision.

Textbook Costs

There are so many variables that affect textbook costs that it is often difficult to determine value for money and equally difficult to prescribe what a good textbook price should be. It is important to distinguish between the cost of individual textbooks and the cost of the system of textbook provision. Thus, an individual textbook may be produced at a reasonable cost but the curriculum prescribes so many subjects and textbook requirements that the cost of providing everything specified becomes very expensive.

The main factors[5] that have an impact on individual textbook unit costs are

- Print runs;
- Piracy (rampant piracy significantly reduces print runs);
- Textbook extents;
- Textbook formats;
- Number of colors;
- Complexity of design and illustrations;
- Origination from scratch or adaptation;
- Physical production specifications;
- Whether the textbooks are imported or locally developed (generally, imported textbooks are designed and priced for a developed world market and are very expensive in terms of local affordability; textbooks designed for local market conditions are usually much cheaper, but the motivation to develop books for local market conditions depends upon market size and reliability of funding);

- Print locations and print price competitiveness;
- Speed of payment (for example, in Ghana publishers may have to wait for up to two years for payment for bulk supplies to the MOE and this has to be taken into account in the setting of prices);
- The use of price as a factor in evaluation for textbook approval;
- Distribution costs—are they included in the textbook price? and
- Level and nature of corruption—some countries have much higher corruption-related costs than others.

The main factors that have an impact on system costs are

- The curriculum specifications—specifically the number of required textbooks and teachers' guides and the density of the syllabuses, which impact on extent;
- The languages of instruction, (LoI) (too many LoIs will significantly increase origination costs and can fractionalize print runs and thus increase costs);
- Number of approved textbooks (too many approved textbooks fractionalizes print runs);
- Nature and quantity of other specified TLMs;
- The textbook–pupil supply ratios;
- Target classroom life;
- Loss and damage rates;
- Distribution effectiveness; and
- School management and conservation effectiveness.

Good system design can have a major impact on both individual and system costs. Thus, in 2002 when the Department for International Development (DFID) was supporting primary textbook system reforms in Uganda, the unit cost of textbooks was reduced by the new evaluation and approval system by 56 percent while production specifications were upgraded and the amount of color used in the textbooks was increased. Although it is a complex task to compare textbook costs in different countries, there should be no reason why primary and secondary textbooks should not be made available at reasonable costs if the system design is well performed and if print runs are large enough to achieve reasonable cost benefits. On this basis, primary textbook unit costs of US$2 to 3 and secondary textbook costs of US$4 to 6 should normally be achievable, but these figures cannot necessarily be achieved in every case.

Costs and Print Runs

There is a growing assumption among project managers that the longest possible print runs achieve the lowest possible costs. Figure 8.1 demonstrates that textbook cost savings plateau and that above 35,000 to 50,000 copies for four-color books the cost benefit from long print runs quickly becomes marginal. For one-color textbooks the cost plateau is often reached after 7,500 to

Figure 8.1 Long Print Run Cost–Benefit Curve

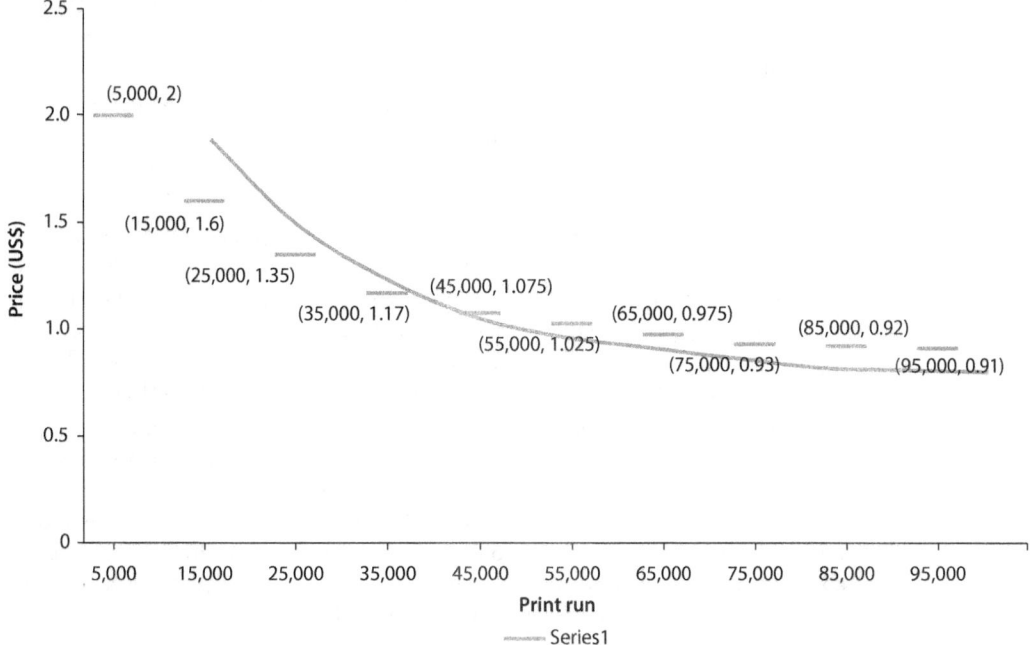

10,000 copies. Only small population countries are likely to derive significant cost benefits from single monopoly textbook policies designed to reduce costs. Most countries have sufficient school enrollments to provide some level of choice of alternative competing textbooks at economic prices.

A Summary of Key Issues

- The major cost components of school textbook retail prices are generally bookseller discount (or distribution costs if publishers are supplying direct and not using a retail book chain) and publishers' overheads, and these are the areas where cost savings theoretically are possible.
- The annual amortized cost of four-year book life is much lower than the annual costs of one-year book life, and wherever possible it makes more financial sense to opt for long book life rather than short book life.
- Modern printing technology makes it possible to achieve significant economies of scale at relatively low print run levels—about 35,000 to 50,000 for four-color books and 7,500 to 10,000 copies for one-color books.
- There are many variables that affect the costs of textbooks and the cost of textbook provision system design and this makes it difficult—if not impossible—for the nonspecialist to compare textbook costs and prices between one country and another.

Notes

1. These percentages are taken from an actual textbook costing of a 96-page primary textbook printed in four colors with durable production specifications intended for retail sale provided by a leading African textbook publisher.
2. Because long book life is a critical factor in achieving amortized cost reductions, some approved list criteria require minimum physical production specifications to ensure that all titles on the approved list will have similar book life expectations. This is a strongly recommended approach.
3. Physical specifications comprise text paper and cover card or board, cover finish, binding style, and sometimes book format. Presentational specifications normally comprise type font and size, number of colors, number and type of illustrations, and sometimes book format. Book formats are sometimes included in physical specifications because large book sizes, particularly in landscape formats, are often considered to be not durable. Landscape and A4 formats are therefore often specifically excluded.
4. For example, King's College Budu in Uganda had a number of textbook sets that were more than 20 years old. Each book had been rebound and regularly repaired, but the annual cost of provision was very low because the textbooks had been made to last for so many years. Of course, there is a down side to maintaining textbooks for very long periods because the content can become dated and irrelevant. A reasonable balance between cost and longevity is desirable and a target six-year book life at secondary would seem to strike a reasonable balance.
5. These factors are not the same as the textbook price components nor are they the same as the links in the Book Chain.

Reference

Jones, B., and N. Sayer. 2013. *Annual Review of the South Sudan Textbook Project*. Juba: DFID.

CHAPTER 9

Procurement, Bidding, and Evaluation

Sole Sourcing versus Decentralized Competitive Textbook Selection

In recent years the switch from monopolistic sole sourcing from the private sector to approved book lists and decentralized financing, selection, and ordering by schools has removed the need for competitive bulk procurements of teaching and learning materials (TLMs) organized by ministries of education (MOEs), which were often problematic in the past. The use of notional school purchasing power budgets, rather than cash budgets, and annual school ordering on official order forms where the orders are bulked up centrally by the MOE and passed on to publishers along with detailed distribution schedules, have been effective in getting rid of price markups and fund misappropriation. Rwanda is a good current example of such a system. Kenya, Lesotho, Malawi, and Namibia are among a number of countries where commercial supply and distribution have been developed with reasonable success in recent years, although there are still problems in management, monitoring, and supervision that need to be overcome. The introduction of sophisticated, computerized textbook and teaching and learning materials (TLM) management systems and databases in Rwanda and Namibia demonstrates that the operational problems—particularly in ordering, distribution, and confirmed delivery, need not be insurmountable.

Where notional purchasing power budgets are not used as the vehicle for school-based selection and ordering, there will still be schools where the head teacher asks for money from publishers in return for ordering their books, or from booksellers in return for the school order. Overpricing and even misappropriation of funds through invoicing for materials that are never delivered will still be a problem in some systems. There have been well-documented cases of district education officers being paid to change school orders in favor of one or two publishers, or of district education officials establishing their own bookshops through relatives and then pressuring schools to order through these favored outlets. The solution to these problems lies in regular and thorough inspection and supervision and regular school audits. In Kenya in 2003–04 when the Free Primary Textbook Project was launched, the Department for International Development (DFID) funded PricewaterhouseCoopers to conduct random school audits for the first two years. Booksellers and publishers have reported since that the random auditing kept the system free of corruption and misappropriation. It was only when the random auditing stopped and schools and districts gradually became accustomed to lax supervision and long intervals between audits that the system became corrupted.

Although decentralized competitive systems are increasing in anglophone Sub-Saharan Africa (SSA), they are still relatively uncommon in francophone Africa where textbook printing bids are also still common. Centralized bulk procurement can still exist even within decentralized financing systems when bilateral or nongovernmental organization (NGO) donors decide to order titles (usually supplementary or reader titles) in bulk for distribution to schools. The World Bank and the Asian Development Bank (ADB) maintain model bid documentation to cover this type of transaction. However, although considerable thought and effort has gone into the design of model textbook bid documentation, the real need is for adequate and detailed supervision of the evaluation and award processes because this is where problems most commonly occur.

An example of the problems that can occur in procurement, even when established model systems and documentation exist, is illustrated in Ethiopia.

> The failure by publishers to meet contractual delivery deadlines and long delays in paying off and closing textbook supply contracts has been identified as a matter of concern. The following factors are reported to be the main causes of delay:
>
> - Frequent re-tendering of contracts by MOE. Thus the Chemistry package for Grades 9–12 was not awarded in the original February 2010 tender; it was retendered in December 2010 but not awarded; retendered again in 2011 and not awarded; retendered again in January 2012 and finally awarded in September 2012. Environmental science and integrated science were tendered, cancelled, retendered once and then withdrawn in favour of local non-competitive development;
> - The contracts included in the bid documents were not the contracts that publishers were asked to sign. Changes included changes in the production specifications and the transfer of copyrights and reprints to the MOE (Clause 18.2) although Clause 32.3 confirming publishers' right to reprint was left in the contract.[1] Disputes over the changed contracts led to delays in contract signature;
> - The approval of publishers' proofs for printing by the MOE was sometimes long delayed—in some cases until the contracted delivery deadlines had been passed;
> - There were some long delays in clearance at the port of entry; delays of 4–5 months were reported with associated expensive demurrage charges being incurred. Publishers claimed that MOE inexperience in clearance requirements was the main cause of the problem;

- Disputes over completed deliveries, which led the MOE to withhold full payments and to fail to close contracts. Some of these disputes are of long standing and are the major cause of failure to close contracts. Publishers claim that the disputes are often over relatively small quantities. One publisher reported that the delivery of contracted stock to the 628 WEOs had been completed in 5–6 weeks but that minor delivery problems amounting to a few hundred books had led to non-payment of the final tranche and an ongoing dispute. (Read 2013)

Evaluating and Establishing an Approved List of Textbooks and TLMs

The creation of an approved list of textbooks from which schools may select the titles that they want is the basis of almost all decentralized competitive textbook systems. The general rule is that publishers and their authors should be provided with the maximum amount of information to enable them to meet the MOE requirement for textbooks and other TLMs. This information should always include

- The national curriculum framework;
- The relevant syllabuses;
- A list of key skills, competencies, values, and attitudes required by the curriculum and by individual subjects and grade levels;
- Any subject standards that have to be met;
- Any cross-cutting issues that need to be included (for example, gender equity, environmental issues, concepts of globalization, HIV/AIDS, maternal reproductive health, and so on); and
- Desired teaching and learning methodologies.

The specification should state what materials should be submitted for evaluation such as a textbook and teachers' guide or a textbook, teachers' guide, and ancillary materials or a textbook, teachers' guide and access to additional materials via a website. Guidance may be needed on exercises, activities, methodological approaches, and assessment requirements. Alternatively these may be left to the discretion of individual publishers.

It is often helpful if publishers are provided with sample lesson plans produced by members of the curriculum/syllabus groups so that publishers can see how information is combined with activities and student-oriented working methodologies to develop the skills and competencies specified by the curriculum.

There are two broad approaches to evaluation:

- A *threshold evaluation*, in which all titles that meet minimum standards are approved for competitive selection by individual schools.

- *Competitive evaluation,* in which a predetermined number of titles may be approved if they achieve the minimum standards specified. The number of titles approved can vary from just one (monopoly supply) up to three, four, or even six (Kenya). The list of approved titles is determined entirely by the competitive evaluation scores with the top-scoring qualified titles up to the established limit achieving approved status.

The threshold evaluation often leads to problems when too many titles are approved; this can confuse teachers, fractionalize print runs, and increase unit costs as a result. All approved lists should be time bound so that they are regularly rebid and refreshed with new and improved titles. This prevents inertia in the system and provides losing publishers with the opportunity to improve their submissions and succeed in the future. It benefits no one if publishers are excluded from the market for long periods.

There are normally some minimum requirements in the evaluation of submissions for approved lists. These are usually conformity to curriculum and an overall average mark on all criteria. Thus, it is common to require that any evaluated textbook approved for use in schools should have a minimum 80 percent conformity with the national curriculum. It is also common that all other criteria should be scored to a minimum level of 60 percent or higher to ensure that all of the critical components of a textbook and teachers' guide achieve good minimum standards.

There are normally three bands of evaluation criteria as follows:

Compulsory Criteria

These cover qualification and eligibility to bid according to the rules of the tender plus the achievement of the minimum production specifications set down in the tender documents and tested as part of the evaluation process. The minimum physical production specifications are meant to ensure that every textbook approved will have the same level of durability. All compulsory factors are scored as a straightforward pass or fail. Submissions that fail on the compulsory factors are not considered for further evaluation stages.

Qualitative Criteria

There can be some variation in the qualitative criteria but the most common categories are

- Conformity to curriculum;
- Suitability of content to the needs of teachers and students;
- Quality of writing and editing and suitability for age and interest levels;
- Quality of page design and illustrations and the relevance of illustrations to the subject;
- Methodologies, including the use of exercises, activities, and practical work, that encourage the development of skills and competencies; and
- Teachers' guide and the help provided to the teacher.

The qualitative evaluation would normally be conducted by a team of trained evaluators who would be supervised by a nonscoring neutral moderator or chair. There are established methodologies, evaluation instruments, and scoring regimes that are available and that can be used to ensure maximum objectivity and transparency. For example, in recent years it is common for submissions to come from publishers with no covers, no authors or publishers names, and no identifying logo so that evaluators can evaluate without knowing the name of the publisher or the names of the authors. All titles that pass the qualitative evaluation are then evaluated for price.

Price Evaluation

The art of good textbook publishing is to achieve the right balance between the qualitative components and price. Experience suggests that a price mark representing 25 to 30 percent of total evaluation marks usually provides a good balance.

With careful evaluation management and well-trained evaluators and moderators this system has been proved in many countries to produce high-quality results in terms of content, presentation, durability, and competitive pricing. Where the evaluation criteria for the creation of an approved list do not include minimum physical production specifications or price, both durability and price competitiveness are likely to be undermined.

In Rwanda and Kenya the award of approved status to a publisher is the subject of a contract between the publisher and the MOE that specifies the obligations of each party. One of the articles in the contract prohibits publishers from individual price increases and requires all requests for price increases to be submitted by the Rwanda Publishers and Booksellers Association, which is required to provide hard documentary evidence of input cost increases in excess of 10 percent since the publishers' prices were submitted for evaluation. This clause maintains a degree of price control for the period of the approved status. Any individual price increases not approved by the MOE can be a reason for the removal of approved list status. Other types of TLM (for example, readers, dictionaries, atlases, and so on), require different types of evaluation schedules.

The design of a TLM evaluation methodology, criteria, instruments, and marking or scoring system is a specialist task and needs experienced specialist consultancy inputs. Good examples of sole-source textbook procurement documentation are available from World Bank model textbook bid documents. Examples of good bid documentation for the creation of an approved list as the basis for decentralized competitive textbook supply can be found in Kenya, Malawi, Rwanda, and Uganda.

Bid Supervision

While good examples of different types of procurement documentation are available, the most critical input in achieving good outcomes is detailed supervision of the process by professionally qualified specialists. The lack of supervision can lead to abuses. The availability of supervision will reinforce good awards and the achievement of good pricing. It should be noted that the combination of a well-designed evaluation system with tight supervision in Uganda in 2001 led to quality improvements and substantial price reductions in excess of 45 percent.

A Summary of Key Issues

- In recent years in anglophone SSA there has been a shift towards decentralized textbook supply systems based on MOE-approved lists and school-based choice from school per capita purchasing budgets. This shift has been less pronounced in francophone Africa.
- All procurement bids should include minimum physical production specifications and price as part of the evaluation criteria. Failure to do this leads to shorter book life and higher costs.
- Good examples of bid documentation and evaluation methodologies, instruments, and criteria for different types of procurement are readily available.
- Good procurement requires good, professional supervision.

Note

1. The current supply contracts need to be tidied up to make them consistent.

Reference

Read, T. 2013. *Ethiopia: The Textbook Component in GEQUIP 1 and GEQUIP 2.* A World Bank Study. Washington, DC: World Bank.

CHAPTER 10

Distribution, Storage, and Management

Basic Teaching and Learning Materials Requirements for Effective Distribution

The basic requirements for operating effective teaching and learning materials (TLM) distribution systems are very well known. They are the same for both state and commercial systems. They are

- Adequate, timely, and predictable financing of textbooks and other TLMs;
- Reliable information on school locations, grade level roll numbers, and TLM requirements;
- Effective, trained, and experienced management using good (and preferably computerized) management systems;
- Access to adequate and appropriate storage and transportation facilities;
- Effective monitoring and supervision of the whole process; and
- The willingness and ability to be accountable and thus to correct errors quickly and at no cost to the schools.

In most state textbook distribution the key tasks are usually restricted to collecting information on needs, ordering from the publisher(s) and allocating supplies to districts and schools, and moving supplies in good time and in acceptable condition to widely dispersed school locations in fulfillment of school requirements. In theory, it should be possible for state distribution services to subcontract stock procurement, consolidation, warehousing, and transportation and thus to avoid the substantial capital investment needed to create these within state institutions. In practice, state textbook distribution in Africa has only rarely contracted out the warehousing, consolidation, and transportation functions to professional private sector companies. Governments, frequently supported by development partners (DPs), for many years combined to fund state-owned central, regional, and district level warehouses plus fleets of trucks; but it was rare that any of the state textbook distribution organizations had access to professionally trained and experienced logistic experts and basic inventory control and stock movement systems. Typically, the management and staffing of state distributors usually comprised teachers transferred from schools or bureaucrats on short-term postings. Distribution as a professional skill has not been appreciated in Sub-Saharan Africa (SSA). Despite significant investment in Education Management Information System (EMIS) in many SSA countries, basic information on school roll numbers and needs often has not been available at the time it is needed or has been inaccurate or out of date.

The Coca Cola Argument[1]

There is a view that textbook distribution in SSA should be much easier than it is and that the process of national textbook distribution is in urgent need of demystification. According to this view, which has been perpetuated for many years without exposure to serious analysis, Coca Cola, matches, rice, sardines, tomato paste, exercise books, pens, and the like[2] are easily accessible to almost every village throughout Africa. Thus, if these articles can be reliably distributed on a national basis at acceptable cost, then it should be possible for ministries of education (MOEs), publishers, distributors, and booksellers to learn from the companies that distribute these articles and to establish equally reliable and comprehensive systems.

There is validity in the argument that textbook distribution in SSA should have been much more effective than it has been. But there are many differences between the commercial distribution of Coca Cola and the commercial distribution of textbooks. These differences invalidate the argument that the successful distribution of one product automatically ensures that the successful distribution of a different product is possible. Thus,

- Coca Cola is a product in daily demand; textbooks are highly seasonal.
- If Coca Cola supplies are late, the market for the product still exists; the late availability of textbooks can significantly reduce sales.
- Consumers of Coca Cola will purchase very regularly, perhaps more than once a day; consumers of textbooks will purchase only occasionally, perhaps once a year.
- Sales of Coca Cola are high-priority purchases for an established, even addicted, clientele; textbooks are rarely high-priority purchases for most of the population.
- Coca Cola sales are predictable; textbook sales are usually unpredictable.[3]
- Because Coca Cola is a reliable "sale," petty traders are prepared to operate on a firm-sale, cash-with-order basis; commercial textbook distribution can only rarely operate on a firm-sale basis. Thus credit is not a serious problem for Coca Cola but it is a major issue for commercial textbook distributors. This usually leads to serious understocking of textbooks, particularly in rural areas, because commercial textbook sales are far less certain and predictable and there are few local traders who can afford to invest in textbook stock to the

extent required.[4] As a result, there are frequent cases of textbook nonavailability, simply because of poor stock levels in local booksellers. The Uganda case study provides an example of this factor in the use of school-based capitation funds allocated for supplementary reader purchase. A high proportion of these very large funds are not used for their designated purpose because basic levels of appropriate book stock are not available in local bookshops.
- Coca Cola is never dependent upon unreliable government financing; primary school textbooks are dominantly dependent upon government or donor financing in most African countries—and it is the unreliability and inadequacy of this funding that underpins many of the distribution problems.[5]
- Coca Cola is not forced to attempt deliveries to high-cost, low-return, difficult-access, whereas textbook supply is expected to reach every part of a country, no matter how remote, difficult to access, or costly and often without compensatory price increases to cover additional costs.
- Coca Cola is not expected to achieve on-time, total national supply; textbook distribution is judged on its ability to achieve on-time, national coverage once a year—often in the rainy season when many communication links are impassable.
- Coca Cola in bottles or cans is a durable product that is not subject to weather damage or deterioration in store; textbooks are made largely of cellulose (paper and cover card) and are thus highly susceptible in use and in store to water (including humidity), fungus, dust, insects, direct sunlight, and vermin.
- Coca Cola distributes three or four different branded products; a typical primary school textbook and teachers' guide requirement might require up to 100 different titles, thus requiring more complex stock records and picking or packing systems.
- Coca Cola users are not required to achieve long life, do repairs, practice conservation, and protect against loss or damage to achieve affordability; all of these are important for textbook system affordability.
- Coca Cola staff are well trained and supervised because Coca Cola is profitable; none of these advantages apply to textbook distribution.
- Coca Cola distribution is not subject to swings in national policy; textbook distribution policy is frequently in a state of flux and change (see Guinea case study, below).

Textbook distribution in SSA is a unique problem and solutions must be based on a clear understanding of the special characteristics in each country that need to be addressed, even though there are common causes of distribution failure found in many countries.

Distribution Performance in SSA—Some Case Studies

The scale of losses in normal annual textbook distribution in many SSA countries is often not fully appreciated by either governments or donors. In 1991 a summary of nine Book Sector Studies in Africa reported that

In the majority of countries studied there is a consistent failure to provide a cost effective distribution system that delivers the books and maintains them efficiently and reliably. (Buchan, Denning, and Read 1991)

In 2001 Amadou Waziri (Waziri 2001a) reported:

In all Sahelian countries the inefficiency of the book distribution systems causes very large losses in stock, time and money. Typically, the state takes on the responsibility for textbook distribution, but the state rarely has the skills and the required human, material and financial resources to fulfil the role adequately. The state also underestimates the costs of distribution because its own employees handle it and the costs are absorbed into salaries. (*Read, Denning, and Bontoux 2001*)

As examples, the case studies revealed 67 percent textbook stock attrition in warehousing and transportation in Guinea, between 50 and 60 percent in Niger, and close to 50 percent in Chad. No education system could afford to live with this level of stock loss. The main causes of the stock losses were identified as follows:

- Delays of several months in shifting stock from HQ via districts to schools
- Poor planning and management (for example, no inventory control or movement systems)
- Inequity in supplies to rural and urban areas
- Lack of funding to pay for suitable transport
- Poor security in transportation and in storage
- Poor storage in districts and schools without either security or weatherproofing
- No funds in schools to collect books from districts
- Failure to inform schools that stock was available for collection
- The coincidence between the main distribution period and the rainy season
- The lack of professionally qualified and trained staff
- No supervision of the system
- Widespread theft and corruption and resales to private schools

In 1998 the Canadian International Development Agency (CIDA) (Fearnley 1998) commissioned a report into the distribution operation of the Malawi School Supplies Unit (SSU) after supplying large consignments of primary textbooks. Extracts from the report are provided below:

the cartons being used are only a single flute, and not a ... carton suitable for export conditions.... 5% of stock is being damaged due to inadequate cartons. All stock is manually handled from loose loaded containers to school delivery which can consist of ... up to 10 handling movements.... [D]uring the rainy season cartons are subject to water damage in leaking warehouses and during transit..., which accounts for another 5% of damage.... [T]here are shortages in the cartons, which has led to schools receiving fewer than the required number of books, for which they have to account.... From entry stage onwards the system does not work. The main problem is the Blantyre warehouse. This is rented ... and as a result of the frequent MOE cash-flow problems there is constant tension between the leasee and the leasor ... resulting in extended storage and demurrage costs.... The warehouse is capable of handling ... 2–3 containers at a time. Thus when a large consignment is delivered, the warehouse cannot manage and the books cannot be warehoused, incurring additional demurrage charges from the transporter. When the CIDA consignment arrived in December 1996 it took 17 months before the consignment could be expedited by the Blantyre warehouse.... The main warehouse is inadequately equipped and staffed to handle the current level of consignments.... There is inadequate stock management apart from stock cards, which are rarely completed within the working day. Redistribution to the four regional warehouses is very slow, due to lack of basic warehouse equipment and transport. Further delays occur, due to the lack of payment to the transport company. As the transport company is also the owner of the warehouse, this often results in the company refusing MOE access to the warehouse until payment is received. This stage of the supply chain has been identified as being the main "bottleneck"... distribution to the DEO's is causing problems as there are few district storage facilities.... There are 31 districts and approx 315 zones, a zone meaning between 10-20 schools.... The delivery to the zones is another link ... which requires funding, storage and additional vehicle movements. There is inadequate provision also at this level.... The final link ... is rudimentary and is dependent upon the school collecting the books from the Zone.... The CIDA consignment (54 containers) arrived in Malawi in Dec 96. 10 containers were released in August 97, a further 10 in September, a further 2 in October and the balance of 32 was released in April/May 1998. Demurrage was charged at the rate of US$6.00 per day per container (Source: Supplies Unit. 17/7/98).[6] The system is clearly ineffective.

The problems with textbook distribution described above are not isolated cases. In 2007 a report on textbook provision in Zanzibar (Read and Ibale 2007) found serious flaws in storage and distribution—and Zanzibar must be one of the easiest countries in SSA for textbook deliveries.

The current textbook store is managed by a Storekeeper, trained in stores management assisted by two staff without formal training. The stores are not suited for textbooks but they are unnecessarily disorganized with no proper shelving or lighting, poor ventilation and no system of stacking or caring for books. The same stores are used for other supplies apart from textbooks e.g., mattresses, wheelchairs etc. The poor condition of the store and the low level of management and care of the stock were reported on 10 years ago in a previous visit but little seems to have changed. Textbooks are stored here before they are distributed to schools. The stores still maintain large quantities of textbooks that are now irrelevant to the schools since the change of curriculum. The stores were noticeably damp, which is not a good situation where paper is being stored[7] and as a result many copies of textbooks had been damaged, largely because the ink and varnish of the covers were stuck together. In addition, many of the loose textbooks were dusty and curling because they had not been repackaged after being removed from the cartons. Many boxes were stacked on the floor or thrown on top of each other in no organized way making it difficult to identify individual titles. There was very little space for movement within the store and no space at all to be used as a packing area, so that much of the packing was done outside. The store keeper reported that there was no schedule for deliveries and these were handled as they came in. If there was more than one consignment at a time then it was difficult to handle since in most cases there is only one person attending to everything, e.g., looking for the titles, counting them, filling-in the delivery form, updating the stock ledger book and packing the books etc. At present it is impossible to estimate the regular level of stock loss and damage incurred in storage, but it must be considerable.

In 2010 a distribution tracking survey in Ghana (GNECC 2010) reported that 29 percent of English language stock for primary schools could not be accounted for. This included a loss rate of 57 percent for primary English Book 3. The report noted particularly,

- Inadequate finance at district level to move stock to schools;
- Poor quality of district-level storage in terms of security and weatherproofing;
- Poor record keeping;
- Lack of supervision;
- Nongovernmental organizations (NGOs) and churches intervening to support their own schools and taking stock that should have been allocated to other—usually more remote—schools;
- District education officer (DEO) and head teacher sales of free textbooks to private schools, which were in many cases owned by DEOs and senior district officials;
- High costs of collection from the districts for remote and difficult-access schools; and
- Inequity in costs of collection and level of supply between urban and rural schools.

This survey repeated the main findings of a previous National Audit Office survey in Ghana in 2005. The 2010 survey indicated that the system had deteriorated since the 2005 survey.

Textbook supply to South Sudan[8] (Jones and Sayer 2013) effectively came to a halt in 2008 in the wake of a corruption scandal in which attempts were made to influence the outcome of a World Bank textbook bid. In response the World Bank reallocated its funding away from textbooks to school construction. As a result, 1.9 million children in South Sudan did not receive textbooks in 2009, 2010, and 2011. The 2010 school census identified the lack of textbooks as one of the key causes of school dropouts. Even those textbooks supplied in 2008 often did not reach schools but were kept in county offices, often in poor storage conditions, because of the lack of financing to support onward movements from counties to schools. In 2011 the Department for International Development (DFID) provided funding for the supply of primary school textbooks for Grades 1–3 in textbook–pupil ratios (TPRs) of 1:1 and upper primary textbooks in TPRs of 1:3. It also agreed to finance the distribution of the textbooks to individual schools using a commercial distributor selected by competitive bid, because government did not have the finance or systems to manage the distribution exercise themselves.

Because of the postconflict situation, the poor condition of the road network, and a heavy rainy season that makes travel to many parts of the country impossible, distribution costs in South Sudan will be high for the foreseeable future. As part of the DFID project, consolidation and distribution costs from Mombasa in Kenya[9] to schools throughout South Sudan represented 75 percent of the total costs of provision and were three times higher than the total textbook manufacturing costs plus the costs of delivery to Mombasa from the Republic of Korea, where the manufacturing took place. Under these circumstances long book life, which reduces the requirements for frequent deliveries, is an important objective in cost-reduction strategies in South Sudan. More accurate EMIS data could reduce the costs and operational difficulties associated with overreporting of school enrollments and thus the need for post-delivery stock redistribution. The fact that the distribution cost in South Sudan is three times higher than manufacturing costs is an indicator of the areas where cost reduction should be focused.

It should also be noted that losses in distribution and in school book care and management have a significant impact on system costs over time and that the delivery of books that are not well used or even not used at all is a significant waste of scarce financial resources. Thus additional investments in school-level training in book care, stock management, and TLM usage and the encouragement of more effective supervision and monitoring are all important components in the creation of a cost-effective and cost-efficient system of TLM provision.

In Ethiopia textbook stock is delivered by publishers direct to 628 Woreda Education Offices (WEOs) but there is no information available on what happens to the stock after it arrives at the WEOs. The packing instructions contained in the bid documents make it clear that each publisher or printer is delivering bulk stock to each WEO so that each consignment of publisher cartons has to be broken down and repackaged to create the stock allocations for each individual school. The 2010 Early Grade Reading Assessment (EGRA) study (Piper 2010) noted significant differences in local language textbook availability in different regions, with Tigray and Harar recording around 95 percent availability but Somali recording only 43 percent availability. These data suggest that either distribution or school management might not be working as well in some regions as in others. It is well known that the district-to-school part of the distribution system is the most problematic operation in almost every SSA country. Governments typically underfund textbook distribution and particularly at the critical district or school level where storage and delivery present common difficulties. Publishers supplying to WOEs in Ethiopia report that they have been assured by the MOE that there will be functioning store rooms and trained storekeepers in every WOE to accept deliveries and publishers report that in general they have had no serious problems in finding a WOE official to accept and sign for stock, although some of the more remote WOEs were not easy to reach.

However, the reported high levels of staff turnover in WOEs suggest that there could be problems in maintaining well-trained staff in place and thus effective systems.

The case studies above demonstrate a number of common problems as follows:

- Underfinancing of the distribution system, particularly at district levels
- Lack of adequate and well-maintained storage facilities at district levels
- The lack of basic stock control, movement, and management systems at every level
- Lack of trained storage and distribution staff, particularly at district levels
- Lack of effective monitoring and supervision
- Absence of auditing
- Lack of up-to-date and accurate information on the number of schools, their location, and the number of enrolled students in each grade requiring TLMs
- The lack of accountability—in the examples quoted above there was no real incentive for district offices to deliver equitably and on time and to correct errors
- High levels of loss and damage through poor security and weatherproofing
- Repeated examples of theft during transportation or district-level storage and by head teachers; much of the theft is associated with sales of free textbooks to private schools either in-country or in neighboring countries
- The lack of an effective TLM management system[10]

Textbook distribution in SSA is not universally bad and there have been some success stories, for example, in Kenya, Lesotho, and Uganda and more recently in Rwanda.

The Textbook Rental Scheme and Textbook Revolving Fund (TRS/TRF) in Lesotho was inaugurated in 1982 and launched in a mountainous pilot district with severe distribution difficulties in 1983 before being extended to national coverage in 1984. Although Lesotho is a small country, its distribution challenges can be formidable with high mountains, swift running rivers, many without bridges, and severe winters. Despite these problems the TRS/TRF ran successfully, providing textbooks for all students in all subjects at all levels, until 2005 when it was replaced by free primary textbook distribution funded by a World Bank project. Throughout its long life the scheme was affordable to parents and succeeded in getting primary textbooks more or less on time every year to every student in every primary school in every part of the country. Lesotho's success can be attributed to the following:

- It established strong management and monitoring systems and reviewed them regularly and amended them as required to ensure that the system continued to be effective.
- It had well-trained staff with consistent management who remained in post for long enough to become thoroughly familiar with their work and their responsibilities.

- It consistently reviewed its own performance, identified problems, and proposed solutions to address the problems.
- Every three or four years it commissioned an external independent review to report on progress and efficiency and it took decisive action on the recommendations.
- It consulted regularly with teachers, the school managers (mostly churches), head teachers, and parents and took notice of their criticisms and suggestions.
- It maintained a group of field officers who reported regularly on the real conditions of schools and kept the SSU focused on the real issues.

As a result it maintained rental fees at levels sufficient to guarantee funds for replacements when required, it streamlined its distribution practices and constantly considered ways and means to improve feedback from schools, and it maintained collection rates at high levels. Table 10.1, below, shows how every time the collection rate started to fall there was an introduction of new ideas to bring them back up to a sustainable level. The Lesotho experience contrasts with a similar rental scheme and revolving fund in the Gambia which failed to increase rental fees in line with inflation and replacement costs and failed to prevent collection rates from falling. As a result the Gambia revolving fund deteriorated, adequate replacement copies were not procured, and the scheme failed to prosper.[11]

In Kenya, a decentralized textbook provision pilot project funded by the Royal Netherlands Embassy (RNE) from 1997 to 1999 provided decentralized capitation grants to primary schools in Laikipia and Machakos districts. Three methods of decentralized financing were tested. These were

- Cash grants transferred direct into school bank accounts;
- Local purchase orders; and
- Decentralized ordering via school order forms followed by centralized order consolidation and centralized procurement.

Table 10.1 Annual Textbook Rental Fee Collection Rates in Lesotho

Year	Collection as % of invoices
1983	85.5
1984	84.7
1985	87.4
1986	92.5
1987	87.3
1988	86.2
1989	93.4
1990	80.4
1991	79.6
1992	89.4
1993	90.2

The distribution mechanism was via the private sector retail book trade, which was, and remains, unusually strong and comprehensive in its experience, professionalism, creditworthiness, and national coverage. Unfortunately, these critically important characteristics are found in very few other SSA countries. The results of the pilot project were very encouraging and the Ministry of Education, Science, and Technology (MOEST) selected direct electronic transfer of cash grants into unique primary school textbook bank accounts as the method of decentralized financing for the national Free Primary Education (FPE) project funded by the World Bank, which was launched in 2004. The decision to use cash grants was based on the evidence from the pilot project (Read and Mugiri 1999). The bookseller performance was reported in an Interim project report in 2001 (Buchan et al. 2001).

> Some larger established booksellers, and some "briefcase" booksellers operate over a number of different districts…. Some booksellers specialise in schools in remote and difficult access areas. For example, Dol International, based in Isiolo District travels to the remote—and sometimes dangerous—district schools and nomadic seasonal schools where no other booksellers wish to operate…. Most booksellers offer a 10% discount to schools. A few booksellers started by offering 15% discount, but had to reduce this to 10% when they discovered the actual costs involved. One bookseller that was very successful in winning contracts offered discounts ranging from 6 to 15%, depending on the value of the order and the distance to the school. Some booksellers typically offered small discounts but added other incentives, such as stationery. Discounts in stationery, furniture, sports equipment etc. cannot be checked for value, because none of these items has a fixed price (unlike the books on the approved list)… some head teachers and/or SMC chairs are demanding personal payments as a condition of awarding a supply contract to a bookseller. In a recent monitoring report on the WB/DFID SPRED 3 textbook funding a named bookseller openly admitted that some schools had demanded as a condition of contract that their discount should be provided partly in cash and partly in textbooks…. a majority of booksellers are over-discounting in the scramble to win school orders. In this situation, briefcase booksellers with minimum operational overheads are probably better placed to win school orders than established booksellers. This is not desirable for the long-term development of the Kenyan book trade. Transport of books to the school was cited as a critical aspect of marketing. For schools in remote areas, free delivery of books can be a very important factor.
>
> There was no evidence even in remote areas that booksellers were charging schools more than the listed prices. Most booksellers offered free delivery to schools. However, delivering books may wipe out the majority of the bookseller's profit, especially if more than one trip to a school has to be made (for example, if there is no-one to sign for the books on delivery). It is frequently impossible for a bookseller to arrange delivery by phone. The result has been that for some school orders, booksellers have offered free delivery and then failed to provide it.

Some booksellers reported delays of up to 2 months in receiving payment from schools, but these delays may be partly a result of schools ordering before their textbook allocation had actually become available to spend. (In some cases, schools ordered a month before their allocation became available in their bank accounts.)

Project monitoring was provided by PricewaterhouseCoopers (PwC) who reported that the majority of schools had received their orders in good condition and in reasonable time. Schools and booksellers were maintaining and operating all the required systems although many primary schools had problems in understanding how to maintain a cash book. Overall, schools were delighted with the services that they received from booksellers and compared them very favourably with their previous experiences with state distribution. In particular, schools were pleased that they were empowered to make their own selection decisions and to negotiate the terms and conditions of supply and that booksellers were prepared to deliver in most cases direct to their premises and that booksellers corrected errors and damages quickly and efficiently. The success of textbook distribution via retail bookselling in Kenya was based upon the following:

- Strong but simple management systems designed to create a clear audit trail for monitoring the system
- Extensive training of DEOs, Zonal Inspectors of Schools (ZISs), Teachers' Advisory Centres (TACs), schools, publishers, and booksellers in the required systems
- The availability of basic system management handbooks for schools and the book trade
- Rigorous external monitoring (via PwC) on a random basis intended both to support and train DEO staff and HQ staff in system monitoring
- On-time release of decentralized funding
- The incentives for efficient performance created by payments to booksellers only *after* correct delivery, in stark contrast to the Kenya School Equipment Scheme (KSES) where there was inadequate funding for the task and there were no incentives for good performance
- The strength and national coverage of the Kenyan book trade

There were problems, particularly in the lack of effective auditing by districts. There were also examples of corruption, and some DEOs and head teachers (or their families) opened their own bookshops and then applied pressure to schools to place their orders there. Overall, however, the retail book trade performed creditably and to the satisfaction of the schools and the MOEST. They continued to perform the TLM distribution function satisfactorily up to 2009 when there were reports of large-scale diversion of school per capita textbook funds away from schools and into personal pockets. This led to the arrest of a number of MOE officials and the withdrawal of all DP support for textbooks and the collapse of a successful textbook provision system.

In Uganda the MOES adopted a different approach to textbook distribution by advertizing competitive tenders for professional consolidation and distribution services. These generally worked quite well, particularly down to district offices, but there were examples of consignments delivered to districts and left for school collection, thus perpetuating the traditional disadvantages and bottlenecks of state-run distribution services.

Planning and Management Problems

Liberia installed a management database to plan and control textbook distribution. However, its effectiveness was undermined by a host of human management problems. A report by a book distribution specialist identified a wide range of planning and management problems, which are also typical of many other textbook distribution systems in SSA (Burchell 2010).

> The MOE recognises that the implementation of programmes is problematic for them, due… to the lack of depth in its line managers. Many of the latter have little or no management experience or expertise. Within the Ministry's HQ, internal communication across the three Departments, comprising the Ministry's structure, is poor and is a significant contributing factor to poor performance…. There are circa 140,450 textbooks and teacher's guides in store…. This is a reflection on the quality of information on school enrollments provided by the EMIS…. The Ministry's procurement/warehouse staff had not been trained in the handling of textbooks and textbook procedures. If untrained staff work with the textbook stock, the warehouse will quickly revert to disorder. The rapid turnover in CEOs and DEOs has led to a lack of continuity. Information imparted during training workshops has been lost. An analysis of the CDN[12] schedule shows that the many EOs are not following the procedures for handling the distribution paperwork making it virtually impossible for them to monitor the performance of the schools in their jurisdiction. Similarly not all EOs are maintaining an [instructional materials] file (i.e., holding all the documentation relating to distribution)…CEOs spend much of their time in Monrovia due to the lack of adequate housing in many of the districts and a lack of funds to fuel their motorbikes. DEOs are unlikely to spend more than three days a week in their districts… many schools are rarely visited by the DEO… consequently nobody has any (knowledge) of what is really happening…. The situation in schools is much more fluid, with considerable variation in performance and standards within the same district. The high turnover in School Principals … was frequently given as the reason for not following the guidelines/procedures specified in the IMMH and on which all School Principals received training. A survey of the CDNs revealed shortages and overages. One school had a shortage of 300 textbooks, but since no school in this County had submitted their CDNs, details of this shortage would not have reached the Ministry.

In 2010 Rwanda launched a specially designed TLM system management database which contained details of all schools and grade level roll numbers, all approved textbooks, teachers' guides, and supplementary materials and allocated budgets for school-based TLM procurement. The system monitored school ordering against their individual capitation budgets, consolidated all school ordering into individual title print orders and provided all publishers with distribution schedules based on Confirmed Delivery Notes (CDNs), which have to be signed and stamped by every school as proof of successful delivery. The system also maintains records of TLM inventory in every school and calculates five-year forward projections of the annual financing required to achieve and maintain official TLM targets. If these projections are unaffordable then the system enables government to amend its supply assumptions in order to bring annual financing back within acceptable limits. By extending school inventory records to the inspectorate and requiring inspectors to complete a short five-minute questionnaire on their visits, the database can calculate loss and damage rates and can identify storage and usage problems in schools. In 2012, Read noted that

- Rwanda has a TLM provision profile that supports curriculum objectives by ensuring the availability of textbooks, teachers' guides, and other TLMs.
- Schools-based TLM selection and ordering is now established.
- The system prints and supplies each school with its own order forms annotated with their official capitation allocation calculated by the system.
- TLM system management capacity is developing well.
- The Rwandan Ministry of Education (MINEDUC) now has detailed information on TLM provision in every school in Rwanda.
- MINEDUC can now project TLM financing requirements five years ahead.
- Cycle 1 achieved 98.6 percent successful school ordering and 98.3 percent successful delivery direct to schools at no cost to the schools—even to difficult-access schools in remote areas where delivery had to be achieved via head porterage. The motivation for this performance was that the publishers could not be paid until they had demonstrated successful delivery. This contrasts with years of ineffective state distribution.
- Prices are controlled for five years as a condition of approved status.
- All TLMs are tested annually for conformability with production specs.
- All data entry into the system has been successfully devolved down to district level.

A similar system was requested by the Namibian MOE in 2013 and is being funded by the Millennium Challenge Corporation (MCC) office in Windhoek and will become fully operational in 2014.[13]

A Summary of Emerging Key Issues

The key issues identified in the brief country case studies provided above could be replicated in the majority of SSA countries in both anglophone and francophone SSA. The levels of stock losses reported are not necessarily extreme examples. The following key issues therefore apply:

- Many textbook and TLM distribution systems in SSA are seriously dysfunctional, leading to very high levels of stock loss and damage.
- The stock loss and damage lead directly to substandard TPRs in a majority of SSA countries.
- Most governments and DPs are unaware of the extent of wastage caused by poor national distribution systems because of the lack of good management information.
- Despite the serious impact of substandard distribution there are relatively few examples of sustained, well-planned, professional project components aimed at upgrading book distribution capacity and performance in-country.
- Textbook distribution is still maintained as a state or MOE activity in many countries; but MOEs rarely have the finances, facilities, equipment, knowledge, and skills to perform this job.
- Commercial book trade involvement is constrained in most countries because of the lack of creditworthy wholesale or retail outlets in rural and remote areas.
- Distribution is generally underfunded by governments and particularly at the critical district levels where storage and delivery from districts to schools represent very common problems in most SSA countries.
- Effective planning is constrained by out-of-date and inaccurate data; many countries may not even be sure how many schools there are or where they are located.
- Distribution management requires well-designed computerized databases and management systems and staff who are trained to use them. TLM distribution management systems are generally weak. The creation of well-designed database management systems would improve the situation dramatically in most countries.
- There is a lack of simple, professional management and monitoring systems designed to ensure that schools receive and maintain the supplies that they require.
- Most distribution staff are untrained; training is more difficult with high staff turnover in schools, districts, and HQ departments responsible for distribution management.
- System supervision and inspection is ineffective in a majority of countries.

The list of problems provided above may seem daunting, but there are examples of SSA distribution systems that work and there is no reason why distribution should not be effectively upgraded in most SSA countries so long as experienced professional assistance is sought in analysis, system design, training, supervision, and initial implementation and accurate assessments of the true costs of distribution are agreed. A number of DPs have invested in warehouses and transportation in the past, but without investing in good system design and without considering the alternatives to state management. Three alternatives always need to be considered:

- Use the existing wholesale and retail book trade if it is has the necessary capacity, national coverage, finance, and professionalism.
- Ask publishers to include distribution costs to schools in their tendered prices and pass the distribution burden to publishers.
- Tender school-level distribution to professional haulage companies.

But for any of the above three solutions to work the MOE must have the right information to give to subcontractors and must have management and monitoring systems in place to make sure that the subcontractors have performed satisfactorily. One of the most powerful incentives for good performance is the incentive of payment only on confirmed delivery.

Notes

1. Extracted from Read 2001.
2. These are all consumer priority products throughout SSA where daily sales are pretty much guaranteed and are usually highly predictable.
3. In Kenya, in January 2000, the school textbook selling season was brought to an abrupt halt two months early because of public debate following the publication of a report on the possible introduction of a new curriculum. Although the curriculum reform was two or even three years away, public fear of purchasing redundant textbooks halted sales immediately. Pleas from booksellers and publishers to the Government of Kenya (GOK) to provide a positive statement that would resolve the uncertainty fell on deaf ears and substantial losses resulted.
4. As an example, a village primary school in a rural area with an enrollment of 400 students might require a starting stock of 2,400 books (six textbooks per student) at an average unit cost of US$3 per book. This would require a local trader to invest in stock to a value of US$7,200 less 25 percent discount = US$5,400 in order to fulfill the needs of one average-sized village school. The average annual income of such a trader in a rural village might be only US$300 to 400. Obviously, such an investment level (or even one-tenth of this level) is impossible for an underfinanced village trader, even without the risk element involved in the purchase of textbook stock on a firm basis. In contrast, the village trader might purchase six cases of Coca Cola per week (144 bottles/cans) at an average investment of US$0.25 per can = US$36. Within a week the trader knows from past experience that all stock will be sold. At a profit of US$0.05 per can the trader has recouped the original investment, has made a profit of US$7.20, and is ready to reinvest in stock for the next week. This activity will provide a safe and reliable income for the trader of US$374.40 per year. This example illustrates graphically the illogicality of the *commercial* comparison between Coca Cola and school textbook distribution. The trader *knows* absolutely that the investment in Coca Cola will sell quickly and that the initial investment is both safe and affordable. The trader has no idea how long it will take to sell the textbook stock (or whether it will sell at all), even if the finance was available to underwrite the purchase, and finance on the required scale generally isn't available. This example also illustrates the critical roles of credit, stock financing, and risk in the development of commercial textbook distribution networks. It also illustrates the benefits of small daily or weekly sales in comparison to a narrow annual selling season.

5. For example, any distributor who invested in a distribution network to serve the 14 districts of the RNE primary textbook project in Kenya would have suffered badly when the project was prematurely cancelled by the donor after one year despite generally very encouraging results.
6. Total demurrage charges were estimated at approximately US$200,000.
7. Paper absorbs water, even from the atmosphere, which is why good ventilation is essential in a book store.
8. This section is taken from Jones and Sayer 2013.
9. Mombasa was the shipping point of entry for supplies to South Sudan, which is landlocked.
10. In Guinea the *Horizon d'Afrique* textbook, donated in large quantities by *Agence Internationale de le Francophonie* (AIF), should have been sold at one third of its actual price (that is, US$2). In a very short time it was no longer available in Guinea, but was widely available in the pavement bookshops of neighboring countries at US$6.50.
11. Case studies of the Lesotho and the Gambia revolving funds can be found in Da Cruz et al. 1998.
12. Confirmed delivery note.
13. It is interesting to note that, although the Namibian learning materials management system was based on the Rwanda system, the differences between the two systems required that the 16 modules used in the Rwandan system had to be increased to 21 modules in Namibia to cope with the different national system requirements. This underlines that, although there will always be common elements in the design of computerized management systems for different countries, it is unlikely that a system designed and successfully implemented in one country could be "parachuted" intact into another country.

References

Buchan, A., V. Bontoux, C. Denning, E. Mugiri, and T. Read. 2001. "Towards a National System of Instructional Materials Provision in Kenya." Department for International Development East Africa for MOEST, Nairobi.

Buchan, A., C. Denning, and A. Read. 1991. *African Book Sector Studies Summary Report*. Windsor, United Kingdom: International Book Development for World Bank African Ministers of Education Conference.

Burchell, K. 2010. *An Evaluation of the Distribution of Primary Textbooks in Liberia*. Monrovia: Open Society Foundation for MOE.

Da Cruz, A. J., T. A. George, F. Z. Gnahare, F. Z. Kouakou, P. Mendonca, C. Schlabi, M. Simao, and A. Read. 1998. *Financing Textbooks and Teacher Training Materials*. Perspectives in African Book Development Series. Paris: Working Party on Books and Learning Materials, Association for the Development of Education in Africa.

Fearnley, R. 1998. *Primary Textbook Distribution in Malawi*. Lilongwe: International Book Development for Canadian International Development Agency (CIDA).

GNECC (Ghana National Education Campaign Coalition). 2010. *Tracking Survey for Textbooks, School Uniforms, Capitation Grants, School Infrastructure and Teachers*. Accra: GNECC.

Jones, B., and Sayer, N. 2013. *Annual Review of the South Sudan Textbook Project*. Juba: DFID.

Piper, B. 2010. *Ethiopia Early Grade Reading Assessment: Data Analysis Report*. Research Triangle Park, NC: RTI International for USAID.

Read, N. 2012. *Interim Report on the TLM Reform Project*. Windsor, United Kingdom: International Education Partners for UNICEF and NCDC.

Read, T. 2001. "Introductory Essay." In *Upgrading Book Distribution Systems in Africa*, edited by T. Read, C. Denning, and V. Bontoux. Paris: ADEA.

———. 2010. *Ghana Learning and Teaching Materials Policy Review*. Accra: DFID for MOE.

Read, T., C. Denning, and V. Bontoux. 2001. *Upgrading Textbook Distribution in Africa*. Paris: ADEA, 174–75.

Read, T., and A. Ibale. 2007. *Zanzibar Textbook Policy and Financing Study. A World Bank Study*. Washington, DC: World Bank for MOEVT.

Read, T., and E. Mugiri. 1999. *Final Report of the Decentralized Textbook Provision Pilot Project in Laikipia and Machakos Districts*. Nairobi: Royal Netherlands Embassy.

Sow, M. A. E. Brunswic and J. Valerian. 2001. "Guinea Case Study." In *Upgrading Book Distribution Systems in Africa*, edited by T. Read, C. Denning, and V. Bontoux. Paris: ADEA.

Waziri, A. J. P. Leguere, and G. Stern. 2001a. "Niger Case Study." In *Upgrading Book Distribution Systems in Africa*, edited by T. Read, C. Denning, and V. Bontoux. Paris: ADEA.

———. 2001b. "Chad Case Study." In *Upgrading Book Distribution Systems in Africa*, edited by T. Read, C. Denning, and V. Bontoux. Paris: ADEA.

CHAPTER 11

Managing and Using Teaching and Learning Materials in Schools

School and Classroom Storage

Many schools in Sub-Saharan Africa (SSA) have substandard storage for books. Conditions are generally worse in primary than in secondary schools and worse in rural and remote areas than in urban areas, although slum districts in urban areas can have storage conditions that are worse than in many rural or remote areas. Typically storage may be insecure, leading to theft; poorly managed and untidy, leading to loss and damage; not weatherproof, leading to damage through rain and dust; or infected with fungus, vermin, and insects. Mice, termites, silverfish, and so on are all capable of seriously damaging, even destroying, book stock if not checked on a regular basis. The level of loss and damage through poor storage and book care is impossible to generalize but annual teaching and learning materials (TLM) stock losses in SSA schools of 10 percent are not unusual and annual stock losses of 30 to 50 percent have been recorded in some primary schools in some SSA countries.

In primary schools the book storage is often in the head teacher's office or in a room adjoining the office. In schools where the head teacher is often absent the stock may not be accessible to teachers because the keys have travelled with the head teacher. Thus textbooks and other TLMs can remain unused for many days, weeks, or even months through simple lack of access. In Ghana in 2010 visits to schools indicated considerable variations in levels of storage, usage, care, and conservation of TLMs. A long-established, prestigious secondary school maintained its textbook and library stocks in good condition, maintained good management procedures, and demonstrated good basic conservation techniques to identify damaged textbooks at an early stage and to initiate repairs before the textbooks or library books became irretrievably damaged. Library books were routinely covered with heavy-duty plastic covers as protection. However, a relatively newly established rural secondary school nearby had completely inadequate textbook storage and poor to nonexistent management and conservation systems and the textbooks were in significantly worse condition and inevitably had a much shorter useful life as a result. Nevertheless, both secondary schools were actually using the TLMs that they had received. In three primary schools visited storage was in the head teacher's office and in one case the quality of storage was so poor that there was evidence of serious water damage to many of the textbooks held in the head teacher's office (Read 2010).

A further problem is the widespread lack of classroom storage in primary schools. Few primary classrooms in many SSA countries have lockable built-in cupboards to provide secure storage for textbooks and reading books that desirably should be used every day. Many primary teachers are reluctant to issue books to lower primary children to take home because of the risks of loss and damage. At the same time the burden of having to collect book stocks every day from a central store and then carry them to class and then return them at the end of the day becomes tiresome; and many teachers stop using TLMs in class sets on a regular basis, particularly when frequent head teacher absences are typical so that there is no access to the book stocks anyway. Lockable classroom storage would greatly improve access to book stocks and would encourage more frequent TLM use in class, particularly of reading books. Unfortunately, even in 2014 a majority of classroom designs from both public works departments (PWDs) and development partners (DPs) do not specify built-in, lockable classroom storage.

TLM Management Issues

The management of TLM stock in schools is also widely substandard and often completely lacking. This often means that schools have no records—or only imperfect records—of issued stock and thus have no means of retrieving stock at the end of the term or year. The Liberia report quoted in chapter 10 confirms the basic TLM management problems.

> No school visited knows how to use the Stock Register and Stock Issue Register. Frequently, neither was available for inspection. Those schools, which were using the registers, were not using them correctly. A number of School Principals volunteered that "school administration" is not their strong point and that further training is required. (Burchell 2010)

This situation probably could be found in a majority of primary and even secondary schools in SSA. Part of the problem is the rapid turnover of senior staff in schools and the failure to have proper handover periods between departing and newly appointed head teachers and deputy head teachers. Thus newly appointed head teachers often have no knowledge of the basic systems that once applied. The rapid expansion of both primary and secondary education has also had an impact because of the demand for large numbers of new senior staff to run newly created schools. Secondary school heads in Kenya in 2007 claimed that prior to their appointments they had received no training in school inventory management and maintaining school accounts (Read and Read 2008).

A related issue is the infrequency of school inspections and audits, particularly at primary level in rural and remote areas. Unless systems are monitored they will inevitably fall into disuse, and if they are not maintained losses will increase. One school in Ghana reported a 50 percent stock loss of new textbooks in one term because students would not return the textbooks issued to them. When the school tried to apply penalties, the parents complained to the district education officer (DEO) who ruled that no penalties should be imposed. As a result the school no longer issues textbooks on loan despite the fact that it is government policy to do so (Read 2010).

Once again it is not possible to estimate even an approximate figure of the extent of stock losses through poor school management. There are good and bad schools and arriving at an average applicable over different national systems is not possible without extensive survey work. There is a clear need to provide all primary schools with some basic guidelines on the management, conservation, and usage of TLMs in order to achieve value for the substantial sums being invested in TLMs. But training and handbooks will not work if management systems are not monitored regularly and this depends upon inspection from experienced supervisory staff, which in turn depends upon sufficient numbers in the inspectorate, adequate inspectorate training, the availability of the means to travel to schools as required, and the capability of following up where substandard facilities and systems are identified.

Patterns of TLM Usage in the Classroom

Even where adequate stocks of teaching and learning materials exist in schools there is no guarantee that this will result in effective classroom use. A study undertaken by the Swedish International Development Agency (SIDA) as part of the Pilot Project for Publishing in Tanzania discovered that there were huge discrepancies between the availability of good class sets of textbooks in schools and their use in the classroom. A national survey undertaken in 1999 revealed that although almost 40 percent of schools surveyed had class sets of textbooks, only four percent of schools were actually using them. In many SSA countries poor textbook supplies over many years have conditioned teachers to operating without textbooks and many teachers may prefer that textbooks are not issued in order to avoid students knowing as much as the teacher. There is certainly evidence to indicate that many teachers may have forgotten (or never learned) how to use textbooks and other TLMs. For example, in Cameroon in August 2013 (Buchan 2013) it was reported that

> In the Extreme Nord region, UNICEF and other sources report that there are areas where primary schools have no textbooks at all, and have not had them for so long that none of the children have ever used a book. Teachers in these schools have become accustomed to never using textbooks and therefore have no knowledge of how to use them in class.

A similar situation was reported in South Sudan (Jones and Sayer 2013).

Many teachers have been without books for so long that they no longer know how to use them effectively. The high percentage of untrained teachers, estimated at

14,000 out of a total of 26,000 teachers (54%), plus a significant proportion of only partially trained teachers also require help in basic usage skills. 70% of teachers are more familiar with teaching in Arabic rather than in English and there has been a fragmented approach to teacher training by local NGOs. It is reported that some teachers are reluctant to issue textbooks to students because they fear being asked questions about an unfamiliar language that they can't answer.

Similar reports on poor textbook usage in the classroom and the reluctance to even issue textbooks to students have been reported as well from the Democratic Republic of Congo, Ethiopia, Ghana, Guinea, Namibia, Rwanda, Sierra Leone, and Uganda in the past two or three years; and this kind of reporting has been a feature in many other countries in SSA for at least the past 15 to 20 years. In these circumstances, a crash course in usage techniques, or at least a simple usage guide book for teachers, could have some benefit.

Because many of the teachers no longer know how to use textbooks in class to the best effect, the teachers' copy of the textbook is often written on the blackboard (or sometimes just dictated) and the students copy from the blackboard into their notebooks (if they have notebooks). This means that the expensive illustrations, use of color, and page designs employed by publishers and authors for the benefit of students are often not seen by the students at all.

> Many teachers ... simply copy the textbook onto the blackboard for the children to copy into their note books with no explanation. The biggest problem is that children don't learn to read and write properly, so when they sit exams, whilst they might know the answers, they can't read the question or write down the answer. (Coughlan 2014)

Even when textbooks and other TLMs are successfully delivered to schools and are reasonably well maintained in storage there is a common problem in SSA that many teachers do not issue the materials to their students. A 2013 World Bank Uganda study (Wane and Martin 2013) reported as follows:

> No textbooks were used by students in 86% of the classes in public schools. While the observed use of textbooks by students in public schools was very low at 14%, public schools—contrary to expectations—actually fared better than private schools, where the use was virtually non-existent at 3%.[1]

The reasons for nonissue are not easy to determine and many causes have been postulated over the years; it is probable that all of the causal factors listed below may be valid in some schools in many countries. These include the following:

- The effort of issuing books at the beginning of a class and then collecting them afterwards is a burden for many teachers, particularly where there is no adequate classroom storage and books have to be collected daily from a central school store, which may not always—or even often—be open when required.
- Schools are often reluctant to issue TLMs to students because they fear loss, damage or theft. This is a particular issue in exam classes in the last year of schooling.

- Teachers are reluctant to issues books to students if they are likely to be held responsible for losses and damage. Similarly, parents may be unwilling to accept textbooks issued to their children if they are to be held financially responsible for losses or damage.
- Failure to achieve reasonable textbook–pupil ratios (TPRs). Many teachers appear to find it difficult to cope with textbook provision if there is less than a 1:1 TPR despite the fact that there is research to indicate that acceptable results can be achieved with 1:2 or even 1:3 ratios.
- Teachers often prefer to use one textbook as a teachers' copy and do not issue the other textbooks to students. This is widely reported to be associated with teachers' fears that students may come to know as much or even more than the teacher if the textbooks are made available to students.
- Teachers may not fully understand all the subject content in the textbook and thus do not issue the textbooks in case there are student queries that they cannot answer. This tends to be a common issue in math and science or even in a second language where teachers are not confident of their language skills.
- Teachers no longer know how to use textbooks effectively in class and thus do not issue them.
- Teachers are uncertain that current textbook stocks will be reliably replaced and thus develop a hoarding mentality in which textbooks are maintained in stock rather than issued to students.
- Teachers are not taught how to use TLMs effectively as part of their pre-service training.

Even when textbooks and other TLMs are issued to students for use in class there still may be problems caused by the ineffective use of the materials by teachers. A review of classroom practice in South Sudan in 2014 (Mikulska 2014) reported as follows:

> In South Sudan, late enrollment, no enrollment, and school drop-outs are common. For every hundred primary-age children, only 62 get enrolled in school. Out of these 21 drop-out before they reach grade 2 and only 17 stay at school till grade 8.... Paradoxically, teachers are unable to meet the cost of educating their own children; so they seek additional employment, which contributes to teacher absences (World Bank 2012). Very few teachers spend their time teaching. Most sit in the staffroom marking learners' books. Teachers in the classrooms spend most of their time copying textbooks onto the chalkboard and tasking learners to memorize the text by copying it to their copy-books which are then collected for marking, on which teachers are reported to spend up to 15 hours a week. Recent distribution of free textbooks and supplementary readers lowering the student-textbook ratio from 60:1 to circa 2:1 has not changed classroom practice because most teachers prefer to keep the textbooks safe in store rather than give them to students. Nobody challenges the current practice or models more effective learning approaches. Head-teachers spend their time dealing with paper-work and reporting statistical data to school supervisors who at most offer schools a liaison service rather than a

pedagogical challenge. Their main job seems to be delivery of circulars to schools and collecting EMIS data. Local government tries to manage the education system to 60 schools but without vehicles, operational budgets and demands from development partners and the government.

In a recent training workshop on effective textbook and TLM use in Namibia (Hiddleston and Hovelmann 2013) the following styles of common classroom textbook use were reported by Education Officers, subject specialist Advisory Teachers, and ordinary subject specialist classroom teachers.

- Some teachers use the textbook by reading a passage and then working through the passage with the class, sentence by sentence, providing explanations for meaning. They then give the activity to the students as stated in the textbook, often with no preparation other than the description of the activity in the textbook.
- Some teachers read the textbook at home and summarise the topic. They ask learners to open their books and copy the vocabulary into their notebooks. They give the class a different activity from the one in the textbook and then give the activity in the textbook as homework.
- Some teachers will ask learners to read a chapter from the book silently in class. Then they will ask questions that learners are required to answer from their silent reading.
- Sometimes learners are asked to read the textbook aloud in class.
- Some teachers formulate and put questions on the board. Then learners read the passage in the textbook and attempt the answers to the questions in the passage.
- Learners are required to summarise the content of the topic in the textbook.
- Some teachers encourage learners to identify difficult words in the topic and then find out the meaning and the correct pronunciation.
- Immediately after coming to class a teacher will say 'Open at page ...' and then start reading from the textbook word for word.
- Some teachers use the textbook to present a lesson and then ask learners to open to a certain page and do an exercise.
- Some teachers will come to class with a short summary derived from the textbook.
- Some teachers will ask the class to memorise a chapter for homework and will then set a test the next day.

The Master Trainers at the workshop concluded that many of the examples of teachers' textbook use quoted above were inadequate and would impact adversely on students' learning outcomes and that there was little evidence of the creative use of textbooks and supplementary materials in the pursuit of curriculum learning objectives. The Master Trainers also recognized that most teachers were not preparing their lessons in advance and were relying on the textbook alone to get them through unprepared lessons and that teachers' manuals were not sufficiently used in lesson preparation. In support of this viewpoint a leading editor of textbooks for use in SSA recently commented in a discussion on appropriate TLMs that she had never met a teacher who had used any of the teachers' guides designed to accompany and support the student textbooks. The Master Trainers also noted that teachers were far more concerned with student acquisition of facts and were far less concerned with the development of student skills and competencies despite the fact that these were quoted as important required learning outcomes in both syllabuses and textbooks. A significant part of the problem was considered to be teachers' lack of confidence in their own knowledge of the subject content and the skills and competences specified by the syllabus. Thus the textbooks when they were used in class were most often used in ways to *conceal* the teachers' lack of subject knowledge, competencies, and skills, which in turn led to poor learning outcomes, student demotivation and pronounced classroom passivity, and the rapid development of a lack of enthusiasm for school and learning.

Namibia is not the only country where these kinds of problems are common and clearly not all schools and teachers are performing badly in the use of TLMs in class, but the textbook usage practices described above are widespread in probably a majority of SSA schools. The twin problems of the nonissue of textbooks and other TLMs to students and the widespread poor use of textbooks and TLMs in class when they *are* issued combine to undermine the cost effectiveness of textbook and TLM provision systems. The development of simple but effective school-based TLM management systems, the more rigorous and regular training of schools and teachers in the management and usage of TLMs,[2] plus efficient and regular monitoring and supervision of what happens in schools are the obvious solutions. The free issue of printed stock inventory ledgers and stock issue registers to all schools would also support a common national school management system and would support improved management practices at school level and this should be considered widely as a sensible and cost-effective investment.

The Namibia report referred to above also commented on the lack of alignment between curriculum and syllabus objectives—often poorly defined—and textbook content and approach and felt that there was a need for more detailed textbook specifications when invitations were issued to publishers to submit bids for evaluation and selection. The issue is not just a concern over the authorship and publishing of textbooks but also the realism and specificity of curriculum objectives. Of particular concern is the wide variation in contact hours between schools in many SSA countries, which are almost never officially recognized by curriculum developers, by ministries of education (MOEs), or by development partners; so guidance on how authors and publishers should respond to handling in their TLMs the significant differences in contact hours and the many other disparities in trained teachers, equipment, electricity supply, internet connectivity, furniture, and so on in terms of textbook and teachers' guide design and content is almost never provided.

Many of the textbooks approved for use in schools—particularly secondary schools which are dominated by second language (L2) learning—are probably too difficult in language for many teachers and students and particularly so for those lacking in L2 competency. Professor John Clegg, an expert on content and concept acquisition by students using a second language, has commented on the potential teaching and learning problems as follows:

> Students learning in a L2 are doing more things, cognitively speaking, than they would do if they are learning through their L1. They are learning subject-matter, knowledge and skills, but they are also concurrently learning the language which is the vehicle for that subject learning. This means that they have less mental processing capacity available than when learning through the L1 [first language]. They cannot therefore do some classroom tasks without help. Teachers can give help where it is necessary either by making the task conceptually easier, so that the students can focus more on language; or they can make it linguistically easier so that the students can focus more on the concepts. It is not a good idea to make tasks conceptually easier very often: students—and other stakeholders such as parents and teachers—may get the idea that CLIL (Content and Language Integrated Learning) is too easy and not as good as the L1-medium version. So teachers need to learn the skill of providing language support and at what points in a lesson they need to do that. (Clegg 2013)

Unfortunately, many teachers lack both the L2 skills and the content knowledge and competency skills to provide L2 students with the additional help that they need. Thus, the burden of addressing this problem is usually assumed to be the responsibility of the textbook author and publisher—but these in turn are only very rarely provided with the right kind of guidance from curriculum developers and MOEs to address the issue of additional help for L2 learners through the provision of the right kind of language.

Clegg (2013) recommended that CLIL teachers should explicitly teach the most important learning strategies and study skills and should expect students to use them regularly. These should include note taking, using dictionaries and atlases, doing research, planning for writing, and developing TLMs vocabulary through consciously learning and using new words. It was suggested that curricula and textbooks written for L2 students and teachers should pay more attention to the regular use of these basic learning skills.

From the above brief analysis it seems clear that there is still considerable conceptual work required in SSA countries on the effective alignment between textbooks, teachers' guides, supplementary materials, classroom usage of materials, curricula and syllabuses, assessment, contact hours, and language competency.

Conservation and Reuse

It is arguable that standards of book care have deteriorated seriously in schools in SSA countries over the past 40 to 50 years. For example, in the 1960s and 1970s virtually every primary and secondary school in Africa insisted on textbooks issued to students being properly covered in strong brown paper and maintained in good condition by the students. Now there are many schools where covered textbooks are a rarity and basic standards of book care and book conservation, including book repairs, are almost entirely absent. The key objective of a school book conservation policy is to keep books in good condition so that they can achieve their targeted classroom life and thus contribute to maximum cost amortization and minimum TLM costs to the system. Well-cared-for books are also pleasanter to reuse for succeeding students.

To simplify even further, perhaps the single greatest objective is to keep the covers on the textbook in order to protect the page block. Regular inspections of textbooks by teachers can often identify damage at an early stage so that remedial action can be taken. A simple set of book care and conservation practices is provided below. Because teachers can become overwhelmed by the scale of conservation activity that may be required it is often suggested that schools should try to involve parental groups in ensuring good book care and undertaking regular repairs. Not all damage can be repaired in school but there are a range of simple repairs that are within the range of teachers and parents and these should be well known to all teachers and informed to all parents.

Where textbooks are loaned to students a clear loss and damage policy is required. Some systems believe that any kind of penalty charge for loss and damage will discourage effective textbook use.[3] Other systems and schools can levy quite severe charges in order to guarantee proper care. But a national textbook loss and damage policy that has been discussed and agreed with representative groups of teachers and parents is recommended.

A Summary of Emerging Key Issues

School level management and use of TLMs is seriously substandard in many SSA countries and is responsible for potentially large percentages of TLM loss and damage, which in turn reduces the effectiveness of TLMs in schools and increases the costs of effective provision.

In order to reduce the TLM loss levels in schools and to ensure the proper use of the TLMs provided, the following actions are suggested:

- Upgrade storage facilities in schools to meet minimum criteria of (a) security; (b) weatherproofing; and (c) cleanliness—that is, freedom from infestation by vermin, insects,[4] and fungus.
- Provide classroom-based storage in primary schools and in particular in lower primary (P1–P3) classrooms.
- Design simple TLM management systems for schools using stock registers and stock issue registers, which should be provided free of charge to schools every year in the same way that student attendance registers are provided free in many school systems.
- Produce and publicize loss and damage policy guidelines to all schools.
- Produce a TLM Management Handbook for all schools, teachers in training, DEOs, and the inspectorate.
- Produce a simple guide to the effective classroom use of all TLMs.

- Provide in-service and pre-service training to teachers and inspectors in the use of TLMs in the classroom and school TLM management systems.
- Ensure that a review of TLM management systems should be a requirement of all inspection visits to schools.
- Where decentralized financing mechanisms for TLMs are in use, ensure regular auditing of school accounts.
- Undertake regular surveys (for example, every 3–4 years) of TLM availability in schools to ensure that provision targets are being met and maintained and take corrective action on the results of the surveys as required.
- Provide better and more precise textbook and TLM specifications when publishers are invited to submit for evaluation and approval; these should include clear and unambiguous definitions of standards, concepts, skills, and competencies that are required to be achieved and guidance on how these should be measured.
- Ensure more rigorous textbook evaluation mechanisms before textbooks are approved for use in schools.
- Reconsider the issue of the additional help required by L2 students in subject content and skills learning.
- Provide clear guidance to publishers on how to handle variations in national contact hours.

Book Care Rules for Students

1. Always make sure books are well covered.
2. Keep books away from water and damp.
3. Always carry books to and from school in a waterproof and dustproof bag, which is big enough for the books that you have to carry. Even a plastic carrier bag provides some protection and is better than nothing.
4. Take care not to put too many books in a bag at the same time. Paperback textbooks can be strong and durable but they suffer if pushed roughly into overcrowded school bags.
5. Never fold books or push them roughly into bags which are too small.
6. Keep your books clean. Most of them should have varnished or laminated covers and the covers can be wiped clean with a slightly damp (not wet) cloth.
7. Always use your books with clean, dry hands. The dust, grime, and sweat on your hands will damage the text pages unless your hands are washed before books are used. Paper is easily damaged by water and damp, so never use a book with wet or sweaty hands.
8. Always open books carefully using the top outside edge of the page to avoid tearing.
9. Never bend books back against the spine.
10. Never press out the gutters to make books stay open when flat.
11. Never use books as weapons or missiles.
12. Never write in your textbooks.
13. If your textbook is damaged in any way show it to your teacher so that it can be repaired before the damage gets worse.

Notes

1. This study also reported an average textbook–pupil ratio of one textbook per 14.4 pupils. However, in 2006 after 12 years of reforms in Instructional Materials provision funded by USAID, the World Bank, the Department for International Development (DFID), and the Royal Netherlands Embassy (RNE), the average reported primary TPR was 1:2 and donors and MOES expected to achieve a 1:1 TPR. (See Ward, Penny, and Read 2006). It would be instructive to discover why there has been such a major collapse in the TPR in Uganda by 2013 after the very substantial reform achievements recorded in 2006.
2. Many pre-service teacher training syllabuses provide no training on TLM management and TLM classroom usage. However, in Namibia, the training materials on textbook and TLM usage originally developed for in-service teacher training are now being included in the pre-service teacher training course programs at the University of Namibia (UNAM).
3. In Guinea the imposition of penalties for textbook loss and damage led to parents refusing to allow their children to use the textbooks.
4. Antitermite paint is widely available and cheap and provides good protection for a reasonable period against termites if applied for 30 centimeters above ground level to walls and the legs of bookcases and cupboards used for TLM storage.

References

Buchan, A. 2013. *Cameroon Textbook Sub-Component Report: Cameroon Equity and Quality for Improved Learning Project Pre-Appraisal Document*. Windsor, United Kingdom: International Education Partners for the World Bank.

Burchell, K. 2010. *An Evaluation of the Distribution of Primary Textbooks in Liberia*. Monrovia: Open Society Foundation for MOE.

Clegg, J. 2013. *Providing Language Support in CLIL*. jclegg@lineone.net.

Coughlan, S. 2014. "Tackling Uganda's Lack of School Places." *BBC News*, January 8.

Hiddleston, P., and W. Hovelmann. 2013. *Master Trainers Training Workshops for Textbook Use for Maths, Science, and English*. Windhoek: MCA-Namibia.

Jones, B., and N. Sayer. 2013. *Annual Review of the South Sudan Textbook Project*. Juba: DFID.

Mikulska, A. 2014. "School Teaching and Learning: The Challenge of Education in South Sudan." *NORRAG News*, June.

Read, T. 2010. *Ghana Learning and Teaching Materials Policy Review*. Accra: DFID for MOE.

Read, T., and N. Read. 2008. *Free Day Secondary Education in Kenya: Tuition Vote Management Training and Research Report*. Windsor, United Kingdom: International Education Partners for the World Bank and MOEST, Kenya.

SIDA (Swedish International Development Agency). 2000. *Textbook Usage in Tanzanian Schools: The Results of a National Survey*. Pilot Project for Publishing.

Wane, W., and G. H. Martin. 2013. *Education and Health Services in Uganda: Data for Results and Accountability*. A World Bank Study. Washington, DC: World Bank and African Economic Research Consortium.

Ward, M., A. Penny, and T. Read. 2007. *Education Reform in Uganda—1997 to 2004: Reflections on Policy, Partnership, Strategy and Implementation*. London: DFID.

World Bank. 2012. *Education in the Republic of South Sudan: Challenges for a New System*. Washington, DC: World Bank.

PART 3

e-Alternatives to Hard Copy Textbooks

CHAPTER 12

The Potential Impact of Information and Communication Technology Solutions on Textbook Provision

Information and Communications Technology for Education as Competition to Hard Copy Teaching and Learning Materials

Increasing frustration with the difficulties experienced in most Sub-Saharan African (SSA) countries in achieving affordable and sustainable textbook provision (and other essential teaching and learning materials [TLMs]) has led many ministries of education (MOEs) and development partners (DPs) to a consideration of the possible introduction of electronic alternatives to traditional print-on-paper solutions. The proposed e-solutions range from the use of Digital Printing On Demand (DPOD) equipment sited in regional or district level locations to print textbooks from online pdf sources, to the use of e-readers as vehicles for textbook provision (Kindles, and so on), to the use of tablet computers, low-cost laptops, the enhanced use of existing school-based PCs and the future role of mobile phone technology and Personal Digital Assistants (PDA).

The advent of information and communication technology (ICT) as a major budget line in many SSA education systems and schools is an additional cost component of education budgets that are already typically thinly spread. Because there are perceptions that ICT provision could solve TLM provision problems there is also the possibility that ICT and print-based TLM could compete in the future for the same funding. For this reason it is important to understand the nature of ICT provision in many SSA countries and the potential benefits and constraints that currently apply to ICT operations in schools.

The current TLM-related issues raised by ICT provision to education in developing and transitional economies are quite well known but are summarized in appendix B, which provides information on ICT and student achievement, the total cost of ownership (TCO), current constraints to ICT use, and a consideration of the One Laptop per Child (OLPC) initiative.

e-Alternatives to Textbook Provision

Using DPOD for Textbook Provision

It has been suggested that cheaper textbook provision costs in SSA countries could be achieved by locating DPOD equipment in district offices and printing from one-color textbook files in pdf format made available online.

DPOD equipment specifications can be as simple as a photocopier linked to a laptop. Alternatively it can be a sophisticated piece of printing equipment costing US$15,000–50,000[1] and upwards. The exact specification will depend upon the volumes required, the speed of manufacturing, and the binding requirement. However, the nature of digital DPOD needs to be taken into account. DPOD is designed to be used to print a limited number of items for a fixed cost per copy, regardless of the size of the print order. Thus, the unit price of each physical copy printed is always higher—often significantly higher—than with medium-to long-run offset printing, but the average cost is lower for very small print runs, because setup costs are much higher for offset printing. Quality control with DPOD is also considered to be less rigorous than with offset or letterpress printing. However, DPOD has other benefits besides the lower costs for small print runs. These are the following:

- Technical setup is usually quicker than for offset printing.
- Large inventories of a book or print material do not need to be kept in stock, reducing storage, handling costs, and inventory accounting costs.
- There is little or no waste from unsold products.

The unit cost of DPOD will always be higher than offset or letterpress printing whenever there are medium to large print runs required and in most SSA countries even the district level requirement will generally require volumes that will make DPOD uneconomic compared to traditional printing. For example, in a district with 50 schools with an average enrollment of 500 students per school and an average requirement of eight textbooks per student, the total number of textbooks required will be 400,000 copies at a textbook–pupil ratio (TPR) of 1:1 or 130,000 copies at a TPR of 1:3. This kind of volume would make DPOD uneconomic compared with traditional printing, particularly when all district textbook requirements could be consolidated into large national print runs, thus achieving the lowest possible manufacturing costs.

In addition to the cost issues, the following also should be taken into account:

- There would be no saving on distribution costs because sufficient paper (and toner) would have to be transported to district centers and the distribution costs of textbooks are always directly related to the paper weight.
- Paper costs would be higher because the paper used would be supplied in pre-cut reams rather than in large sheets or in reels.
- The DPOD printings would require some form of binding, which would increase the printing equipment specs and also the unit costs of provision.

Alternatively, ring binder files could be used, which are much more expensive than traditional durable textbook bindings. Failure to provide some form of protection to the printed sheets could lead to significant losses in onward distribution and in storage and usage in schools and thus would result in very short book life and increased cost.
- Printing in district centers would still require the textbooks to be moved from district centers to schools and this is widely recognized in most SSA countries to be the most difficult link in the distribution chain.
- Although the training requirements for operating DPOD equipment are much less rigorous than for traditional printing processes there are certain to be maintenance problems, which will require the procurement of expensive spare parts and the availability of machine-specific servicing engineers, who may not be resident in-country. Most District Education Offices (DEOs) suffer from inadequate operational budgets so there could easily be problems in paying for the servicing requirements and thus maintaining DPOD plant in operational condition.
- The textbook printing requirement in each district would normally be concentrated into a few weeks prior to the beginning of the school year. Thereafter it is unlikely that many districts, particularly in rural areas, would have very much demand during the rest of the year to justify the capital investment. With a relatively short window in which to produce the textbooks, the sort of maintenance downtime experienced with sophisticated digital presses (two to three weeks is not uncommon even when spare parts and specialist engineers are readily available) could prove a serious problem.
- Single-shift operations and lack of district-based demand apart from textbooks would reduce the impact of plant cost amortization, which would increase overall costs and add to the adverse price differential between DPOD and traditional textbook printing.

The combination of factors listed above makes it unlikely that district-based DPOD would be either cheaper or more efficient than traditional printing methodologies and it would not resolve the problems associated with textbook distribution cost and effectiveness.

E-readers
In 2012 the display of the standard Amazon Kindle had a diagonal measurement of six inches and used e-Ink technology to create electronic paper. The pixel resolution of the display was 600 by 800 at 167 pixels per inch (ppi) with a four-level gray scale. The overall size of the reading device was 7.5 inches by 5.3 inches by 0.7 inches and the weight was only 10.3 ounces. It had an internal storage capacity of 256 megabytes but a secure digital (SD) memory card slot was available that could support an SD memory card capacity of four gigabytes. Higher specification versions are becoming available but at increased prices.

The basic Kindle has a black-and-white display screen that simulates the readability and physical appearance of printed papers. The light reflection in the display is similar to that of ordinary paper. There is no backlight in the device, thus there is no glare in the display. It is as easy to read in direct sunlight as indoors. Readers can move from one page to another freely due to the full-length and vertical page-turning buttons that are found on both sides of the reading device. Both left-handed and right-handed users can navigate and use the unit comfortably with one hand. The latest Kindle version has sound and a backlight capacity to enable night time reading. The Kindle is thinner and lighter than a standard paperback. Up to 3,000 titles can be stored on each Kindle; an SD memory card can provide access to many more. The size of the text can be changed easily by a button to the desired text size, but for textbooks increasing the type size reduces the view of the full page layout. The use of an e-reader would make it easy for children to transport multiple textbooks and reading books to and from school; at the same time the possession of an expensive piece of hardware in poor countries could make school children a focus for mugging.

Worldreader uses the Amazon Kindle in its pilot projects, although there are other cheaper (and smaller) e-readers currently available and more will come to market in the future. France has developed its own e-reader, the FNAC Book, which has an even smaller screen size than the Kindle. At the time of writing there is no information that e-readers have been piloted in francophone Africa. The problem areas with e-readers that need to be reviewed and resolved can be summarized as follows:

1. *Wi-Fi connectivity*—how effective will Kindles be in accessing new content in rural areas? Limiting Kindles to urban areas only would increase the domestic digital divide (DDD). A more expensive version of the Kindle gives access via third generation (3G) mobile phone networks, which is obviously more suitable for African classrooms than downloading content via the Internet but there is no information available so far as to how long downloads would take if bandwidth in rural areas is limited or interrupted. Also, most rural mobile phone users in SSA use very basic pay-as-you-go models and would not yet be able to afford 3G versions on any scale to access new content. Current e-reader pilots come preloaded with content and accessing new content in SSA conditions has not yet been reported on at the time of writing.
2. *Power requirement*—although the Kindle is a low power user it still requires charging up at regular intervals[2] so would have limitations in some rural areas where access to power is a problem, although the Worldreader pilot project in Ghana reports that recharging has not been a significant problem, perhaps because the piloting has not taken place in areas with no easy access to power supply.
3. *Durability*—field tests will provide information on how well the Kindle performs and survives in harsh rural environments. This has been a problem with the extension of ICT into rural areas and might also limit the usefulness of the Kindle. The Worldreader pilot in Ghana reported that breakage had been a problem and that more rugged e-reader specifications were required.[3] Trucano (2014) reports an example of disproportionate numbers of e-reader

devices breaking because students had been told to keep them clean and, as a result, decided to wash them in a local river. The need to amortize expensive capital costs over the longest possible period prior to replacement emphasizes the need to establish realistic durability parameters.

4. *Investment cost*—the cheapest Wi-Fi Kindle currently costs around US$90 retail in the United States and the 3G version around US$200 retail with additional costs for a carrying case. On the assumption that the e-reader would survive for a target life of five years, the basic version still represents an annualized investment cost of US$16 per student per year, which is around double the average annual amortized per student costs for textbook provision calculated in chapter 3, Textbook Unit Costs at Primary, Junior/Senior Secondary Levels in 11 Sub-Saharan African Countries. If the expected average operational life comes down to three years then the annualized investment cost would be around US$30 per student per year. Even the most simple e-readers with generous durability assumptions would use up most of the total per child educational expenditures (excluding teachers' salaries) in the most developed SSA countries; their annualized cost could consume more than the full per child expenditures in the poorest countries, including teachers' salaries. Kindle costs are projected to continue to decrease, but the current small screen size militates against textbook use where good user-friendly design of the information provided tends to require larger page formats. There may well also be a demand for a color facility for textbook use. The demand for larger e-reader formats with a color capacity as a suitable vehicle for textbooks will tend to drive e-reader costs up as other factors drive costs down.

5. *Content cost*—the purchase price of the e-reader has to be supplemented by the cost of purchasing the content to go on the reader.[4] Although cheaper than printed books to download the current commercial content is still developed world oriented with title costs between one-half and two-thirds (on a random average basis) of the original published prices. On the assumption of a 50 percent cost reduction for textbook provision, a per pupil cost for six primary school textbooks made available via Kindles would still cost approximately US$7.50 plus the investment cost in the hardware. Thus content to the value of US$7.50 would require a US$150 plus delivery vehicle. Textbook delivery via e-readers would then only be cost effective if combined with a collection of supplementary reading materials, which would increase the content cost. Two hundred reading books added to the textbooks might cost an additional US$100 to provide. On this basis, special pricing would be needed to make content prices affordable for SSA, and special content for primary and secondary schools from African publishers (and perhaps even in local languages) would need to be generated before the Kindle could be considered fully appropriate and affordable in content. However, Worldreader pilot projects in Ghana, Kenya, and Nigeria have loaded the Kindles with locally relevant textbook and supplementary reader content with the support of local publishers, so the ability to deliver relevant content appears to be demonstrated.

6. *Accessing Content*—all content has to be either preloaded and included in the initial purchase price or has to be paid for by credit card for post-purchase upgrading. For most of SSA this is likely to be a big problem. Very few schools have access to credit cards (which is also a main cause of lack of antivirus software on PCs). A primary classroom library of 50 single copies of readers (cost around US$50) would provide sufficient reading for every child to read a different book every week for a year, and with reasonable care the reading books could be maintained in use for four to six years. Providing Kindles for every child in a class of 50 would have an investment cost of US$5,000 without including the content costs.
7. *Screen Size*—The current screen size is smaller than a standard paperback and the standard model provides only a one-color image, although color e-readers are available but at a significantly higher cost (the FNAC Book has an even smaller screen size). The screen size would prevent the effective regular use of the Kindle for textbooks and the small size means that good reader design suitable for young children would not be possible. The small screen size and the limitations of one-color presentation probably mean that the Kindle as currently presented would be more suitable mainly as a text vehicle.

Kindle-type devices have been piloted in rural areas in the Landes Département of South west France and were abandoned because of durability issues and cost. Attempts to use the Kindle for whole-class reading via a projector were considered to be counterproductive by both teachers and children. E-readers will certainly fall in price but for use as textbook vehicles they should ideally be larger format and provide color as well. Both of these characteristics will require an increased price. The Kindle Fire at a U.S. price of around US$150 provides color via a 3G/4G Wi-Fi Internet connection and an eight-hour battery life and provides access to movies, games, music, apps, and books.

Extensive and carefully designed pilot testing and the calculation of accurate cost implications are essential before any expensive investments are made in an unproven technology with many questions still to be answered. In SSA, pilot projects on the use of e-readers are underway in Ghana, Kenya, and Nigeria and are under consideration in the South Africa. There is obvious potential for the use of e-readers as vehicles for a wide range of TLMs, but hardware costs will need to come down before they are likely to provide a cost-effective solution. Additionally, the current small screen size and one-color presentation are not ideal, and larger formats and color would be preferable for textbooks and for illustrated children's books for younger children. In urban areas in Africa all children are now fully sensitized to the use of color in the presentation of ideas and information through TV, videos, computer games, cinema, display advertising, packaging, newspapers, magazines, and so on. One-color presentations of school materials would run the risk of making them less attractive. Durability of the hardware is also certain to be a critical factor in cost projections. Even the most ardent advocates of e-readers in SSA countries recognize that there are many problems to overcome and an entire supportive infrastructure to construct before e-readers can be seen as a practical and cost-effective alternative to current print-on-paper solutions. It may well be also that as costs continue to come down a new generation of tablet PCs with larger screen size and color capability could have a role to play in textbook and illustrated children's book presentation in e-formats. The iPAD2 with a larger screen (9.7 inches compared to the Kindle's seven inches), Wi-Fi and 3G Internet connectivity, a battery life of almost eight hours, and a capacity of up to 64 gigabytes with cameras front and back has a current price (2014) of close to US$600.

In spite of the issues raised above a recent research review reports that

> the strongest evidence of changes in learning outcomes and classroom practice came from the use of mobile devices (such as eReaders). (Power et al. 2014)

In a review of e-reader and tablets used to support literacy a number of research studies have reported that

> Several programs presented evidence of improved learning outcomes (in terms of increased reading fluency in the mother tongue or English) that combined provision of e-readers and eBooks for students with TD programs on phonics-based literacy instruction. (Power et al. 2014)

However, none of the studies reviewed the affordability and cost effectiveness of the use of e-readers on a national scale and this is obviously a critical issue in any decision to significantly expand the use of e-readers as vehicles to provide enhanced access to reading books on a national scale. DFID's *Educational Technology Topic Guide (2014)* noted that

> value for money (VFM) analysis is non-existent in most studies

and recommended that VFM metrics and cost-effectiveness analyses should be carried out as part of all project design and evaluation. However, the Primary Math and Reading Initiative (PRIMR) programme in Kenya implemented and compared the effectiveness and costs of three different interventions—tablets for teacher trainers, tablets for teachers, and e-readers for students. Similar gains in student learning outcomes were shown for all three variants, with no statistically significant difference between the approaches. However, the study demonstrated that while the outcomes were similar, the costs for teacher or tutor tablets were much lower than for class sets of e-readers, making the cost-effectiveness of teacher or tutor tablets approximately an order of magnitude greater (Piper and Kawumba 2014).

Mobile Phones, Smart Phones, and PDAs

There have been a number of mobile phone–based learning materials and information projects for school and student access in poor countries. In the Philippines the Text2Teach project (sponsored by Nokia) uses mobile phones and monthly prepaid load allowances supplied by Nokia and Globe, in order to provide public schools with access to a library of science, English and math videos provided by Pearson and SEAMEO-Innotech. Each video was supported by targeted lesson plans that integrated exercises and activities already linked to the curriculum. The project required an upfront school payment of 100,000 pesos (US$2,500) to join. Videos could be downloaded from mobile phones onto school computers and then made available via data projectors or TVs for classroom use. Effective access to the e-materials thus required significant ICT equipment investment.

In the South Africa Nokia sponsored the MobilED and MXit schemes. In MobilEd students could send low-cost short message service (SMS) messages to a dedicated number and order text resources, which could be turned into speech for transmission by mobile phone using Nokia Text to Speech software. The MXit scheme is a specialized chat room where students can discuss learning issues with other students and seek peer group assistance. Closely associated with the MXit scheme, the Dr. Math program provided mobile phone contact and support between students and math teachers. In Pakistan mobile phones were used to provide upper secondary students with educationally related objective multiple choice (OMC) tests.

The English in Action (EIA) program in Bangladesh has reported positive impacts on student learning outcomes and classroom practice from using mobile phones to support English language teaching (ELT) teachers. Mobile phones provide access to audio resources for classroom use, particularly for primary teachers. Mobiles are also used to provide access to teacher development materials, including videos of classroom practice. Materials are not broadcast, or downloaded, but are provided as a library of digital resources on a memory card.

Observations of classroom practice showed significant increases in students' talk time (including talk in pairs and groups), and students' and teachers' use of English (the target language), compared with baseline studies (EIA 2012).

The BridgeIT programme in Tanzania provided evidence of improved learning outcomes from teachers' use of smartphones to play video lessons for their classes via flat-screen TVs or data projectors. Teachers also had activity guides to support or extend the video lessons. Students showed average gains of 10 to 20 percent over control groups for math and science. However, while some groups of students excelled, others showed only modest gains, if any (Enge 2011).

In developed countries where high specification mobile phones are common their use in schools is more sophisticated.

> (Mobile phones) are being used as mobile computers. They have a big advantage over lap top computers in the classroom because they are cheaper, more portable and almost as sophisticated. Using camera phones, students develop their literacy by capturing images, writing about them, and emailing the work to friends, families and teachers. In some variations ... students receive plans from the teacher via the devices, and record evidence of their work.... [O]ne of the key rationales behind the project is that students are using technology they value and with which they feel comfortable.... [M]any educators view these phones as a huge distraction, dreadful intrusions and tools of the evil "snapperazi." But as with all tools of learning, once a purpose is established, mobile devices will have a role to play.... The principal of one participating school had been looking for something to excite disengaged students, and had been "overwhelmed by the resulting enthusiasm" when projects incorporated cell phones. And for students who are reluctant to put pen to paper, the phones

appear to be opening the door to literacy because they are being used to write stories. The project is using 20 high-tech phones provided by Nokia in Finland. They contain a 10 megapixel camera, and can record up to 10 minutes of video. They can access the Internet, have 8MB of memory—and make calls. (Hartnell-Young 2005)

A review of the possibilities indicates hundreds (perhaps thousands) of potential uses for mobile phones as learning tools in the classroom and outside school. In the developed world the enhanced use of mobile phones depends to a large extent on high-end specifications that provide high-definition photography and video capability and the ability to link to the Internet, download, save, and print (if the right software apps are loaded). Amazon can now download e-books direct to iPhone users as well as to laptops.

In 2008, Hartnell-Young (Hartnell-Young and Heym 2008) listed the following potential uses for mobile phones in UK schools:

- Timing experiments with stopwatch
- Photographing apparatus and results of experiments for reports
- Photographing development of design models for e-portfolios
- Photographing texts or whiteboards for future review
- Bluetoothing project material between group members
- Receiving SMS and e-mail reminders from teachers
- Synchronizing calendar and timetable and setting reminders
- Connecting remotely to school learning platform
- Recording a teacher reading a poem for revision
- Accessing revision sites on the Internet
- Creating short narrative movies
- Downloading and listening to foreign language podcasts
- Logging into the school email system
- Using GPS to identify locations
- Transferring files between school and home

In 2011 discussions with teachers in the United Kingdom provided the following very similar common examples of mobile phone use in learning in the classroom and at home.

- Using the mobile phone to take videos for use in projects and presentations
- Recording lectures or lessons for exam revision purposes
- Taking lesson notes using SMS (most students in 2011 can use SMS faster than they can write)
- Reading books purchased from Amazon and downloaded direct on to iPhones
- Storing textbooks for revision purposes
- Writing essays using Speech-to-Text software apps
- Using mobile phones in foreign language learning to improve pronunciation
- Accessing information for homework from school virtual learning environments (VLEs)
- Communicating with peers or even teachers via SMS to answer or resolve queries

Most of the teachers consulted had ambivalent views about the educational use of mobile phones. While most saw the use of mobiles as potentially beneficial in controlled situations, the uncontrolled use of mobile technologies, particularly in school and classroom situations, was seen as disruptive and a barrier to good learning and the development of concentration on the task in hand. Most teachers also had strong reservations about the excessive use of mobile phones for reading textbooks and other books because of concerns about the impact on student eyesight and also because of the loss of detail in photographs and illustrations. Many textbook publishers have been approached for individual textbook licensing of e-versions of textbooks but generally have restricted licensing of e-versions to schools and not to individuals. Licensing fees are considered by many schools to be high and have to be repurchased as new editions are released. However, there are a number of Indian websites which have made illegal pdf copies of U.K. textbooks and these are sold back to individual European and U.S. students, often direct to mobile phones, which are then downloaded onto PCs or laptops at home. Teachers also report that mobile phones are preferred to laptops by students for working in schools because they are lighter and easier to carry. In any case, most U.K. schools have adequate provision of PC work stations at school, which makes carrying laptops to school redundant when mobile phones can provide record and storage facilities.[5]

Mobile phone use has spread rapidly even in rural Africa and sponsored links can provide low-cost access to information in rural areas. Mobile phone ownership for secondary school students is quite widespread although primary student access in rural areas is much more limited. At present the mobile phones typically tend to be of the most basic pay-as-you-go type. In the context of textbook and reader provision the major problem with using mobile phones and PDAs is the small screen size, which makes direct extended textbook reading and use problematic, uncomfortable, and potentially detrimental to student eyesight. It also undermines the learning gains achieved in the past 50 years through the use of large-format page size, color, and professional design and layout in the presentation of information and ideas. However, basic mobile phones can be used to order TLMs or to access speech-based information and advice, but access to good and effective visual presentation will normally depend on the ability to download onto a PC and print[6] or view. Thus, while mobile technology has many current and potential applications for student learning, it is currently unlikely to provide adequate access to textbooks without linked 3G mobile phones and PC or print access. High-end mobile and smart phone technology is not cheap. Typical Nokia and Blackberry models capable of accessing and using visual information were priced at between US$150 and US$600 retail in 2014. It should also be noted that the mass printing of textbooks and readers by schools using photocopiers and A4 paper is significantly more expensive and significantly less durable than purchasing professionally printed, bound, and finished textbooks.

Most proponents of m-learning currently see it as a useful supplementary tool rather than as central to the learning process.

E-textbooks Plus

In January 2012 Apple announced in the United States the launch of a series of fully interactive, multimedia e-textbooks developed in association with mainstream textbook publishers for use on the Apple iPad. Critical reviews were generally very enthusiastic with the new e-textbooks widely described as "educational game-changers." The concerns were almost entirely related to the costs of hardware provision and the costs of the textbooks themselves.

Prior to the Apple launch a number of developed country publishers had adopted "blended learning" strategies in which hard-copy textbooks were closely linked with additional supplementary e-materials available either on disk or online. Good schools with developed ICT infrastructures and well-trained teachers generally found the blended learning approaches to be positive.

Some developing and transitional economies have also invested in the development of their own e-textbooks with wide variations in approach and quality. At the lowest level some e-textbooks are merely digitized versions of existing hard-copy textbooks with little interactivity. Others can be much more sophisticated but are often developed without adequate pilot testing and rarely take note of successful approaches developed elsewhere. Many teachers still appear to be more comfortable with traditional hard-copy textbooks than with e-format textbooks.

It seems obvious that e-textbooks will emerge as standard pedagogic materials, but for developing countries the infrastructural and cost implications of hardware and software procurement, maintenance and replacement, and the associated substantial recurrent operational costs will continue to inhibit the rapid and widespread introduction of e-textbooks as standard learning materials, which in turn will tend to increase both the international and the domestic digital divides in teaching and learning approaches.

A Summary of Emerging Key Issues

There is clear evidence that investment in the provision of ICT facilities to SSA education systems has been increasing rapidly, particularly from 2003/2004 onwards. The motivation for this increased investment often appears to be more political than educational, with heads of government closely involved in the promulgation of policy statements and the establishment of provision targets. The investment objective is almost universally perceived to be investment in hardware, which is widely considered to be a beneficial end in itself. The educational benefits of ICT provision are usually expressed as generalities and there is a very widespread lack of a clear vision as to how ICT will actually be used in schools and the precise educational benefits that will accrue from it. When benefits are specified they tend to be attitudinal and behavioral rather than performance related. This is not surprising because policy makers are almost universally from a generation without close personal experience of educational technology and its use in the classroom as part of the teaching and learning processes. But teachers, lacking in adequate and well-targeted training, and lacking also in the confidence and the practice time needed to use the hardware and software provided, are left with no clear guidance on how to use ICT effectively in their classes.

It is not remarkable that national educational and economic progress should be closely linked with access to, and familiarity with, computers and other e-technologies. Computers are a major and growing part of every aspect of modern life and no country can afford to be without clear national and educational ICT policies, which in turn often aim to provide universal access to ICT facilities to all students. It has been estimated that up to 75 percent of jobs in developed countries over the next 20 years will require some level of computer proficiency. The demand for national ICT policies and national ICT provision probably comes from every parent and student, although by no means from every teacher. There is an increasing view that access to computers is fundamental to better employment possibilities and thus to a good job and a better life. For young people the link between computers and gaming and mobile phones and peer group communication and status are also significant in increasing popular demand for access to computer facilities in schools. Politicians are very aware of these parental and student aspirations, hence the strong political angle in the development of national policies and targets.

However, it is also clear that the provision of hardware is not the same thing as the effective educational use of the hardware (and software) provided.

> Technology of itself doesn't enhance learning! It depends how the technology is designed and implemented; how teachers are supported to use it; how outcomes are measured; what communities are in place to support it.[7]

Effective edtech programs are characterized by:

- a **clear and specific curriculum focus** (e.g., communicative language learning, early literacy or remedial mathematics)
- the use of **relevant curriculum materials** (classroom audio, video, eBooks, research resources, radio programs)
- a focus on teacher development and pedagogy
- **evaluation mechanisms that go beyond outputs** to look at outcomes in terms of changes in teaching and learning practices, or learning outcomes. (Power et al. 2014)

Unfortunately, very large sums of scarce resources are increasingly allocated to hardware procurement in many SSA countries, which in turn tends to be badly maintained, underused, badly used or even, in the worst cases, not used at all because the most basic and most essential support services have not been made available to schools and teachers. These essential support services include:

- Financial support in terms of adequate operational budgets at school level to support the effective use of the hardware provided.
- Teacher training—both pre-service and in-service: perhaps the greatest current teacher training problem is the concentration on in-service training to provide

a minimalist familiarity with computers, combined with the lack of any coherent policy towards ICT training in pre-service institutions, so that many new teachers continue to enter the teaching profession with underdeveloped ICT skills. Most countries with "ICT across the curriculum" policies aren't investing enough to ensure that all teachers—or even teachers in targeted priority grades and subjects—have sufficient ICT skills directly related to their specialist subjects and also have confidence and a genuine operational grasp of the possibilities of ICT use in the classroom.
- Reliable power supply—this is still a problem in many rural areas for all of the reasons listed above.
- Connectivity to the Internet—still not reliably available to many SSA schools in rural and remote areas, and can be too costly to use if it is available. There is also a recognition that there is a significant difference in operational terms between access to the Internet and *effective* access to the Internet (that is, the ability to download easily useful data from the Internet or MOE specialist portals).
- Access to good, professional, and affordable maintenance and support services. This is an issue with strong rural and urban implications. Maintenance services in urban areas are generally more likely to be professionally competent, more accessible, and cheaper (because of the distances involved). Maintenance in rural and remote areas is often less professionally competent, much more expensive (because of the distances involved), and therefore much less affordable and accessible to schools as a result. The inevitable outcome is that hardware in rural and remote areas tends to be more difficult and expensive to maintain and thus to have a much higher downtime component. Many schools in rural areas recognize that they are more likely to incur additional damage to sensitive hardware in transporting it over rough roads to the nearest maintenance center.
- A curriculum and subject syllabuses that clearly define the roles and possibilities of ICT at different levels and in different subjects and that provide the framework in terms of syllabus space and time for the gradual development of ICT both as a subject and as a teaching and learning tool in other subjects.
- An assessment system that recognizes and identifies the required ICT-based skills and outcomes and knows how to test them. The failure to test ICT skills in high-stakes examinations is a disincentive for teachers to use ICT in their classes.
- Appropriate software and educational learning environments that provide the right kind of teacher- and user-friendly e-materials (including e-textbooks) in the right languages.
- Clear guidelines for the effective management of ICT in schools. The widespread absence of antivirus software, the lack of uninterrupted power supply (UPS) protection, the failure to establish school-based networks, the lack of policies on student use of flash disks, and the failure to establish adequate passwords and protection for student work are all examples of an endemic lack of knowledge and guidance on how to manage ICT in schools.

ICT provision on any reasonable scale is expensive for any educational system. In SSA, ICT investments have been made, and continue to be made in most countries, with no clear idea of the on-cost implications in terms of recurrent budgets, replacement (depreciation) costs, and associated costs (teacher training, curriculum and assessment reform, support services, supervision and monitoring, e-materials development, and so on). As a result, the educational outcomes achieved so far as a result of ICT investments are probably tenuous at best. Teaching ICT skills has probably improved as a result of hardware provision (although this in turn depends upon a range of associated issues such as curriculum design, teacher training in ICT skills and knowledge, individual student time on task, assessment, and so on), but the use of ICT as a teaching and learning tool in other subjects has almost certainly made little progress outside individual schools and there is little evidence available of an impact on student performance resulting from ICT investments. Indeed there is little evidence that there is much concern for establishing or even measuring such a link.

> [T]here are examples of large-scale investment in edtech—particularly computers for student use—that produce limited educational outcomes. (Power et al. 2014)

> Several studies showed that increasing students' access to computers of itself has little discernible impact on teaching or learning practices. (Power et al. 2014)

Thus,

- Computers are often not used for teaching and learning purposes. (EdQual 2011)
- While 98 percent of publicly supported schools in Chile have increased access, "ICT is not frequently used at school." (Hinostroza et al. 2011)
- Although New Partnership for Africa's Development provided schools with 20 suites of desktop computers, satellite connectivity, wireless networks, smartboards, and health software, "teachers are not in general using the Healthpoint software for purposes of health promotion." (Rubugiza et al. 2011)

A 2014 national ICT audit and TCO calculation in Rwanda (Read 2014) concluded as follows on the current and projected costs of ICT provision to primary and secondary schools:

> ICT4E [ICT for education] is expensive. The current ICT audit and TCO calculation gives a good idea of just how expensive the cost of sustainable provision might be with a 5-year projected TCO of RWF63,138,165,588 (approx. US$93.55 million) based on existing policy assumptions simply to sustain the level of hardware provision achieved in Rwanda up to October 2013. If [Government of Rwanda] policy to provide every child in P4–6 with an OLPC device by 2020 is taken into account there will be a need for an additional procurement of approximately 810,000 XO machines at a current cost of around USD162 million and the operational cost of sustaining these could be four times higher than existing operational costs. If the cost of expanding hardware provision to secondary schools is added on to the OLPC future investment programme the annual capital investment, operational and necessary infrastructure costs for ICT4E in Rwanda obviously will be very significantly higher.

It is also becoming obvious that education systems worldwide are increasingly the focus of major marketing efforts by hardware and software manufacturers and the number and variety of new pieces of "kit" increase annually. For governments, MOEs, and ICT spending departments there is a constant temptation to invest in new pieces of equipment and new approaches to teaching and learning, particularly if these investments may seem to place the country and education system at the cutting edge of new technology in education. Even in developed countries there is often uncertainty about the benefits that will or might accrue from this kind of investment.

Donor organizations must also take their share of the blame. Few DP project inputs address the full range of policy and operational issues that need to be resolved in order to ensure the basic success of the hardware investments made to date. Donor ICT component design is also frequently hardware led and is more often than not lacking in national on-cost projections. Where DP investments have focused on teacher training or e-materials development, there is typically a lack of coordination with other DPs providing similar inputs. A survey of ICT teacher training in one country revealed multiple overlapping donor and NGO activity in ICT teacher training with no sign of effective donor or MOE coordination. As the pace of ICT-related investment picks up there is an urgent need to formalize the approach to ICT component project design—perhaps via the provision of a national policy checklist and guidelines to essential basic components of project design and the development of national policies. The development of a national "ICT in Basic Education Strategy" is perhaps a starting point.

Perhaps the single most important conclusion is the overwhelming need for the priorities and requirements of education to be clearly articulated *first* as the basis for national ICT development and investment strategies. So far, it is clear that education requirements have had to follow behind the national hardware (and, to a lesser extent, software) investments, which tend to be politically and commercially rather than educationally driven. Too often the hardware has been provided but without any of the support mechanisms needed to make the hardware usable by teachers and students.

> One of the enduring difficulties of technology use in education is that educational planners and technology advocates think of the technology first and then investigate the educational applications of this technology only later.... It is believed that specific uses of ICT can have positive effects on student achievement when ICTs are used appropriately to complement a teacher's existing pedagogical philosophies.... ICTs are seen to be less effective (or ineffective) when the goals for their use are not clear. While such a statement would appear to be self-evident, the specific goals for ICT use in education are, in practice, often only very broadly or rather loosely defined. (Trucano 2005)

> Provision of ICT in schools is only the first step. For ICTs to become a tool for improving teaching and learning ... they need to be supplemented by teacher professional development. (EdQual 2011)

The effective use of any learning technology is bound up in pedagogy, curriculum, purpose, roles and activities. If new technologies are introduced without changing any of the other aspects, nothing different is happening.... Historically, programs that incorporate edtech have focused on the distribution of hardware and programme evaluations have measured the number of devices in the hands of teachers or students. This approach is very limited. It fails to measure the extent to which edtech has changed the process of teaching and learning, or the impact on learning outcomes, and thus prevents decision-makers from evaluating the effectiveness and cost-effectiveness of edtech. Programmes that move beyond access to hardware both in programme design and evaluation are still relatively rare. Equally, few programme evaluations focus on capturing improvements in the teaching and learning process or measuring improvements in learning outcomes. (Power et al. 2014)

There are fundamental questions that education systems need to address. How much ICT do we want or need to have in the education system? What is an acceptable balance between ICT as a subject and ICT as a teaching and learning tool? What kind of learning does ICT support? What impact does ICT have on student performance and behavior? How do we measure and assess ICT competencies as a subject and as part of the learning process in other subjects and areas of knowledge? How important is access to information? What kind of curricula and syllabuses support the effective use of ICT in education? How much teacher training is required and how often to ensure the effective use of the hardware provided? What are the opportunity costs of ICT? What proportion of the national education budget should be spent on ICT? How much do we want our children to watch rather than to do? How much will it cost to do ICT4E properly and how can the cost be afforded?

Education systems need to start the process of addressing the kind of issues outlined above. It is not necessarily possible to resolve these issues prior to major investments in ICT, but at the very least these issues and questions should form an important part of the thinking that should underpin the development of national strategies. This is not happening in very many, if any, SSA countries but until these issues are addressed and resolved it should not be assumed that ICTs will yet provide an affordable, sustainable, or effective—and certainly not a cheaper—alternative to print-based teaching and learning materials.

Notes

1. If web-fed presses (to increase speed) and inline binding and finishing (for durability) are specified, the costs will be very much greater than US$50,000.
2. A one-hour charge is reported to provide two to three weeks of normal play time.
3. The Ghana pilot project reported in 2012 that 50 percent of the e-readers suffered from breakage during the course of the pilot. If each reader costs in the region of US$100 then a class of 30 will require a capital investment of US$3,000. A breakage rate of 50 percent per year would require an annual replacement budget of US$1,500 per year, which makes for very expensive support to reading.

4. The free titles currently provided on commercial sale e-readers are mostly out-of-copyright titles. No current textbook or relevant supplementary title is likely to be out of copyright and would therefore have to be purchased.
5. Derived from conversations with teachers in the United Kingdom on the learning uses of mobile phones.
6. Smartphones with appropriate software are required to print directly from a mobile phone.
7. http://tel.ac.uk/about-3/2014.

References

EdQual. 2011. *Implementing Educational Quality in Low Income Countries: Final Report*. Bristol, United Kingdom: University of Bristol. http://r4d.dfid.gov.uk/PDF/Outputs/ImpQuality_RPC/EdqualFinalReport.pdf.

EIA (English in Action). 2012. *The Classroom Practices of Primary and Secondary School Teachers Participating in English in Action*. Dhaka: EIA, http://r4d.dfid.gov.uk/pdf/outputs/misc_education/Large-scale_quantitative_Study_2a2_14_03_2013.pdf.

Enge, K. 2011. *Elimu kwa Teknolojia: Summative Evaluation*. International Youth Foundation.

Hartnell-Young, E. 2005. "What's in a Name? Why We Can't Teach with Mobile Phones" *Professional Educator* 4 (3): 18–21.

Hartnell-Young, E., and Heym, N. 2008. *How Mobile Phones Help Learning in Secondary Schools*. London: BECTA.

Hinostroza, J. E., C. Labbe, M. Brun, and C. Matamala. 2011. "Teaching and Learning Activities in Chilean Classrooms: Is ICT Making a Difference?" *Computers and Education* 57 (1): 1358–67. http://www.sciencedirect.com/science/article/pii/S0360131511000376.

Piper, B., and D. Kawumba. 2014. *Kenya Primary Math and Reading Initiative (PRIMR): Endline Report*. Research Triangle Park, NC: RTI International for USAID.

Power, T., R. Gater, G. Grant and N. Winters. 2014. *Educational Technology Topic Guide*. London: HEART for DFID.

Read, N. 2014. *Calculating the TCO of ICT4E in Rwanda*. London: Capacity Development Fund for DFID.

Rubugiza, J., E. Were, and R. Sutherland. 2011. "Introducing ICT into Schools in Rwanda: Educational Challenges and Opportunities." *International Journal of Education Development* 31 (1): 37–43. http://www.sciencedirect.com/science/article/pii/S0738059310000866.

TEL (Technology Enhanced Learning). 2014. "About." http://tel.ac.uk/about-3/2014.

Trucano, M. 2005. "Knowledge Maps: ICT in Education." *Edutech* (blog), Washington, DC. http://www.infodev.org/en/Publication.8.html.

———. 2014. "In Search of the Ideal Educational Technology Device for Developing Countries." *Edutech* (blog), January 11.

PART 4

Teaching and Learning Materials Policy Issues and Options

CHAPTER 13

Options in the Development of National Teaching and Learning Materials Policies

Private Sector versus Parastatal Textbook Producers

State textbook provision in most countries has had an adverse impact on commercial bookseller networks, the viability of commercial educational publishing houses, and the activities of local commercial printing plants, which often had to transition into jobbing commercial printers because the dominant books work was reserved to state companies. The track record of state textbook provision via state publishing, state printing, and state distribution companies has not been good; and by the end of the 1980s most state textbook provision systems were in serious difficulties. During the 1990s up to the present, state textbook provision systems have widely been replaced by the involvement of the private sector and in particular by private-sector publishing. Private-sector bookselling has been much more difficult to rehabilitate than publishing and in-country private-sector printing still has to demonstrate its competitiveness outside Kenya, Nigeria, and South Africa.

The main failures were widely perceived to be

- Poor quality textbooks;
- Inertia;
- Poor physical production standards;
- Irregular, inaccurate, and ineffective book distribution;
- School complaints and
- Poor financial management.

Private-sector textbook publishing in many developing countries has a good track record of support for local children's and general book publishing out of the profits from the textbook sector. As a result, it actively supports the development of local culture and provides support for literacy in local, regional, and international languages. The availability of a number of diverse local publishing companies also provides an opportunity for the expression of different political, economic, and social viewpoints, which underpins an active democracy. A single state textbook publisher would only rarely reinvest in children's book publishing, and it would never provide the same plurality of viewpoints as the private sector book trade.

Centralization versus Decentralization

In its simplest form centralized supply is associated with monopoly textbook provision systems (either commercial or state) and is based upon a central authority deciding how many titles and copies each school in the country requires. Obviously it is impossible for a centralized authority to know the current supply situation in every school in the country and thus centralized supply tends to be characterized by considerable inaccuracy and thus a waste of scarce resources. Many Education Management Information Systems (EMIS) attempt to collect data on school textbook stocks but practical experience suggests that the data are rarely accurate and are open to considerable interpretation. Also, the cost and management stress of maintaining individual school stock records centrally can be high.

Decentralized supply tends to be associated with competing alternative textbooks and school-based selection and ordering (although it can equally well apply in a monopoly textbook situation) and requires that a school orders what it needs within the limits of an annual per capita purchasing budget. There have been occasions when no limit was placed on the number of titles and the quantities that schools could order (for example, textbook supply in the former Soviet Union prior to about 1985). However, in most developing or transitional economies finances are sufficiently constrained that some limitations are imposed either in the allocation of central procurement funds or through annual per capita budgets for individual schools.

As a general rule, decentralized ordering by individual schools tends to be a more accurate reflection of school needs and to be less wasteful of scarce resources. Decentralized ordering and supply requires accountable distribution systems where the distributors are paid on proven successful delivery. If there is no accountable distribution system then decentralized ordering can be negated by a distribution system that fails to provide the materials ordered by the schools.

Local Language Policies and Literacy

It is generally recognized that children will perform better and learn faster if early education is conducted in a familiar language, although the issue is not necessarily as straightforward as this and considerable care is needed in developing an effective and practical policy for the selection, use, and development of local languages within the primary curriculum. If reading in the local language is badly taught by teachers with little formal training in either the local language itself or in the teaching of literacy, or if it is not well supported by appropriate teaching and learning materials (TLMs) (for example, local language readers), it could undermine progress towards basic literacy, the development of learning in other subjects, and the later acquisition of literacy in the national or official language and thus effective access to education in upper primary grades and in secondary school. In small countries the use of local languages as languages of instruction (LoI) can lead to very small print runs and thus to potentially high costs if high-quality reproduction is required (for example, in Botswana and Namibia).

Many countries have many potential LoIs and thus the selection of a local language to use as the LoI in lower primary grades has a number of implications, which need to be taken into account in the development of a local language policy for education. These include the following:

- *Financial implications*—the use of too many local languages could fractionalize print runs for essential learning materials, which in turn would increase the costs of educational provision. Too many languages operating with small enrollments, and thus print runs, could be a disincentive to potential publishers of educational materials in local languages. There is a risk that smaller language groups would be less well served than larger language groups. The cost inflation factor would be far greater if other primary curriculum subjects such as math, social studies, science, and agriculture also required textbooks in multiple local languages. However, if local language textbooks are developed and printed in one color, cost benefits can be achieved at relatively low print runs in order to support local language publishing.
- *Staffing and training implications*—instruction in local languages also requires teachers trained to use the local language. Too many LoIs will increase the costs and the complexity of teacher training in local languages and could have implications for the posting, selection, and promotion of teaching staff between different language areas.
- *Political implications*—the selection of a local language as the LoI is not just a pedagogic issue but also has cultural and political implications, particularly in districts where there are a number of different, and sometimes rival, language possibilities.

Local languages operate at different levels of development. Some local languages are widespread and highly developed with an established orthography; a flourishing supportive literature of newspapers, magazines, fiction, children's books, poetry and drama, and radio and TV stations; and a cadre of trained language speakers, readers, and teachers. Other languages may be used by only a few villages, have no established orthography, little or no supportive literature (or even print of any kind), and no trained language teachers.

There is also an obvious difference in the early childhood exposure to written languages between urban and rural areas. Thus, in urban areas all children are constantly exposed to written language in the form of shop and street signs, product packaging, advertisements, newspapers, magazines, TV, cinema, bookshops and libraries, and so on. In many rural areas none of the above exists and there is little (or even no) cultural conditioning and exposure to written language as the foundation for the basic decoding of letters and words into sounds and meaning. Many rural children arrive at school for the first time from home environments that are almost entirely oral and thus with little or no print awareness. In this situation the absence of any supporting literature for a language selected as an LoI could have a damaging impact on the acquisition of literacy.

In the circumstances described above, is it preferable to use a regional local language not favored by a local community but which has trained teachers, a known orthography and reading books, textbooks, and a supportive background literature? Or is it preferable to use a community-favored minority local language, but without an accepted orthography, trained teachers, reading materials, a background literature, and so on?

Monopoly versus Competitive Supply

There are a range of options as follows:

- *State-published monopoly textbooks*—these are characterized as being open ended in duration, often for extended periods without review, revision, and updating.

- *Private-sector monopoly textbooks*—these are usually achieved as a result of invited submissions by government or development partners (DPs) to private-sector publishers. This is sole-source textbook supply. The submissions are subjected to an evaluation methodology and criteria and the best evaluated textbooks for each subject and grade level are granted monopoly status. In some cases there is a formal contract that specifies the rights and obligations of approved status on both the publisher and the ministry and which also specifies the duration of the approved status. In other cases there is no formal letter of contract setting out the mutual obligations and no specified duration for the approved status. Sole-source supply, unless professionally supervised, provides opportunities for corruption because large sums of money are available on the basis of a single national decision.

- *A limited approved list of textbooks*—in this scenario governments or DPs initiate an invitation for submissions which are then "competitively" evaluated and a limited list of textbooks that reach acceptable marks is established. In some countries small populations and small print runs limit the number of approved textbooks to no more than two (for example, Armenia). In other cases the number of approved titles can be three, four, or six (Kenya). With a limited approved list schools are free to choose from those titles awarded approved status. It should be noted that many publishers are not keen on limited approved lists because they fear being excluded from the market if they do not make the cut.

- *Unlimited approved lists*—these result from a "threshold" evaluation in which all titles that meet minimum criteria are automatically awarded approved status (for example, Tanzania). The basic problem with unlimited lists is that they frequently have no fixed duration for the approved status and often no way of removing books from the approved list once they have been established. Thus the number of approved textbooks tends to grow year by year as new books are submitted by publishers. Eventually, the number of approved books can be so large that it actually becomes confusing for schools. Although approved lists without limitations are often supported by publishers, because everybody gets a chance to participate in the market, they tend to fractionalize print runs, increase unit costs, increase the costs of textbook provision, and decrease profitability for participating publishers. Many publishers claim that unlimited lists are the basis of a "pure" free-market textbook supply system. Unfortunately unrestricted free-market textbook competition and supply is difficult to sustain in poor countries with limited purchasing power.

On balance, there are considerable advantages with a choice of textbooks over a single monopoly textbook simply because it is extremely unlikely that a single textbook can meet the requirements of widely differing school environments in the same country. A textbook that suits the needs of a well-funded, well-resourced, well-equipped urban school with relatively small classes, well-qualified teachers, and good classrooms and furniture that can easily be moved to support group work and pair work situations will not easily fulfill the needs of an overcrowded, under-resourced rural classroom with untrained teachers where many students will be sitting on the ground and where desks and benches are at a premium and are not easily manipulated into different learning configurations. Multiple textbook choice can provide something for each of these extreme situations, which is not available in single choice textbook environments.

Also, there is evidence that schools have greater ownership of textbooks that they choose themselves. Finally, in multiple choice situations competitive pressures tend to force publishers to upgrade their textbooks to meet the standards set by rival publications and also to compete actively on price.

Cost-Reduction Strategies

There are a number of standard textbook cost-reduction strategies that could be considered in order to make textbook costs more affordable to either government or parents. These are the following:

- Fewer curriculum subjects and thus fewer textbooks (this requires a curriculum review but generally provides the greatest cost saving)
- Reduced page extents (review of syllabus content requirements; many syllabuses are overloaded and as a result textbooks can provide too much content that often cannot be completed in the time available)
- Textbooks turned into books of core content by shifting material into teachers' guides (supplied at one book per class rather than one book per one, two, or

three students) or into library books (supplied in small multiples to school libraries rather than in class sets). This strategy will depend for its effectiveness on consistent library funding but it is clear that good school libraries and core content textbooks are potentially much cheaper and more effective in terms of learning outputs than no school libraries and overlong textbooks.

- Extended book life (review of minimum physical production specifications)
- Book sharing and thus reduced textbook–pupil ratios (TPRs) (for example, 1:3 rather than 1:1)
- Reduced use of four colors
- Reduced wastage in manufacturing, warehousing, distribution, school storage, and school usage (this can be very substantial; annual loss rates of up to 50 percent have been recorded in some countries and 20 percent annual loss and damage is not unusual)
- Use of textbook loan or rental systems
- Reduced page formats (large formats use more paper and are frequently less durable)
- Short-term rather than long-term student loans in order to reduce annual rates of loss and damage (short-term loans provide more control than long-term loans but require more teacher management time)
- Tax exemptions for book manufacturing raw materials (finished books are usually imported duty free under the terms of the Florence Agreement on the Free Flow of Books and Information, but printing equipment and paper often attract duty, thus making local printers more expensive than external printers)
- Greater control over input costs from publishers and printers (review evaluation and approval mechanisms and conditions to ensure that price is a significant factor in evaluation and approval and that pricing is closely monitored in parent purchase situations)
- Increased use of teachers' guides

Very few countries have explored the full range (or even a limited range) of the cost-reduction possibilities available to them.

Country Comparisons

Table 13.1, below, provides country comparisons of five key textbook issues in 10 countries. The following notes provide an overview of the key factors relating to the five major issues covered by the country comparison.

Authorship, Publishing, and Copyright
The evidence seems clear that local authorship is now widespread for primary up to and including some junior secondary textbooks. In some cases experienced foreign authors or editors may be attached to inexperienced local authorship teams to provide support and guidance. In general, this is a positive practice because it creates and professionalizes fledgling local capacity. At senior secondary

level many countries in both anglophone and francophone Africa continue to import titles written for other national or international markets. The development of local authorship in junior secondary textbooks is probably closely related to the growth in enrollments in the junior secondary subsector resulting from the increased pressure on secondary school places created by Universal Primary Education (UPE) policies. Increased enrollments create larger markets that are of more interest to publishers and particularly to local African publishers. Eventually local authorship may extend into some senior secondary areas as enrollments grow but at senior secondary local content (except for subjects such as history, biology, literature, and local languages) is likely to be less significant than at lower educational levels. International editions where local content is not a significant factor will always tend to have larger print runs and thus lower production costs than national editions and thus to be potentially price competitive.

Of the ten countries represented in table 13.1, eight are now sourcing textbooks from the private sector. The three state publishing countries are Burundi, Djibouti, and Malawi (for primary textbooks but not for secondary). The shift back to private-sector publishing results from growing unhappiness with the performance of state publishing from the 1980s onwards but is also related to the growing strength of local and regional African publishing, which has managed to launch effective lobbying campaigns in support of access to the profitable national textbook markets for local businesses. It is perhaps significant that anglophone countries have made more progress in private sector access than francophone countries because local educational publishing companies tend to be better developed and financially more viable in anglophone countries. In most Sub-Saharan African (SSA) countries local, regional, and international publishing manage to coexist. In a recent bid in Rwanda, out of 15 bidding publishers, two were Rwandan companies, two were Ugandan, five were Kenyan, one was French, and five were British. In Ghana and Nigeria there are legal requirements for locally owned companies to supply textbooks, although this is not applied strictly at junior and secondary levels.

The issue of copyright ownership of the textbooks has tended to disappear with the growth of private-sector access. When manuscripts are commissioned, paid for, and then published by the private sector, government requirements for copyright ownership have tended to disappear.[1] In those countries where private-sector access to the national textbook market is well established, ministries of education (MOEs) have experienced no negative aspects from the retention of copyright by authors or publishers, particularly when there is competitive textbook supply and school-based selection. Copyright typically becomes a cause of dispute in two situations, both of which tend to be more common in francophone than in anglophone countries. These two situations are

- Publishers attempting to secure publishing rights for a textbook manuscript authored by a national curriculum development center and
- MOEs trying to license reprint rights for textbooks originated by commercial publishers.

Copyright and licensing problems are usually exacerbated by a limited understanding of the concept and practice of copyright, publishing rights, and licensing, resulting in substandard contracts, which provide plenty of scope for misunderstanding and dispute. Common problems (not an exhaustive list) include the following:

- *Uncertainty over copyright ownership*—this tends to occur when MOEs try to negotiate not just institutional royalties but individual authorship royalties as well. This practice can lead to high levels of royalty payments from publishers and thus to increased costs.
- *Failure to limit the licensing of publishing rights*—licensing rights are normally limited by time (for example, five years from date of contract), by printing (for example, up to 200,000 copies), or by default (for example, the rights revert to the copyright holders if the title is out of stock for 12 months or if license fees have not been paid). Some publishers have attempted to enforce unlimited licences granted up to 20 years previously.
- *Using a license to establish a monopoly textbook supply situation*—there have been cases where an unlimited license has been used in an attempt to halt curriculum reforms on the grounds that the curriculum reform would be contrary to a monopoly license.
- *Disputes over access to film or digital printing disks*—this occurs because the copyright in the manuscript is not the same thing as the copyright in the presentation of the manuscript (page design, typesetting, artwork and layout, and so on). When publication rights revert to an MOE there is often an assumption that this automatically includes the publisher's work on the presentation and unless this is clearly specified in the contract there are likely to be disputes.

The simple solution to these problems is to use specialists to draw up contracts between MOEs and publishers.

Procurement

Six of the ten countries have approved textbook lists from which schools can choose the textbooks that they wish to use from decentralized textbook procurement budgets. The approved lists are selected from international bids where publishers submit titles for evaluation and the objective of the bid is not procurement and purchase but approval and thus access to the market. After approval publishers can market direct to schools and decentralized school ordering provides the market. Publishers have to work harder and spend more money on competitive marketing in these situations but generally prefer the approved list system to monopolistic approaches. Schools certainly prefer the opportunity to exercise their own choice, despite a number of MOEs believing that primary schools in particular do not have the ability to exercise rational selection decisions. Not all approved lists are selected on the same basis. Some include price as a criterion for selection; others do not. Some specify minimum physical production specifications; others do not.

Printing

The factors that determine textbook manufacturing are

- Price;
- Quality;
- Capacity; and
- Reliability.

It is difficult for many local printing industries to compete on price with established international printing centers that have large, modern, printing machines operating three shifts a day and with the ability to offer a wide range of sheet sizes and book formats and achieving maximum discounts and thus lowest costs on raw materials because of the size of their ordering. International printing can usually also guarantee high-quality production (or at least production of the required quality) and is usually selected by publishers because it is reliable on delivery dates—a critical component in highly seasonal textbook markets when late stock arrival can attract financial penalties or can result in a loss of market position. Finally, small-scale local printing often cannot provide the full capacity required by the textbook market in the time available. Publishers can use their finance more effectively by manufacturing in multiple locations simultaneously rather than printing in sequence in one location only, which often results in early printings being held in stock for long periods prior to sales. Even in countries with relatively well-developed local printing (for example, Nigeria) a high proportion of textbook printing is contracted to international printing centers for the reasons given above.

The financing of state-owned printing has rarely, if ever, resulted in high-quality, price-and service-competitive printers in Africa. The African state printers financed in the 1960s and 1970s are no longer active participants in textbook production. While there is a clear need for the development of local work opportunities, textbook publishers usually take the position that the education system should not be used to subsidize uncompetitive local printing.

Financing

Nine of the ten countries aim to supply free textbooks to all primary and secondary students. Two of the eleven countries supply textbooks free to primary students, but purchasing or school fee contributions are used to support secondary textbook provision. It should be noted that free supply does not mean that textbooks and teachers' guides are automatically provided and that all students receive the textbooks that they require. Variations in the annual availability of funding often lead to significant variations in supply and in some cases inadequate distribution prevents free textbooks from being supplied equitably to schools.

Distribution

Six of the ten countries now supply to schools using the commercial book trade—either publishers or booksellers if national bookseller coverage is available.

Three countries continue to operate state publishing systems and two countries operate mixed systems (Ghana and Malawi), in both of which primary textbooks are distributed by the MOE and secondary textbooks are supplied via the commercial book trade.

Few MOEs are well equipped to support distribution because they lack storage facilities, equipment, systems, trained staff, adequate budget, and motivation. Commercial distribution tends to work better because the private sector does not get paid until it can demonstrate successful delivery, which is a powerful motivation for fast and accurate supply.

Both Burundi and Djibouti operate state distribution reasonably successfully because the countries are small with adequate transport infrastructures, but inequities occur because of lack of effective monitoring systems. Distribution in most countries would benefit from effective computerization, but of the eleven countries only Rwanda has developed a sophisticated computerized distribution management system for textbooks and other teaching and learning materials.

Textbook system design is a specialized activity requiring good research and an appreciation of the various factors that impact on affordability. Poor distribution has been perhaps one of the major factors over the past 50 years, combined with poor usage, management, and conservation in schools; but different countries will have different strengths and weaknesses and while the basic principles can be specified the unique system problems and solutions have to be resolved on the basis of the circumstances and needs of individual countries.

Table 13.1 **Country Comparisons**

Country	Authorship and publishing	Procurement	Printing	Financing	Distribution
Burundi	Burundi still operates a state publishing regime. BEPEP and BEPES (curriculum development centers for respectively primary and secondary) are mandated to produce their own curricula and instructional materials. Authorship of manuscripts is local. No curriculum has been produced since the 1980s and most textbooks are published under BEPEP/Hachette co-editions. There is no private sector publishing and only one poorly stocked bookshop in the country. Copyrights remain with MOE and publication rights belong to Hachette.	The World Bank PIU (PARSEB) and the Fonds de Soutien à l'Education (BTC-AFD) fund regular printing and editing-printing (whereby a publisher is asked to produce an actual textbook out of a raw manuscript produced by BEPEP/BEPES) bids. Bid management and response lead times could be improved. The reprinted titles are for "core" subjects and thus reproduce textbooks developed twenty or thirty years ago.	In the early 2000s, AFD funded a modernization of the former state-owned printer RPP. It has since been privatised but is not allowed to take part in World Bank bids, because of the subsidies it continues to receive from the government. As a result textbook printing takes place in international print centers selected by the contracted publishers. The MOE had a long dispute with an Indian printer that was resolved only recently.	Textbooks are provided free to students at all levels but not necessarily equitably.	This is either undertaken by the MOE or by the World Bank Project. There are distribution problems, with enormous discrepancies evident between different schools. This may be more due to unreliable enrollment statistics than to the logistics of the distribution system although many aspects of the distribution system may be sub-standard.
Djibouti	State publishing is standard practice via CRIPEN, the national curriculum development center. Heavy financial assistance from DPs has been provided since 2006 in order to "professionalise" CRIPEN's Publishing Unit. Books have been produced in house by local authors often with support from consultant TA for all levels up to secondary, albeit not always on time. Copyrights remain with CRIPEN.	Books are bought by the state from CRIPEN.	Due to high import taxes, in-country manufacturing is only suitable for small print runs and workbooks. The remainder, including all textbooks, are printed in regional/international printing centers, mainly in Dubai.	Textbook provision is free for primary and junior secondary students.	There is state textbook distribution, which is relatively efficient in rural areas (small country, good roads) but is quite inequitable in Djibouti Ville (direct trips to the warehouse by schools on a "first come first served" basis).

table continues next page

Table 13.1 Country Comparison *(continued)*

Country	Authorship and publishing	Procurement	Printing	Financing	Distribution
Ghana	State publishing has been gradually phased out since a new national textbook policy was introduced in 2000. All textbook publishing is now undertaken by private sector publishers in response to bidding procedures organized by the MOE. Textbook publishing in Ghana has been indigenised so that all local textbook publishers are majority owned Ghanaian publishers, although many maintain close contacts with their original owners. Publishers are responsible for identifying and contracting authors, who are mostly Ghanaian nationals. Copyright remains with the commercial publishers. There is some importation of secondary school textbooks.	Textbook requirements are put out to bid by the MOE. Up to five publishers may be approved as a result of the bidding process but there is no school-based selection and ordering because the MOE allocates different titles to different districts on a monopolistic basis in each district. There are aspects of the bidding process that need to be reformed. The evaluation procedures are not considered to be transparent, price is not a criterion for evaluation and selection but is subject to direct negotiation with government and the allocation of districts can be used as a lever to get lower prices. Payment to publishers is typically subject to long delays.	All textbook printing is required to be undertaken in Ghana. In practice the majority takes place overseas at international printing centres in order to achieve best prices, acceptable quality, reliable delivery dates etc.	Textbooks are provided free to students although textbook–pupil ratios vary. The costs of textbook provision are often donor funded.	Secondary school textbooks are delivered direct by publishers to individual secondary schools and this seems to work quite well. At primary, publishers deliver to district education offices that are responsible for onward delivery to schools. Recent distribution surveys suggest that up to 50 percent of districts do not maintain adequate stock control systems and have difficulty in accounting for the textbook supplies delivered to them. There have been reports of state textbook stock being sold to private schools.
Kenya	The curriculum is developed by the Kenya Institute of Education. For primary and junior secondary publishers (mostly private sector but including two state-owned publishers who receive no subsidies or special treatment) are responsible for identifying authors and developing textbooks to meet curriculum requirements. For primary and junior secondary most authors are nationals. Publishers	There is a periodic (every five years) submission of titles for evaluation and selection—up to five or six titles per subject and grade level. The submission documentation has been scrutinized and approved by the World Bank and is up to international standards. Price is a critical factor in evaluation but other criteria include conformity to the curriculum,	Most primary and junior secondary titles are printed in Kenya. Prices are not necessarily cheaper than international sources but quality has improved and publishers find it convenient to deal with local printers face to face. For imported senior secondary titles printing sources are generally	Schools receive per capita cash deposits in specially designated textbook bank accounts and use these funds to order and pay for books from booksellers. Unfortunately there are over 31,000 primary and secondary schools but only 200 district auditors so that monitoring and auditing are not well performed.	Distribution is from publisher to bookseller to school. Prices therefore include the costs of delivery and the booksellers' profit margin. This approach is only possible because Kenya has a very well-developed wholesale and retail bookselling network covering every district of the country—including remote districts. Prices are controlled so that all

table continues next page

Table 13.1 Country Comparison *(continued)*

Country	Authorship and publishing	Procurement	Printing	Financing	Distribution
	are a competitive mixture of 100 percent locally owned companies and subsidiaries/branches of regional and international publishers (including from Uganda). For senior secondary a number of standard textbooks authored and published externally are imported. Copyrights remain with the publishers.	suitability and level of language, methodological approach, relevance and attractiveness of illustrations, help for teachers, etc. There are minimum physical production standards which all submissions are required to meet in order to ensure common durability standards (five years).	international. Some publishers do not employ trained production controllers and are thus more dependent on the printers.	Recent corruption scandals in the provision of textbook budgets to schools are a testimony to the problems of financial control. From 2003 to 2005 when an international accountancy company was retained to undertake random school monitoring the system worked well with no problems.	schools get textbooks at the same price irrespective of location. Distribution is efficient, direct to the school and at no cost to the school.
Malawi	The curriculum is developed by the Malawi Institute of Education (MIE). Primary and junior secondary textbooks are mostly authored by Malawian authors; at senior secondary level standard textbooks are imported. Primary textbooks are monopolistic and are state published. Junior and senior secondary textbooks are competitive based on a limited approved list and publishers are responsible for identifying and contracting authors. Publishers are a mix of local companies and the local offices of international publishers. Copyright in commercially published titles is retained by the publishers/authors. Copyright in primary textbooks is with the MIE.	Junior and senior secondary titles are selected for an approved list by bid procedures which meet international standards. The approved list also includes readers and supplementary materials. There are minimum physical production standards specified in order to achieve four to five years durability.	Printing is mostly external at international printing sources. Primary textbook printing is often donor funded.	Primary textbooks are provided free. Secondary schools charge an MOE approved textbook fee as part of the school fees and this is used to order and pay for textbooks and supplementary materials. Publishers and booksellers complain that schools divert some of the textbook fee to other purposes. Some richer parents pay for textbooks for their own children.	Primary textbook distribution is via provincial, district, and zonal offices. Transportation, storage and systems are all sub-standard and distribution is often slow and incomplete. Junior and senior secondary textbook distribution is via the commercial book trade with a mixture of bookseller and publisher supply. Prices for these titles include distribution costs and provision for booksellers' profit margins.

table continues next page

Table 13.1 Country Comparison *(continued)*

Country	Authorship and publishing	Procurement	Printing	Financing	Distribution
Mali	Mali is the only francophone African country to have moved to a public–private partnership in educational publishing. As a result, it has a relatively sizeable national publishing and authoring community. But French publishers are still very present in the textbook and teaching aid market	Competitive textbook bids are regularly published by the MOE. Accusations of irregularities and corruption had reached such a point that in April 2011 the President changed the Directors of Finances of all ministries.	One of the main Malian publishers, Donnya, is also the country's largest printer and undertakes local textbook printing. Otherwise textbook printing is via international printing centres.	Textbook provision is free to all students.	Publishers are required to deliver direct to schools.
Namibia	The curriculum is developed by the National Institute for Educational Development (NIED); the MOE's curriculum development centre. Private sector publishers are responsible for identifying authors and developing textbooks to meet curriculum requirements. For primary and junior secondary most authors are nationals or South Africans. By law, all primary textbooks have to be published in each of the 13 official Namibian languages of instruction, which creates problems in a small country with a limited pool of translators for some minority languages. The publishing landscape is dominated by subsidiaries/branches of international publishers, with two active national publishers. Copyright remains the property of the publishers at all levels.	Up until 2011, the system for textbook evaluation and approval (no real selection process to speak of) resulted in too many books being approved in the Textbook Catalogue (the official approved book list), with not enough pressure being brought to bear on price reduction. The system was basically publisher driven, and no submission was ever rejected. From 2012 onwards, Namibia will switch to a competitive textbook submission, evaluation, and approval system. The evaluation system's control and trigger will be reverted to MOE and moved away from publishers. Price shall be introduced as a significant factor in evaluation in order to get value for money. The number of approved titles per	Printing is mostly external at regional (Mauritius and South Africa) and international printing sources.	Primary and secondary textbooks are provided free. Schools have a per capita grant that can be used to purchase extra materials, even though it is usually directed at other school expenses.	Traditionally, distribution is tendered out nationally by MOE for a 3 year period. The tender is always won by EduMeds, a school supply distributor belonging to the Macmillan group. It works well logistically, but the belated arrival of MOE funds and school orders, together with the zero risk policy of publishers when it comes to print runs, leads to late deliveries. The current tender was supposed to expire on 31 Dec 2011, but it has been prolonged until March 2012, to give MOE time to think about its policy on distribution.

table continues next page

Table 13.1 Country Comparison *(continued)*

Country	Authorship and publishing	Procurement	Printing	Financing	Distribution
		subject and per grade will be capped at three throughout the system; Once the titles are part of the Catalogue, procurement will be conducted on a Regional basis through the new Regional Tender Boards, whose actual tasks remain to be defined.			
Nigeria	Different Nigerian states operate different systems. In most states textbooks are published by local commercial publishers who are responsible for identifying and contracting authors. Publishers compete for state adoptions or inclusion on state approved textbook lists. A few states (Cross River and Rivers) still operate state publishing systems for primary. All primary and a majority of junior secondary textbooks are authored by Nigerian nationals. Some junior secondary and more senior secondary textbooks are imported and have international authorship and publishing. Local textbook publishing is in the hands of Nigerian companies which were indigenized. Some of these companies have minority overseas stakes but some have now bought out the original foreign ownership. Where commercial textbooks are used copyright remains with the publisher/authors.	Different Nigerian states have different procurement systems ranging from the selection of one monopolistic title per subject per grade to approved textbook lists. Selection procedures also vary from state to state.	Although Nigerian printing is quite well-developed it is estimated that 70 percent of textbook production is performed outside Nigeria in international printing centers, of which India probably has the largest share. Where local printing is used raw materials are imported with Indonesia and Malaysia frequent sources of text and cover card.	There is Universal Basic Education (UBE) across the country and books are purchased from revolving funds and made available free of charge. Senior secondary textbooks are often sold commercially to parents.	Publishers deliver to either local government headquarters, or to UBE warehouses in state capitals. State governments are responsible for delivery to schools and vary in their effectiveness.

table continues next page

Table 13.1 Country Comparison *(continued)*

Country	Authorship and publishing	Procurement	Printing	Financing	Distribution
Rwanda	The curriculum is developed by the Rwanda Education Board's Curriculum and Pedagogic Materials Department (REB/CPMD). For primary and junior secondary, private sector publishers are responsible for identifying authors and developing textbooks to meet curriculum requirements. For primary and junior secondary most authors are nationals. Publishers are a competitive mixture of 100 percent locally owned companies and subsidiaries/branches of regional (from Kenya and Uganda) and international publishers. For senior secondary standard textbooks authored and published externally are imported. Copyright remains the property of the publishers at all levels.	There is a periodic (every five years) submission of titles for evaluation and selection—up to four titles per subject and grade level at primary and three titles at junior secondary. The submission documentation has been scrutinized and approved by donors and is up to international standards. Price is a critical factor in evaluation but other criteria include conformity to the curriculum, suitability and level of language, methodological approach, relevance and attractiveness of illustrations, help for teachers, etc. Prices are fixed for the period of approved status and can only be increased on an industry-wide basis when specific input costs have been assessed. There are minimum physical production standards which all submissions are required to meet in order to ensure common durability standards. The standards are tested and financial penalties are applied for titles which do not meet the required standards.	Local printing capacity is not great and is not considered to be price competitive. Kenyan-based publishers tend to print in Kenya and other publishers use international printing sources in India, the Far East and in the Balkan countries.	All schools receive a per capita textbook budget and there is a separate per capita budget for readers and other supplementary materials. However schools do not receive cash but order on specially designed order forms, which are consolidated centrally so that publishers can be given exact bulk orders. This approach combines school-based selection and ordering with the cost benefits of bulk purchasing. District offices enter orders onto a national database, which checks orders against school capitation budgets to prevent serious over-or underordering. The national database (specially designed for the national teaching and learning materials reforms) provides distribution schedules for each publisher and also provides Completed Delivery Certificates which have to be signed and stamped by schools before publishers can receive	Distribution is undertaken by the publishers because local bookselling only exists in Kigali and doesn't provide national coverage. In 2010, 97.3 percent of Rwandan schools received correct deliveries delivered direct to their premises without payment. Textbook prices include the costs of distribution.

table continues next page

Table 13.1 Country Comparison (continued)

Country	Authorship and publishing	Procurement	Printing	Financing	Distribution
				payment. Publishers receive 20 percent of order value on the signature of the annual supply contract, 40 percent on the provision of advance copies and shipping documents, and 40 percent on completed delivery.	
Sierra Leone	All textbooks are commercially published and publishers are responsible for identifying and contracting authors. At primary and junior secondary most authors are Sierra Leonean. At senior secondary, titles are largely imported and have international authorship. Copyright remains with the publishers. Competing publishers are either U.K. based or Nigerian.	Textbook provision is monopolistic and titles are selected via competitive bidding and selection procedures which have been approved by the donor community and are considered to be up to international standards. All purchasing is handled centrally by the Ministry of Education working together with the Ministry of Local Government.	All printing is from international printing centers.	Textbooks are supplied free to students.	Publishers supply to 19 District Councils who are responsible for onward delivery to schools, with varying effectiveness.

Annex 13A: A TLM Diagnostic Checklist

The checklist provided below will enable ministries of education (MOEs) and development partners (DPs) to determine the basic health of national teaching and learning materials (TLMs) provision and will indicate corrective measures that should be raised with other DPs and the MOE and the Ministry of Finance (MOF).

Issue	Indicators	Recommended action
1. Copyright legislation—is it adequate?	Local Publishers Association should be able to provide briefing and relevant information.	If inadequate, make representations to government for upgrading copyright law to international standards.
2. Piracy—is it an issue that affects school supply?	Local Publishers and Booksellers Associations should be able to provide briefing and relevant information.	If piracy is an issue make representations to government re improving enforcement and increasing penalties.
3. Minimum Profile of TLMs required to deliver curriculum—is there one?	MOE should be able to provide information.	If no clear TLM provision plan then work with DPs and MOE to create this as the basis for future TLM financing projections. *NB: Specialist help may be needed to establish this.*
4. TLM Supply assumptions—are these specified?	MOE should be able to provide information.	If these are not specified then these should be included in the Minimum Profile of TLMs (see chapter 4). *NB: Basic supply assumptions are (a) target textbook–pupil ratios; (b) target classroom life; (c) annual loss and damage rates.*
5. Annual TLM Cost Implications—have these been accurately calculated and projected forward over at least five years?	MOF/MOE should be able to provide information.	An interactive costing spreadsheet is available that can quickly and easily provide an accurate costing and projection. More sophisticated database management systems can be developed to support all aspects of decentralized supply systems and this is recommended.
6. Is there sufficient funding to meet agreed minimum TLM needs?	Compare Minimum Profile cost projections with actual funding releases for TLMs over past five years.	Meet with MOE/Other DPs to discuss creation of minimum funding levels and/or the need to apply standard cost-reduction strategies (see chapter 7).
7. What percent of available funding is actually utilized for TLM procurement?	Public Expenditure Tracking Surveys (PETS) can review this issue and provide data or small sample biennial school surveys can provide data for de-centralized systems.	Available funding allocations for TLMs may need to be adjusted to take account of funding diversion and/or misappropriation.
8. Are TLM funding allocations regularly adjusted for inflation and/or enrollment growth?	Data on annual per capita funding allocations in US$ need to be established. This kind of data is usually available from MOF/MOE.	Many school systems don't adjust for inflation and enrollment growth as often as they should. Agreements with MOE/MOF are needed to review and revise allocations annually.
9. Is textbook supply monopolistic or competitive?	This information is normally easily available and well known and is part of a national book policy.	The answers to these questions might prompt the need for a policy review *where experienced professional input is recommended.* However, although competitive, decentralized, private sector systems generally work best—if properly supervised—there is no silver bullet and different solutions are required for different situations.
10. Is textbook selection centralized or decentralized?		

table continues next page

Issue	Indicators	Recommended action
11. Is the private sector involved in TLM publishing, bookselling, and printing?		
12. Do TLM procurement costs represent "value for money"?	This is not an easy question for non-specialists to answer. Thus, for example, textbook costs in large population countries based on one-color printing cannot easily be compared in value-for-money terms with free-market competitive supply costs for four-color textbooks in small population countries. Also quoted textbook unit costs often contain different combinations of cost components and may not be easily comparable.	*Specialist professional help is always needed to answer this question.* In some countries (for example, many Middle Eastern countries) higher costs are accepted in order to protect high cost local printing industries. In value-for-money terms cost should always be annual average recurrent cost and not actual production cost because high production specifications will be more expensive to provide but will usually last longer thus amortizing the initial costs over longer periods—usually resulting in significant cost savings.
13. Does the distribution system work?	Distribution surveys can be designed and implemented every three or four years to determine whether TLMs are reaching all schools on time, in good condition and in the required quantities? Also whether the distribution system is equitable—that, is do all schools get the same allocations or do urban schools do better than rural and remote schools? Are the costs the same for all schools?	If the distribution system is not working then *specialist assistance will be required to review, amend existing systems or propose new approaches.*
14. Are there storage and conservation problems at school level?	School mapping surveys, small sample surveys or direct observation provide data to answer this question	This is potentially an extremely expensive issue. *Specialist advise is required to provide practical, workable and affordable solutions.*
15. Are TLMs used in schools?	Sample school surveys and direct observation are required.	Solution is the authoring of TLM usage guides for inspectors, schools, and teachers plus in-service teacher training and module units in pre-service teacher training. Interactive web-based training modules can provide useful video coverage of teaching methods with TLMs.
16. TLM availability in schools?	A national TLM availability survey in schools every four to five years is recommended.	Assumptions are frequently made based on what has been supplied. Sometimes, these assumptions fail to take account of loss and damage and under-performing distribution so that actual availability can be worse (or sometimes better) than expected. Regular availability surveys every four to five years—perhaps supplemented by small-scale sample surveys in the interim will ensure that the level of TLM availability will always be known.

table continues next page

Issue	Indicators	Recommended action
17. Is TLM content and presentational quality acceptable and fit for purpose?	Ensure that TLM procurement, evaluation, and approval systems are well designed and properly implemented by independent, trained evaluators, who are well supervised.	Good TLM evaluation and approval systems, particularly if the evaluation is competitive, will usually ensure that content and presentational quality are of an acceptable standard. If there are doubts about the efficiency of the system in place then *specialist assistance is required to ensure that procurement documentation and evaluation/approval systems are up to international standards.*
18. Do the physical production specifications ensure durability and long classroom life?	Ascertain from MOE whether or not there are minimum physical production specifications covering text paper, cover card, binding style, cover finish, and so on.	If there are no minimum specifications these should be established. Existing specifications can be checked for suitability by a production specialist with previous experience of textbook supply in locally applicable conditions.
19. Are there sufficient supplies of appropriate reading books in primary classrooms?	Previous procurement records will reveal whether or not appropriate reading books have been supplied in the past. Sample classroom surveys will also be useful in establishing current availability of reading books and their usage.	At primary level reading books should be available in classrooms to be used effectively but this implies the development of secure, weatherproof classroom storage. This is possible at reasonable cost *but specialist advice would normally be necessary to design an approach.*
20. Are secondary school libraries well stocked and used?	Sample school surveys are useful in establishing current secondary school library situation.	Secondary school library development is a potentially important but expensive exercise. However, good libraries are important in supporting child-centered learning, the development of student research skills, and independent student learning.
21. Is there a national TLM policy?	MOE will provide details.	Needs to be critically reviewed if it exists; if it doesn't exist agreement should be sought with MOE and DPs to develop a national TLM policy. *This will require specialist support.*
22. Are TLMs being used effectively in the classroom after delivery?	Only a series of classroom observations can answer this query satisfactorily.	Simple handbooks on TLM use in the classroom can be effective but most teachers would benefit from being able to see good teachers use TLMs to the best effect. Video or interactive web or disk-based training modules would be more effective.

Options in the Development of National Teaching and Learning Materials Policies 229

Annex 13B: Critical Issues on Upgrading TLM Provision in Africa—A Decision Tree for Policy Makers

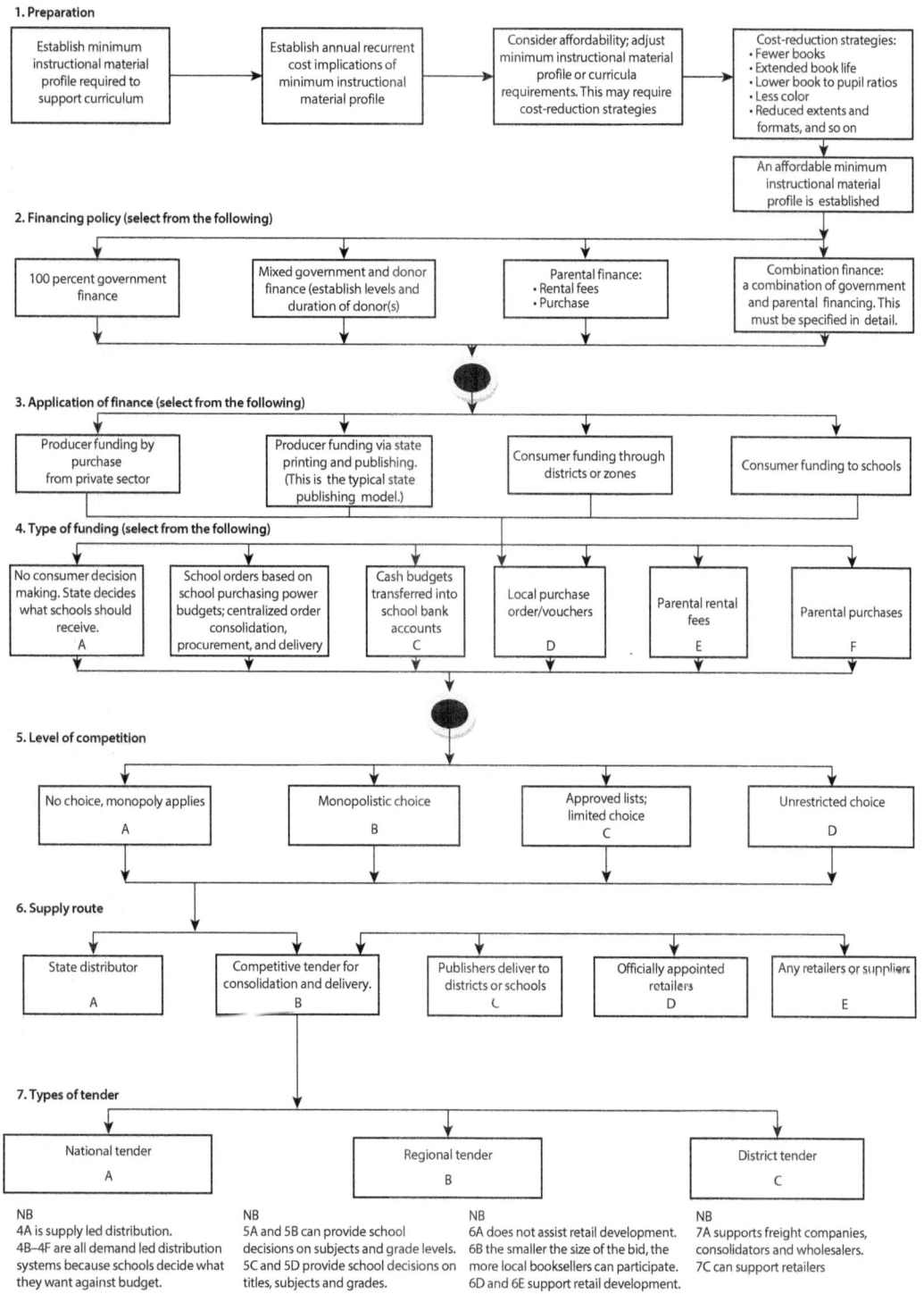

Where Have All the Textbooks Gone? • http://dx.doi.org/10.1596/978-1-4648-0572-1

Note

1. This is not universal. Recent textbook bids in Ethiopia have required private-sector publishers to pass their copyrights to the MOE so that the publishers have no financial interest in any reprints.

APPENDIX A

Statistical Summary of Country Surveys

Table A.1 Textbook Costs for Grade 1

Country	No. of required textbooks	Average unit textbook cost (US$)	Cost of textbook set (US$)	Assumed classroom life (years)	Target textbook-pupil ratio	Annualized amortized cost of a textbook set (US$)
Benin	6	2.70	16.20	n.a.	1:1	n.a.
Burundi	9	1.00	9.00	3	1:1	3.00
Côte d'Ivoire	3	3.00	9.00	1	1:1	9.00
Kenya	8	3.80	30.60	4	1:1	7.65
Madagascar	8	0.75	6.00	2	1:1	3.00
Mali	3	4.50	13.60	2–3	1:1	4.53
Namibia	3	12.00	36.00	5	1:2	3.60
Rwanda	4	2.50	10.00	4	1:1	2.50
Chad	2	5.00	10.00	1	1:1	10.00
Averages	**5**	**5.36**	**19.93**	**2.86**	**1:1**	**5.90**

Note: n.a. = no data available.

Table A.2 Textbook Costs for Grade 6

Country	No. of required textbooks	Average unit textbook cost (US$)	Cost of textbook set (US$)	Assumed classroom life (years)	Target textbook-pupil ratio	Annualized amortized cost of a textbook set (US$)
Benin	6	2.60	15.60	n.a.	1.1	n.a.
Burundi	10	1.00	10.00	3	1:1	3.33
Côte d'Ivoire	7	4.00	28.00	2	1:1	14.00
Kenya	7	4.20	29.40	4	1:1	7.35
Madagascar	8	0.75	6.00	2	1:1	3.00
Mali	4	5.50	22.00	4	1:1	5.50
Namibia	7	25.00	175.00	5	1:2	17.50
Rwanda	5	3.50	17.50	5	1:1	3.50
Chad	5	6.00	30.00	1	1:3	10.00
Averages	**6.6**	**5.84**	**37.00**	**3.25**	**1:4**	**8.02**

Note: n.a. = no data available.

Table A.3 Textbook Costs for Grade 8

Country	No. of required textbooks	Average unit textbook cost (US$)	Cost of textbook set (US$)	Assumed classroom life (years)	Target textbook-pupil ratio	Annualized amortized cost of a textbook set (US$)
Benin	7	5.9	41.30	n.a.	1:1	n.a.
Burundi	15	1.0	15.00	4	1:1	3.75
Côte d'Ivoire	8	9.50	76.00	3	1:3	8.40
Kenya	9	4.60	41.40	4	1:1	10.35
Madagascar	7	n.a.	n.a.	n.a.	n.a.	n.a.
Mali	9	10.00	90.00	5	n.a.	18.00
Namibia	8	20.00	160.00	5	1:2	16.00
Rwanda	8	6.00	48.00	5	1:1	9.60
Chad	5	n.a.	n.a.	1	3:5[a]	n.a.
Averages	**8.4**	**8.14**	**67.38**	**3.9**	**1:1.78**	**9.44**

Note: n.a. = no data available.
a. Chad has a 1:1 ratio for language of instruction, 1:3 for math, and 1:5 for other subjects.

Table A.4 Textbook Costs for Grade 11

Country	No. of required textbooks	Average unit textbook cost (US$)	Cost of textbook set (US$)	Assumed classroom life (years)	Target textbook-pupil ratio	Annualized amortized cost of a textbook set (US$)
Benin	8	4.30	34.40	n.a.	1:1	n.a.
Burundi	16	1.00	16.00	5	1:1	3.20
Côte d'Ivoire	6	13.95	83.70	5	1:5	3.00
Kenya	8	5.00	40.00	4	1:1	10.00
Madagascar	7	n.a.	n.a.	n.a.	n.a.	n.a.
Mali	10	11.50	115.00	5	n.a.	23.00
Namibia	8	20.00	160.00	5	1:2	16.00
Nigeria	n.a.	n.a.	n.a.	n.a.	n.a.	n.a.
Rwanda	15	15.00	225.00	5	1:1	45.00
Sierra Leone	n.a.	n.a.	n.a.	n.a.	n.a.	n.a.
Chad	7	n.a.	n.a.	n.a.	3:5[a]	n.a.
Averages	**9.44**	**10.11**	**96.30**	**4.83**	**1:2.07**	**14.31**

Note: n.a. = no data available.
a. Chad has a 1:1 ratio for language of instruction, 1:3 for math, and 1:5 for other subjects.

Table A.5 Dictionary Costs for Grade 1

Country	No. of required dictionaries	Average unit dictionary cost (US$)	Cost of dictionaries (US$)	Assumed classroom life (years)	Target dictionary-pupil ratio	Annualized amortized cost of dictionaries (US$)
Benin	n.a.	n.a.	n.a.	n.a.	n.a.	n.a.
Burundi	n.a.	n.a.	n.a.	n.a.	n.a.	n.a.
Côte d'Ivoire	n.a.	n.a.	n.a.	n.a.	n.a.	n.a.
Kenya	n.a.	n.a.	n.a.	n.a.	n.a.	n.a.

table continues next page

Table A.5 Dictionary Costs for Grade 1 (continued)

Country	No. of required dictionaries	Average unit dictionary cost (US$)	Cost of dictionaries (US$)	Assumed classroom life (years)	Target dictionary-pupil ratio	Annualized amortized cost of dictionaries (US$)
Madagascar	n.a.	n.a.	n.a.	n.a.	n.a.	n.a.
Mali	n.a.	n.a.	n.a.	n.a.	n.a.	n.a.
Namibia	n.a.	n.a.	n.a.	n.a.	n.a.	n.a.
Rwanda	2	6.50	13.00	5	1:10	0.26
Chad	n.a.	n.a.	n.a.	n.a.	n.a.	n.a.
Averages	**2**	**6.50**	**13.00**	**5**	**1:10**	**0.26**

Note: n.a. = no data available.

Table A.6 Dictionary Costs for Grade 6

Country	No. of required dictionaries	Average unit dictionary cost (US$)	Cost of dictionaries (US$)	Assumed classroom life (years)	Target dictionary-pupil ratio	Annualized amortized cost of dictionaries (US$)
Benin	n.a.	n.a.	n.a.	n.a.	n.a.	n.a.
Burundi	n.a.	n.a.	n.a.	n.a.	n.a.	n.a.
Côte d'Ivoire	n.a.	n.a.	n.a.	n.a.	n.a.	n.a.
Kenya	2	7.15	14.30	5	1:10	0.29
Madagascar	n.a.	n.a.	n.a.	n.a.	n.a.	n.a.
Mali	n.a.	n.a.	n.a.	n.a.	n.a.	n.a.
Namibia	1	10.00	10.00	5	1:10	0.20
Rwanda	2	10.00	20.00	5	1:10	0.40
Chad	n.a.	n.a.	n.a.	n.a.	n.a.	n.a.
Averages	**1.66**	**9.05**	**14.77**	**5**	**1:10**	**0.30**

Note: n.a. = no data available.

Table A.7 Dictionary Costs for Grade 8

Country	No. of required dictionaries	Average unit dictionary cost (US$)	Cost of dictionaries (US$)	Assumed classroom life (years)	Target dictionary-pupil ratio	Annualized amortized cost of dictionaries (US$)
Benin	n.a.	n.a.	n.a.	n.a.	n.a.	n.a.
Burundi	n.a.	n.a.	n.a.	n.a.	n.a.	n.a.
Côte d'Ivoire	n.a.	n.a.	n.a.	n.a.	n.a.	n.a.
Kenya	2	10.50	21.00	5	1:5	0.84
Madagascar	n.a.	n.a.	n.a.	n.a.	n.a.	n.a.
Mali	n.a.	n.a.	n.a.	n.a.	n.a.	n.a.
Namibia	1	10.00	10.00	5	n.a.	n.a.
Rwanda	1	12.50	12.50	5	1:5	0.50
Chad	n.a.	n.a.	n.a.	n.a.	n.a.	n.a.
Averages	**1.33**	**11.00**	**14.50**	**5**	**1:5**	**0.67**

Note: n.a. = no data available.

Table A.8 Dictionary Costs for Grade 11

Country	No. of required dictionaries	Average unit dictionary cost (US$)	Cost of dictionaries (US$)	Assumed classroom life (years)	Target dictionary-pupil ratio	Annualized amortized cost of dictionaries (US$)
Benin	n.a.	n.a.	n.a.	n.a.	n.a.	n.a.
Burundi	n.a.	n.a.	n.a.	n.a.	n.a.	n.a.
Côte d'Ivoire	n.a.	n.a.	n.a.	n.a.	n.a.	n.a.
Kenya	n.a.	n.a.	n.a.	n.a.	n.a.	n.a.
Madagascar	n.a.	n.a.	n.a.	n.a.	n.a.	n.a.
Mali	n.a.	n.a.	n.a.	n.a.	n.a.	n.a.
Namibia	1	10.00	10.00	5	1:1	2.00
Rwanda	1	15.00	15.00	5	1:5	0.60
Chad	n.a.	n.a.	n.a.	n.a.	n.a.	n.a.
Averages	**1**	**12.50**	**12.50**	**5**	**1:2.5**	**1.30**

Note: n.a. = no data available.

Table A.9 Atlas Costs for Grade 1

Country	Average unit atlas cost (US$)	Assumed classroom life (years)	Target atlas-pupil ratio	Annualized amortized cost of atlas (US$)
Benin	n.a.	n.a.	n.a.	n.a.
Burundi	n.a.	n.a.	n.a.	n.a.
Côte d'Ivoire	n.a.	n.a.	n.a.	n.a.
Kenya	n.a.	n.a.	n.a.	n.a.
Madagascar	n.a.	n.a.	n.a.	n.a.
Mali	n.a.	n.a.	n.a.	n.a.
Namibia	n.a.	n.a.	n.a.	n.a.
Rwanda	5.50	5	1:10	0.11
Chad	n.a.	n.a.	n.a.	n.a.
Averages	**5.50**	**5**	**1:10**	**0.11**

Note: n.a. = no data available.

Table A.10 Atlas Costs for Grade 6

Country	Average unit atlas cost (US$)	Assumed classroom life (years)	Target atlas-pupil ratio	Annualized amortized cost of atlas (US$)
Benin	n.a.	n.a.	n.a.	n.a.
Burundi	n.a.	n.a.	n.a.	n.a.
Côte d'Ivoire	n.a.	n.a.	n.a.	n.a.
Kenya	5.00	5	1:5	0.20
Madagascar	n.a.	n.a.	n.a.	n.a.
Mali	n.a.	n.a.	n.a.	n.a.
Namibia	30.00	5	1:10	0.60
Rwanda	5.50	5	1:10	0.11
Chad	n.a.	n.a.	n.a.	n.a.
Averages	**13.50**	**5**	**1:8.33**	**0.30**

Note: n.a. = no data available.

Table A.11 Atlas Costs for Grade 8

Country	Average unit atlas cost (US$)	Assumed classroom life (years)	Target atlas-pupil ratio	Annualized amortized cost of atlas set (US$)
Benin	n.a.	n.a.	n.a.	n.a.
Burundi	n.a.	n.a.	n.a.	n.a.
Côte d'Ivoire	n.a.	n.a.	n.a.	n.a.
Kenya	8.30	5	1:1	1.66
Madagascar	n.a.	n.a.	n.a.	n.a.
Mali	n.a.	n.a.	n.a.	n.a.
Namibia	30.00	5	1:10	0.60
Rwanda	12.00	5	1:5	0.48
Chad	n.a.	n.a.	n.a.	n.a.
Averages	**16.77**	**5**	**1:5.33**	**0.91**

Note: n.a. = no data available.

Table A.12 Atlas Costs for Grade 11

Country	Average unit atlas cost (US$)	Assumed classroom life (years)	Target atlas-pupil ratio	Annualized amortized cost of atlas set (US$)
Benin	n.a.	n.a.	n.a.	n.a.
Burundi	n.a.	n.a.	n.a.	n.a.
Côte d'Ivoire	n.a.	n.a.	n.a.	n.a.
Kenya	12.00	5	1:1	2.40
Madagascar	n.a.	n.a.	n.a.	n.a.
Mali	n.a.	n.a.	n.a.	n.a.
Namibia	30.00	5	1:10	0.60
Rwanda	15.00	5	1:5	0.60
Chad	n.a.	n.a.	n.a.	n.a.
Averages	**19.00**	**5**	**5:33**	**1.20**

Note: n.a. = no data available.

Table A.13 Reader Costs for Grade 1

Country	Average unit reader cost (US$)	Assumed classroom life (years)	Target reader-pupil ratio	Annualized amortized cost of readers (US$)
Benin	2.60	n.a.	2:1	5.20
Burundi	n.a.	n.a.	n.a.	n.a.
Côte d'Ivoire	3.23	1	1:1	3.23
Kenya	2.00	5	2:1	0.80
Madagascar	n.a.	3	n.a.	n.a.
Mali	6.10	n.a.	1:1	6.10
Namibia	5.00	5	2:1	2.00
Rwanda	0.75	5	2:1	0.30
Chad	5.40	n.a.	1:1	5.40
Averages	**3.50**	**3.8**	**1:6**	**3.29**

Note: n.a. = no data available.

Table A.14 Reader Costs for Grade 6

Country	Average unit reader cost (US$)	Assumed classroom life (years)	Target reader-pupil ratio	Annualized amortized cost of readers (US$)
Benin	2.70	n.a.	2:1	5.40
Burundi	n.a.	n.a.	n.a.	n.a.
Côte d'Ivoire	4.16	3	1:1	1.39
Kenya	3.00	5	2:1	1.20
Madagascar	n.a.	3	n.a.	n.a.
Mali	6.10	n.a.	n.a.	n.a.
Namibia	8.00	5	2:1	3.20
Rwanda	2.00	5	2:1	0.80
Chad	5.40	n.a.	1:1	5.40
Averages	**4.48**	**4.2**	**1:66**	**2.90**

Note: n.a. = no data available.

Table A.15 Reader Costs for Grade 8

Country	Average unit reader cost (US$)	Assumed classroom life (years)	Target reader-pupil ratio	Annualized amortized cost of readers (US$)
Benin	7.80	n.a.	1:1	7.80
Burundi	n.a.	n.a.	n.a.	n.a.
Côte d'Ivoire	8.32	3	1:3	0.92
Kenya	5.00	5	1:1	1.00
Madagascar	n.a.	n.a.	n.a.	n.a.
Mali	6.10	n.a.	n.a.	n.a.
Namibia	10.00	5	2:1	10.00
Rwanda	8.00	5	2:1	3.20
Chad	12.50	n.a.	1:1	12.50
Averages	**8.25**	**4.5**	**1:33**	**5.90**

Note: n.a. = no data available.

Table A.16 Reader Costs for Grade 11

Country	Average unit reader cost (US$)	Assumed classroom life (years)	Target reader-pupil ratio	Annualized amortized cost of readers (US$)
Benin				
Burundi				
Côte d'Ivoire				
Kenya				
Madagascar				
Mali				
Namibia				
Rwanda				
Chad				
Averages				

Note: All cells are empty to demonstrate that no country provides reading books to Grade 11 students.

Table A.17 Summary of Annual Amortized TLM Costs for Grade 1

Country	Textbooks	Dictionaries	Atlases	Readers	Total annual amortized TLM costs
Benin	n.a.	n.a.	n.a.	5.20	n.a.
Burundi	3.00	n.a.	n.a.	n.a.	5.00
Côte d'Ivoire	9.00	n.a.	n.a.	3.23	12.23
Kenya	7.65	n.a.	n.a.	0.80	8.45
Madagascar	3.00	n.a.	n.a.	n.a.	3.00
Mali	4.53	n.a.	n.a.	6.10	20.63
Namibia	7.50	n.a.	n.a.	2.00	9.50
Rwanda	2.50	0.26	0.11	0.30	3.17
Chad	10.00	n.a.	n.a.	5.40	15.4
Averages	**5.90**	**0.26**	**0.11**	**3.29**	**9.56**

Note: n.a. = no data available; TLM = teaching and learning materials.

Table A.18 Summary of Annual Amortized TLM Costs for Grade 6

Country	Textbooks	Dictionaries	Atlases	Readers	Total annual amortized TLM costs
Benin	n.a.	n.a.	n.a.	5.40	n.a.
Burundi	3.33	n.a.	n.a.	n.a.	3.33
Côte d'Ivoire	14.00	n.a.	n.a.	1.39	15.39
Kenya	7.35	0.29	0.20	1.20	9.04
Madagascar	3.00	n.a.	n.a.	n.a.	n.a.
Mali	5.50	n.a.	n.a.	n.a.	n.a.
Namibia	17.50	0.20	0.60	3.20	20.90
Rwanda	3.50	0.40	0.11	0.80	4.81
Chad	10.00	n.a.	n.a.	5.40	15.40
Averages	**8.02**	**0.30**	**0.30**	**2.90**	**11.52**

Note: n.a. = no data available; TLM = teaching and learning materials.

Table A.19 Summary of Annual Amortized TLM Costs for Grade 8

Country	Textbooks	Dictionaries	Atlases	Readers	Total annual amortized TLM costs
Benin	n.a.	n.a.	n.a.	7.80	n.a.
Burundi	3.75	n.a.	n.a.	n.a.	3.75
Côte d'Ivoire	8.40			0.92	9.32
Kenya	10.35	0.84	1.66	1.00	13.85
Madagascar	n.a.	n.a.	n.a.	n.a.	n.a.
Mali	18.00	n.a.	n.a.	n.a.	10.00
Namibia	16.00	n.a.	0.60	10.00	26.60
Rwanda	9.60	0.50	0.48	3.20	13.78
Chad	n.a.	n.a.	n.a.	12.50	n.a.
Averages	**9.44**	**0.67**	**0.91**	**5.90**	**12.88**

Note: n.a. = no data available; TLM = teaching and learning materials.

Table A.20 Summary of Annual Amortized TLM Costs for Grade 11

Country	Textbooks	Dictionaries	Atlases	Readers	Total annual amortized TLM costs
Benin	n.a.	n.a.	n.a.	n.a.	n.a.
Burundi	3.20	n.a.	n.a.	n.a.	3.20
Côte d'Ivoire	3.00	n.a.	n.a.	n.a.	3.00
Kenya	10.00	n.a.	2.40	n.a.	12.40
Madagascar	n.a.	n.a.	n.a.	n.a.	n.a.
Mali	23.00	n.a.	n.a.	n.a.	23.00
Namibia	16.00	2.00	0.60	n.a.	18.60
Rwanda	45.00	0.60	0.60	n.a.	46.20
Chad	n.a.	n.a.	n.a.	n.a.	n.a.
Averages	**14.31**	**1.30**	**1.20**	n.a.	**17.73**

Note: n.a. = no data available; TLM = teaching and learning materials.

Table A.21 Average Annual Amortized TLM Costs per Student by Grade Level

Country	Textbooks	Dictionaries	Atlases	Readers	Total
Grade 1	5.90	0.26	0.11	3.29	**9.56**
Grade 6	8.02	0.30	0.30	2.90	**11.52**
Grade 8	9.44	0.67	0.91	5.90	**16.92**
Grade 11	14.31	1.30	1.20	n.a.	**16.81**

Note: n.a. = no data available; TLM = teaching and learning materials.

Table A.22 Types of Textbook Funding

Country	Grade 1	Grade 6	Grade 8	Grade 11
Benin	S	S	P	P
Burundi	S	S	S	S
Côte d'Ivoire	F	F	P	P
Kenya	C	C	C P	C P
Madagascar	F	F	P	P
Mali	F	F	F	F
Namibia	F	F	F	F
Rwanda	C	C	C	C
Chad	F	F	P	P

Note: F = Free government supply to schools; C = purchased by schools with government funding; P = parent purchase; R = textbook rental fee paid by parents; S = government provides limited free safety net supplies.

Table A.23 Types of Atlas Funding

Country	Grade 1	Grade 6	Grade 8	Grade 11
Benin	n.a.	n.a.	n.a.	n.a.
Burundi	n.a.	n.a.	n.a.	n.a.
Côte d'Ivoire	P	P	P	P
Kenya	C	C	C P	C P
Madagascar	n.a.	n.a.	n.a.	n.a.
Mali	F	F	F	F
Namibia	F	F	F	F
Rwanda	C	C	C	C
Chad	n.a.	n.a.	n.a.	n.a.

Note: n.a. = no data available; F = Free government supply to schools; C = purchased by schools with government funding; P = parent purchase.

Table A.24 Types of Dictionary Funding

Country	Grade 1	Grade 6	Grade 8	Grade 11
Benin	n.a.	n.a.	P	P
Burundi	n.a.	n.a.	n.a.	n.a.
Côte d'Ivoire	P	P	P	P
Kenya	C	C	C P	C P
Madagascar	n.a.	n.a.	n.a.	n.a.
Mali	F	F	F	F
Namibia	F	F	F	F
Rwanda	C	C	C	C
Chad	n.a.	n.a.	n.a.	n.a.

Note: n.a. = no data available; F= Free government supply to schools; C = purchased by schools with government funding; P = parent purchase.

Table A.25 Types of Reader Funding

Country	Grade 1	Grade 6	Grade 8	Grade 11
Benin	F	F	P	n.a.
Burundi	n.a.	n.a.	n.a.	n.a.
Côte d'Ivoire	F	F	P	n.a.
Kenya	C	C	C P	C P
Madagascar	F	n.a.	n.a.	n.a.
Mali	F	F	F	n.a.
Namibia	F	F	F	F
Rwanda	C	C	C	n.a.
Chad	n.a.	n.a.	n.a.	n.a.

Note: n.a. = no data available; F= Free government supply to schools; C = purchased by schools with government funding; P = parent purchase.

Table A.26 Types of Textbook Supply

Country	Grade 1	Grade 6	Grade 8	Grade 11
Benin	M	M	OC	OC
Burundi	M	M	M	M
Côte d'Ivoire	LC	LC	LC	LC
Kenya	LC	LC	LC	LC
Madagascar	M	M	n.a.	n.a.
Mali	OC	OC	OC	OC
Namibia	M	M	M	M
Rwanda	LC	LC	LC	LC
Chad	M	M	M	M

Note: LC = limited competition, usually based on school choice from a Ministry of Education list of approved textbooks; M = monopoly textbook supply; n.a. = not applicable; OC = Open competition in which schools can choose from any available textbook.

Table A.27 Estimated Primary Textbook–Pupil Ratios in Urban, Rural, and Remote Locations

Country	Urban	Rural	Remote
Benin	1:10	1:10	1:10
Burundi	2:3	1:3	1:10
Côte d'Ivoire	1:1	1:1	n.a.
Kenya	1:2	1:3	1:5
Madagascar	n.a.	n.a.	n.a.
Mali	n.a.	n.a.	n.a.
Namibia	1:5	1:10	1:15
Rwanda	1:3	1:3	1:3
Chad	n.a.	n.a.	n.a.

Note: n.a. = not applicable.

Table A.28 TLM Distribution Methods

Country	Primary	Junior secondary	Senior secondary
Benin	DEO	Bookseller	Bookseller
Burundi	DEO	DEO	DEO
Côte d'Ivoire	Freighting company	Bookseller	Bookseller
Kenya	Bookseller	Bookseller	Bookseller
Madagascar	n.a.	n.a.	n.a.
Mali	Publisher	Publisher	Publisher
Namibia	Bookseller	Bookseller	Bookseller
Rwanda	Publisher	Publisher	Publisher
Chad	DEO	DEO	DEO

Note: DEO = District Education Office; n.a. = not applicable.

Table A.29 Distribution Performance

Country	Primary	Junior secondary	Senior secondary
Benin	Satisfactory	n.a.	n.a.
Burundi	Satisfactory	Poor	Poor
Côte d'Ivoire	Poor	n.a.	n.a.
Kenya	Satisfactory	Satisfactory	Satisfactory
Madagascar	Satisfactory	n.a.	n.a.
Mali	Satisfactory	Satisfactory	Good
Namibia	Very poor	Very poor	Very poor
Rwanda	Satisfactory	Satisfactory	Satisfactory
Chad	Very poor	Very poor	Very poor

Note: n.a. = not applicable.

Table A.30 Distribution Characteristics

| Country | Primary | | Junior secondary | | Senior secondary | |
	Accuracy	On time	Accuracy	On time	Accuracy	On time
Benin	Inaccurate	Often late	Inaccurate	n.a.	Inaccurate	n.a.
Burundi	Inaccurate	Very late	Inaccurate	Very late	Inaccurate	Very late
Côte d'Ivoire	n.a.	Often late	n.a.	n.a.	n.a.	n.a.
Kenya	Inaccurate	Often late	Inaccurate	Often late	Inaccurate	Often late
Madagascar	Inaccurate	Often late	Inaccurate	Often late	Inaccurate	n.a.
Mali	Inaccurate	Sometimes late	Inaccurate	Sometimes late	Inaccurate	Sometimes late
Namibia	Inaccurate	Very late	Inaccurate	Very late	Inaccurate	Very late
Rwanda	Inaccurate	Late	Inaccurate	Late	Inaccurate	Late
Chad	Inaccurate	Very late	Inaccurate	Very late	Inaccurate	Very late

Note: n.a. = not applicable.

Table A.31 Sources of Authorship, Publishing, Manufacturing, and Raw Materials for Grades 1, 6, 8, and 11

Country	Authorship/publishing			Manufacturing			Raw materials		
	Local	Regional	International	Local	Regional	International	Local	Regional	International
Benin	All grades	Secondary	Secondary	All grades	Secondary	Secondary	n.a.	n.a.	All grades
Burundi	All grades	n.a.	All grades	All grades	n.a.	All grades	n.a.	n.a.	All grades
Côte d'Ivoire	All grades	n.a.	All grades	Primary	n.a.	All grades	n.a.	n.a.	All grades
Kenya	All grades	n.a.	Secondary	All grades	n.a.	n.a.	n.a.	n.a.	All grades
Madagascar	Primary and junior secondary	Upper primary and secondary	Secondary	All grades	n.a.	All grades	n.a.	n.a.	All grades
Mali	All grades	n.a.	n.a.	All grades	n.a.	n.a.	n.a.	n.a.	All grades
Namibia	All grades	Upper primary and secondary	n.a.	All grades	Upper primary and secondary	n.a.	n.a.	All grades	All grades
Rwanda	All grades	All grades	All grades	Primary	All grades	All grades	n.a.	n.a.	All grades
Chad	Secondary	n.a.	All grades	n.a.	n.a.	All grades	n.a.	n.a.	All grades

Note: n.a. = not applicable.

Table A.32 Adequacy, Regularity, and Predictability of Government TLM Budgets

Country	Textbooks			Readers			Libraries			Other TLM		
	Adequate	Regular	Predictable	Adequate	Regular	Predictable	Adequate	Regular	Predictable	Adequate	Regular	Predictable
Benin	No	Yes	n.a.	No	Yes	n.a.	No	No	No	No	No	No
Burundi	No	No	No	No	No	No	No	No	No	No	No	No
Côte d'Ivoire	Yes	No	No	Yes	No	No	No	No	No	No	No	No
Kenya	No	No	No	No	No	No	No	No	No	No	No	No
Madagascar	No	No	No	No	No	No	No	No	No	No	No	No
Mali	No	No	Yes	No	No	Yes	No	No	Yes	No	No	Yes
Namibia	Yes	No	No	Yes	No	No	No	No	No	No	No	No
Rwanda	Yes	Yes	Yes	Yes	Yes	Yes	No	No	No	No	No	No
Chad	No	Yes	Yes	No	Yes	Yes	No	Yes	Yes	No	Yes	Yes

Note: n.a. = no data available.

APPENDIX B

A Summary of Issues in Information and Communication Technology Use in Schools

Information and Communication Technology and Student Achievement

The link between information and communication technology (ICT) use in schools and improvements in student academic achievement remains elusive in all countries—both developed and developing. A 2005 Infodev review of research findings on ICT and student achievement in developing countries summarized the results as follows:

> The positive impact of ICT use in education has not been proven. In general, and despite thousands of studies, the impact of ICT on student achievement remains difficult to measure and open to much reasonable debate. Positive impact is more likely when linked to pedagogy. It is believed that specific uses of ICT can have positive effects on student achievement when ICTs are used appropriately to complement a teacher's existing pedagogical philosophies. Computer Aided Instruction has been seen to slightly improve student performance on multiple choice, standardized testing in some areas. Computer Aided (or Assisted) Instruction (CAI), which refers generally to student self-study or tutorials on PCs, has been shown to slightly improve student test scores on some reading and math skills, although whether such improvement correlates to real improvement in student learning is debatable ICTs are seen to be less effective (or ineffective) when the goals for their use are not clear. While such a statement would appear to be self-evident, the specific goals for ICT use in education are, in practice, often only very broadly or rather loosely defined. There is an important tension between traditional versus "new" pedagogies and standardized testing. Traditional, transmission-type pedagogies are seen as more effective in preparation for standardized testing, which tends to measure the results of such teaching practices, than are more "constructivist" pedagogical styles In many studies there may be a mismatch between the methods used to measure effects and the nature of the learning promoted by the specific uses of ICT. For example, some studies have looked only for improvements in traditional teaching

and learning processes and knowledge mastery instead of looking for new processes and knowledge related to the use of ICTs. It may be that more useful analyses of the impact of ICT can only emerge when the methods used to measure achievement and outcomes are more closely related to the learning activities and processes promoted by the use of ICTs. ICTs are used differently in different school subjects. Uses of ICTs for simulations and modelling in science and math have been shown to be effective, as have word processing and communication software (e-mail) in the development of student language and communication skills..... The relationships between in class student computer use, out of class student computer use and student achievement are unclear. However, students in OECD countries reporting the greatest amount of computer use outside school are seen in some studies to have lower than average achievement (the presumption is that high computer use outside of school is disproportionately devoted to computer gaming). (Trucano 2005)

A review of research studies conducted for the Department for International Development (DFID) in 2014 reached much the same conclusion (Power et al. 2014).

In general, among the studies reviewed, there is little conclusive evidence of measurable changes in teaching and learning practices, through students' use of edtech.

There is some indication that where the focus is upon computers and ICT hardware, rather than subject curriculum and pedagogy, this may do little to improve students' active learning. When it is poorly introduced it may reinforce existing teacher-centred practices and when teachers are not supported in its use it may simply have no contribution to subject teaching. (EdQual 2011)

The finding that extensive use of computers by students may be associated with sub standard performance in math and reading was identified by a research study based on the test performance and background data from the 2000 PISA study involving tens of thousands of students in 31 countries.

Students who use computers a lot at school have worse maths and reading performance. Those (students) using computers several times a week performed sizeably and statistically significantly worse than those who used them less often.... The belief that there is an educational benefit—and not just better work skills—has underpinned huge investments by governments, and many parents, in information and communication technology ... the more computers there were in students' homes, the better their test performance ... but more computers went with more affluent, better-educated families.... [W]hen this was taken into account the more computers in a student's home, the worse the student's maths performance. (Fuchs and Woessmann 2004)

These findings have been challenged by, for example, the U.K. government's ICT agency—BECTA. However, a more recent review of research into the impact of ICT on student performance in U.K. schools was also ambivalent about the benefits. Based on more than 350 research studies the review concluded:

At present the evidence on attainment is somewhat inconsistent, although it does appear that, in some contexts, with some pupils, in some disciplines, attainment has been enhanced. There is a need for more systematically gathered evidence although it is already apparent that, where ICT has been successfully embedded in the classroom experience, a positive impact on attainment is more likely. The body of evidence on the impact of ICT on intermediate outcomes, such as motivation, engagement with and independence in learning, is greater and more persuasive. The benefits identified in the literature include increased collaboration, greater engagement and persistence, more on-task behaviour and better conceptual understanding. Understanding of the extent to which ICT can support creativity, including critical thinking skills and problem solving abilities, is developing, although some of the evidence appears contradictory. In the studies encountered, positive findings were associated with a range of technologies, particularly those with strong visual elements such as digital video, drama-oriented software and multimedia…. much of the evidence of impact on attainment and a range of intermediate outcomes such as motivation and engagement is derived from small scale case studies which are often snapshots of impact early in the life of the implementation of a new technology. The number of different technologies available and the rate at which they are developing provide considerable scope for researchers although this has tended to result in a fragmented and unsystematic evidence base from which to evaluate the impact of ICT more generally…. there is a paucity of large-scale, methodologically rigorous research from which generalisations may be drawn. In general, impact is most clearly observed where tasks have clear educational aims, are designed to maximise the potential of the ICT in use and are perceived as purposeful by pupils. (Condie and Munro 2007)

The same report comments that evidence of positive impact has been reported in mathematics, modern foreign languages, science, history, geography, physical education, and the creative arts. However, much of the evidence for these assertions is the result of small-scale studies, and further more rigorous longitudinal research is needed to determine the extent to which the successes recorded can be replicated elsewhere, and their persistence over time.

The report also notes that in the United Kingdom there has been considerable development in the provision of online resources for teaching across subject areas. Foreign language learning has benefited from the increased availability of online resources as well as technologies such as digital video and photography, while animations and simulations have enabled pupils to grasp more complex concepts in mathematics and the sciences. These have been particularly effective in supporting the understanding of abstract or microscopic concepts and processes in science. Digital video and photography have also been proven to improve performance in physical education, sport, and the dramatic arts where performances can be recorded and watched and skills improvements targeted.

A more recent review of ICT and English language attainment reported its conclusions as follows:

Multimedia e-books and activity-based software can improve literacy attainment in Foundation and Key Stage 1, although not all systems yield benefits. Activity software can improve children's written summarising skills and topic-based writing in primary school children. The spelling performance of children with literacy difficulties can be enhanced by programmes that include text-to-speech feedback or multisensory associations with letters and sounds. Typically, developing children's recreational use of text message abbreviations also appears to contribute positively to children's spelling attainment, although there is no significant educational benefit of giving phones to children per se. Interactive 'listening' toys can benefit children's oral storytelling, and can facilitate peer collaboration in the early years. Multimedia e-books can also foster collaborative learning between peers and story understanding. Adoption of an interdisciplinary ICT curriculum can benefit the English attainment of children in Key Stage 2. (BECTA 2010)

Other recent research reports on the impact of ICT on learning outcomes have provided conflicting results. Banerjee et al. (2007) concluded that exposing grade 4 children to two hours per week of computer-based math instruction improved learning by 0.4 standard deviations but also noted that computers in the control schools were generally unused (a common finding in many Sub-Saharan Africa (SSA) and other developing countries). Barrera and Linden (2009) reported no identifiable gains in child cognitive outcomes as a result of ICT use in schools in Colombia. Malamud and Pop-Eleches (2008) also reported negative impact of ICT use in schools on learning outcomes although some improvements were noted when parental supervision and monitoring were involved.

On the other hand there seems to be little disagreement in a wide range of largely anecdotal reports that ICT use in class can have a beneficial impact on student behavior, attitudes, motivation, and attendance.

The evidence provided above on the links between ICT provision and student achievement are rooted largely in the experiences of relatively rich developed countries where ICT hardware and software are well funded and well maintained, where relevant software is available on reliable Internet links and where teachers are well trained and generally well remunerated and work in well-organized learning environments. However

> in spite of teacher training programmes, an increase in ICT resources and the requirements of national curricula there has been a disappointingly slow uptake of ICT in schools. (Cox, Preston, and Cox 1999)
>
> National survey data from Chile showed that the national ICT education policy (Enlaces) had been very successful in reach (over 98% of the almost 11,000 publicly supported primary and secondary schools had participated by 2009), but found that "ICT is not frequently used at schools." (Hinostroza et al. 2011)
>
> The first large-scale study of the effects of OLPC [One Laptop per Child], carried out in primary schools in Peru, found that despite increasing access to computers by an order of magnitude (from 0.12 computers per student, to 1.18 computers per student), and substantial increases in computer use at home and at school,

there was little effect on motivation (as indicated by enrollment or attendance), time spent on homework, or student reading habits. Computer logs suggested most computer activities were not directed towards educational outcomes. (Cristia et al. 2012)

Fullan (1991) found that

> one of the most fundamental problems in education reform is that people do not have a clear and coherent sense of the reasons for educational change, what it is and how to proceed. Thus there is much faddism, superficiality, confusion, failure of a change programme, unwarranted and misdirected resistance and misunderstood reform.

The introduction of ICT into the education systems of most developing and transitional economies tends to be constrained by all of the problems identified by Fullan (above) plus low personal computer (PC)–pupil ratios, poorly maintained hardware and widespread nonuse of equipment, widely unavailable, Ineffective or unaffordable Internet connectivity, a lack of easy access to relevant software, particularly in local languages, poorly qualified teachers, a widespread lack of well-directed teacher training, inadequate operational funding to support effective ICT use in the classroom, and generally poor classroom environments. In these circumstances, where education is already seriously under funded, the cost implications of ICT provision in poor countries must be a concern, particularly where the benefits of ICT in the upgrading of student performance are difficult to determine—even in well-resourced developed countries. In these situations, cost effectiveness and affordability become major policy issues.

> Affordability at its core in all segments is about the return on investment—the value added—of an educational experience. In some segments, affordability also encompasses a price tag for the educational experience that does not dissuade disadvantaged learners from engaging in an educational opportunity as a right of citizenship. In some segments affordability is measured by the organizational return on investment, often heavily dependent on perceived cost savings in the creation and delivery of the educational experience. Education is expensive to produce and deliver. So lowering costs opens up new possibilities for access. Also, there is usually an affordability benefit associated with more convenient forms of access. (Abel et al. 2007)

ICT Investment and Recurrent Costs and the Total Costs of Ownership

Trucano (2005) summarized the cost issues involved in ICT provision in developing countries as follows:

> Little is known about the true costs of ICTs in education. Few good, rigorous cost studies of ICTs in education exist in LDCs (and surprisingly few in OECD countries as well). Even less is known about cost effectiveness, especially in LDCs. Even fewer studies of cost-effectiveness of ICT in education initiatives in LDCs exist. Opportunity costs are under-studied as well. Little research exists into opportunity costs related to ICT in education investments—this is especially

relevant, and problematic, given the resource scarcities that define many LDCs seeking to meet education-related MDGs. (Trucano 2005)

A four-year research project (Read 2013) on the use of ICT in Basic Education in six Central Asian countries also triangulated the outcomes of the research with reviews of ICT in education policies in other developing countries in SSA, Latin America, and the Middle East. Out of 26 poor countries where ICT education policies were reviewed, only one (Uzbekistan) had attempted to undertake a total cost of ownership (TCO) analysis, which clearly indicated the scale of the costs involved and the need to transfer funds to ICT from other education budget heads.

> The preliminary calculations show that the Fat Client option on the basis of a "10+1" provision per school (student and teacher work stations) with a 1:50 PC/student ratio will require $15.6 million of annual capital investment for 5 years. This option will result in an annual deficit in this budget of US$7.1 million and will exceed the Thin Client option requiring only $11.7 million of investment with a lower annual capital investment budget of $3.2 million. It means that the [Government of Uganda (GOU)] will need to reallocate a considerable amount of other education funding to meet the target PC/student ratio. On the other hand, the GOU target of 1:20 PC/student ratio (Fat Client option) requires nearly $31 million of annual capital investments over the next five years. (Read 2005)

In SSA countries ICT investment in schools is strongly hardware led, even in countries where there is evidence of widespread poor usage or nonusage of the hardware provided. This often means that financing is provided for the purchase of computer hardware (PCs and peripherals) but that many other aspects of essential operational funding are widely ignored. The financing is also typically characterized by being highly centralized. All equipment decisions are top down with schools being the passive recipients of hardware profiles established in central ministries of education (MOEs). Often, there is no regular ICT budget line available to schools to support the hardware provided by government or by donors. Very few SSA MOEs have established adequate school-based operational budgets for equipment maintenance, hardware upgrading and replacement, connectivity, power supply, consumables, and so on, although there are some donors and non governmental organizations (NGOs) that have provided financial support for operational costs to a limited number of schools for a limited period. It is, perhaps, not surprising that donor or NGO ICT projects tend to report higher levels of equipment usage and more impact on classroom dynamics and student and teacher motivation than schools with hardware where additional financial support is not readily available. Similarly, the significantly increased system costs that should be associated with the introduction of expensive ICTs into the school system (curriculum design, teacher training, teacher support, supervision and inspection, assessment and evaluation, and so on) are largely absent from the ICT financial profiles of most SSA countries. There is a consistent mismatch between investment and recurrent budgets. Thus, as an almost universal rule, investment in

ICT hardware does not automatically result in adjustments to school operational budgets. In practice, this means that a school with 20 PCs generally will have the same per capita operational budget as a school with no computers at all, despite the obvious fact that a school with multiple computers needs significant additional funding to operate the computers effectively. The widespread donor and government moves to shift from norms-based school budgeting to per capita–based budgeting have not addressed this very fundamental issue with the result that increases in hardware investments tend to go side by side with increased financial difficulties for schools in operating the hardware provided. And yet the expensive school hardware depends for effective operations, which is surely the most fundamental rationale for its procurement, on adequate operational funding.

In many SSA countries there is an increasing dependence (frequently recognized but more often not discussed at official levels) upon parental charges or contributions to provide most of the school-based operational costs required to make effective ICT use a reality. As a result of this situation, usage at the school level is often undermined by a lack of parental affordability. The persistent failure of governments to provide for adequate school-based operational costs often leads to an emphasis of the digital divide rather than to its removal. Poor rural schools are generally less able to find the operational budget support from parents than are those in richer urban areas—and in any case the costs of connectivity, maintenance, and consumables can be much higher in rural than in urban areas because of the factors of distance and difficulty of access. There is also anecdotal evidence that even when Internet connections are available they are widely underused, particularly in rural areas, because schools do not have the operational budgets to pay the costs of regular connectivity. Where Internet costs are NGO or donor funded there is a typical pattern of Internet use declining or ceasing when the donor or NGO financial support comes to an end.

In situations where schools are largely responsible for raising the funds to support their own computerization (for example, in Ghana, Kenya, Uganda, and others), schools frequently have no understanding of the costs required to sustain effective ICT usage in their schools.

> Visits to secondary schools revealed that the costs of ICT provision and usage were not clearly understood and were often not affordable leading to widespread non-use of expensive hardware and the inability to afford the necessary maintenance costs to keep hardware operational. (Read 2010)

When schools are responsible for funding their own ICT development, there is often a tendency to buy cheap reconditioned or second hand hardware, which frequently has only a limited life expectancy and also, inevitably, has more frequent maintenance and servicing requirements. This increases pressure on school maintenance budgets and leads directly to higher percentages of non-operational hardware. The same problem is also associated with donations of secondhand hardware. One urban school principal in Kigali commented that his school was engaged in a time-consuming permanent pursuit of donations and funding from government, alumni, NGOs, development partners (DPs), and others, in order to replace failing donated hardware. Donated reconditioned hardware, often quite old, may also not be conformable with the operating systems of other PCs in the schools.

Constraints to Effective ICT Usage in Education

There is a remarkable unanimity in the constraints to ICT development in basic education identified in the reviews of ICT provision in developing economies. The following list of problems has been noted in most SSA countries.

- The socioeconomic divide between rich and poor, urban and rural leading to big differentials in the quality of education provided and specifically to radical differences in the application of ICTs to education
- Inadequate hardware provision associated with high percentages of non-operational hardware in schools caused by inadequacy of school operational budgets
- Under developed telecommunications and in particular the problem of the "last kilometer" and the differential access to, and costs of, Internet provision in rural and urban areas
- Ongoing power problems—the fact that a school is connected to the national grid doesn't mean that it is receiving electricity when it is required, that is, during school hours (power surges, brown-outs, unreliable and unpredictable power supply, inadequate uninterrrupted power supply (UPS) and the additional costs of inflated power bills without compensatory additional budget funding are all common issues in addition to the simple lack of access to power)
- Lack of ICT maintenance facilities in rural and remote areas and the increased costs of maintenance in rural areas
- Poor school environments—these range from lack of security, lack of weather-proofing, lack of air conditioning, inadequate furniture with poor ergonomic design, poor computer room design and layout, poor-quality ICT installations, antique (sometimes dangerous) wiring, and so on
- Inadequate financing, particularly for operational costs at the school level for power, Internet connectivity, maintenance, and the purchase of consumables
- Inadequate financing for teacher training, supervision, support services, and so on
- A lack of trained teachers and the problems of teacher resistance to ICT
- Lack of e-materials in local languages (in most countries there is a simple lack of e-materials oriented for educational usage in the national languages, although in most SSA countries this is more of an issue for primary grades than for secondary, where international languages tend to be the languages of instruction)
- Lack of methodological certainty and clarity in national curriculum or syllabus documents) on how best to use ICT in schools and the expected learning outcomes
- Curriculum, syllabus, and assessment policies and strategies not well adjusted to current ICT needs and requirements
- Lack of monitoring of effectiveness

In most SSA countries the problems listed above seriously inhibit the effective use of ICT in classrooms except in good schools (often private schools) in capital cities and other urban centers. The ICT country snapshots provided below cover a range of common ICT policy and operational issues.

Ghana

The provision of ICT to the Ghana education sector is a policy priority of the Ministry of Education, Science, and Sport (MOESS) noted in the draft Fifth Education Sector Policy. In Ghana, the introduction of ICT into the school system is perceived to have three different but related roles as follows:

- A management and administration tool in schools
- Training and familiarization in the use of the most common software applications (for example, word processing, spreadsheets, databases, presentations, desktop publishing, the Internet , and so on
- A teaching and learning tool for all subjects across the curriculum

Because of the cost implications of ICT provision to the education sector there has been an acceptance within the MOESS that major government investment in ICT should, at present, be restricted to senior high schools (SHSs). The 2009 Education Sector Review commented on the effectiveness of ICT in the Ghana education system as follows:

> ICT use in education has not been as effective as expected. Forty-three percent of all computers in Senior High Schools (SHSs) aren't functioning. Most of these were junk, donated to or procured locally by schools. Fifty-four percent of the 501 schools captured in the survey had computers that did not meet the minimum specifications of the Ministry. The national average student:computer ratio is 42 to 1 and this varies from 50:1 in Northern Region to 33:1 in the Volta Region. Within individual schools student:computer ratios varied from 3:1 up to 650:1. Ninety-three point four percent of schools used unlicensed software. Only 89 schools representing 17.7% of the total number of SHSs had internet and 80 of the 89 were in urban or semi-urban areas... only 8.3% of the total number of computers was connected to the internet. Of the majority of computer laboratories, 69.2% are closed immediately after school hours in the daytime. Students generally do not have access to practice skills. There is a big gap between ICT fees collected (from parents) and expenditures on ICT in most senior high schools. (MOESS 2009)

The quotation above summarizes many of the common issues related to ICT strategies and investments in developing and transitional economies as follows:

- ICT development for education is hardware led.
- It is largely unplanned and often uncontrolled.
- A significant proportion of the hardware in schools is not operational or is not used.

- Much of the hardware procured (particularly when schools do their own procurement) is low cost and substandard and is often imported second hand or "reconditioned."
- Donated hardware, particularly from small DPs and NGOs is also often secondhand.
- Secondhand PCs require much more maintenance than new PCs.
- There is no obvious consideration for the full cost implications for both schools and the MOESS.
- Parents tend to be the source of ICT operational costs in schools.
- The fact that ICT infrastructure is currently much more highly developed in urban areas than in rural areas leads to an emphasis of the domestic digital divide (DDD) rather than the reduction in the DDD, which has been widely promised by both hardware and software companies.
- There is little student (or even teacher) access to the hardware after school hours and thus no opportunity for free student or teacher practice and independent work.
- Software programs are dominantly pirated and there is a widespread absence of antivirus software.

Effective ICT use in developing school systems depends, among other factors, upon having sufficient operational budgets to maintain equipment in reliable working order. This means that the investment and recurrent costs of operation need to be clearly identified as part of the TCO. The normal recurrent costs are electricity, Internet access charges, maintenance and servicing, spare parts, consumable supplies, digital content (e-materials), and software (including antivirus software). In addition, investment and replacement costs need to be related to a target classroom life. In rural areas dial-up connections can be far more expensive and far less effective than a high-speed broadband connection in a major city. Maintenance and servicing are much more difficult to achieve in rural areas than in urban areas and are not likely to be as effective. Teacher training costs should never be estimated on the basis of one or two days of "switch on—switch off" basic instruction. If ICT is to be used to teach common software applications and to be used as an effective tool in teaching and learning across a variety of subjects, then teachers have to be competent and confident in their use of ICTs. And yet out of 17,953 teachers in Ghana who responded to the survey questionnaire, 44.1 percent had only basic ICT skills. Fourteen point four percent claimed to have advanced skills (however defined) but only 3.9 percent claimed to be capable of content development and only three percent to networking. In order to develop the confidence and the skills to use ICT effectively in the classroom, teachers should have opportunities to practice and thus to become confident. Few SSA teachers achieve this. Self-study, online courses are typically designed to provide 40 to 60 hours of hands-on experience to achieve an average operational effectiveness. Thus, the potential teacher training costs (including both initial and repeat training) are considerable if the hardware and recurrent investments are to be effective.

The use of ICT in the classroom is a high-cost activity, which at present is almost certainly not producing learning results in line with the scale of the investment in Ghana. The investment in ICT has the potential to divert investment away from other critical areas of education, which is not an argument against investment in ICT but suggests instead that there is an urgent need for a carefully planned and balanced investment strategy, which ensures that basic, high-priority education investments are funded side by side with ICT investment.

Jordan—Education Reform for the Knowledge Economy

Jordan has one of the most heavily funded education reform projects based largely on World Bank and United States Agency for International Development (USAID) funding, which is also strongly supported by the international hardware and software private sector.

Curriculum reform was part of the Education Reform for the Knowledge Economy (ERfKE) project and there are clear indications that the curriculum and traditional textbooks have made an effort to include opportunities to develop cross-curricula skills although an overloaded syllabus content requirement in most subjects and at most grade levels makes it very difficult for classes to undertake the proposed exercises and activities in pursuit of these skills. In addition many teachers do not have the skills, or sometimes even the interest to develop the required skills.

There is a further problem in that the enrichment e-materials produced by the Jordan Education Initiative (JEI) are reported not to be well integrated with the textbooks and teachers' guides despite the fact that the textbooks were generally used as the starting point for the development of the e-materials. A recent research report produced by the National Center for Human Resource Development (NCHRD) (Abuloum and Qablan 2008) indicates that poor quality e-materials are considered by ICT teachers as the main obstacle to the development of ICT as a teaching and learning tool across the curriculum. Ninety-one point five percent of 278 ICT teachers surveyed commented that the major obstacle to the use of ICT in schools was "unfriendly and complicated educational software" and a further 80.9 percent referred to "unfocused educational software." Eighty point nine percent also referred to the "heavy teaching load," which prevented teachers from using ICT resources. Quotations from teachers contained in the report suggested that much of the e-materials duplicated textbook content rather than supplementing or extending textbook content. In some cases teachers commented that the print materials and the e-materials represented two parallel (and competing) approaches to subject syllabuses rather than an integrated approach to the delivery of the syllabuses. The level of active planning and collaboration and coordination between the print and the e-materials development teams varied from subject to subject but overall was rated as inadequate. There was no evidence of a detailed, well-coordinated needs analysis intended to provide an integrated approach to the development and provision of teaching and learning materials (TLMs) in both print and e-formats. Both groups generally had been too busy with their own work to take much notice of what the other group was doing. There was plenty of use of the "blended learning" phraseology but much less hard evidence that "blended learning" actually takes place, or even that it was an objective of the print and e-materials development processes.

The two parallel syllabuses—print and e-materials—were both dominantly sequential. Although the e-materials are described as "enrichment," it is clear that they frequently followed closely the same syllabus sequence as the print materials and could be interpreted as an alternative learning approach. This is certainly the view of the sample of teachers quoted by the NCHRD report. Some of the digitization subject specialists indicated that they were now, retrospectively, trying to build some cross referencing to the textbooks into the e-materials users, guides. In several subjects the print curriculum groups are now proposing their own alternative e-materials because of the perceived problems with JEI materials, the unwillingness of the e-materials publishers to respond to suggestions for change, and digital delivery difficulties. The Digitization Directorate reports that it has provided JEI with feedback and suggestions for revision of the existing e-product, but so far there has been no sign that any revisions will be undertaken.

Almost all successful commercial publishers of core course materials in developed countries now perceive print and e-formats as complementary and thus requiring unified conceptualization, planning, and development. In Jordan the two are perceived in reality, if not in intention, as separate in terms of development. The concentration on the development of comprehensive e-textbooks suggests that in Jordan the e-materials developers perceive e-materials as a replacement for, rather than as supplementary to, existing textbooks and teaching and learning strategies, with which a majority of Jordanian teachers are familiar and comfortable. This is typical of approaches to ICT in education in many developing and transitional economies, which are markedly different to approaches to ICT in education in many developed countries. The concentration on the development of e-textbooks tends to be a symptom of this approach.

> Even in the most advanced schools in OECD [Organization for Economic Co-operation and Development] countries, ICTs are generally not considered central to the teaching and learning process. Many ICT in education initiatives in LDCs seek (at least in their rhetoric) to place ICTs as central to teaching and learning. (Trucano 2005)

> We should not be seduced with the promise that the next emerging technology will deliver our promised educational outcomes. It is only when we combine the capabilities of the technology with teachers' own remarkable skills that we truly make a difference through ICT. (Lynch 1999)

Both of the quotations above imply that ICT is not the silver bullet that will immediately upgrade school quality and student performance and that this can only realistically be achieved by combining new technology with existing (trained) teaching skills in the context of curricula and syllabuses that provide the space and time to use ICT profitably in class and an assessment system that has been designed to measure specified ICT skills, objectives, and learning outcomes.

Associated with the above problems is the issue of computers in schools. The NCHRD report quoted above confirms that Jordan has an average PC–pupil ratio of 1:17, although there are considerable variations between schools, with some schools operating at 1:40 or even higher. These computers are dominantly provided in computer laboratories and there are major scheduling problems reported by head teachers in providing class access to the computer labs at the time it is required. It is not clear from available reports just how much usage computer labs actually achieve, although it is certain that there are wide variations between schools. The data provided by the NCHRD report seems to suggest that a majority of schools are quite seriously under using their computer labs. When the scheduling problem is combined with widespread maintenance problems it is clear that there is a need to consider ways and means to improve the basic ICT infrastructure. The cost of teacher training and teacher support for ICT usage across the curriculum is widely underestimated and yet is a crucial factor in the successful launch of ICT across the curriculum. Bearing in mind the high-profile role that e-materials and ICT usage have in the Jordanian curriculum and education reforms, it is surprising that no detailed TCO for the provision of ICT facilities and the use of e-materials in education has so far been undertaken. The NCHRD report found that 89 percent of ICT teachers felt that teacher inability to use e-materials was a major obstacle to the use of ICT in schools, which tends to underline the issue that teacher training in the use of ICT across the curriculum remains a problem area.[1]

Kenya

In August 2008 a survey of ICT provision in 20 secondary schools was undertaken as part of the preparation for the World Bank–funded Free Day Secondary School Project (Read 2007). The 20 secondary schools surveyed were located in five provinces and in 11 different districts. Sixty percent of the secondary schools surveyed were rural schools.

Thirty-three percent of the rural schools surveyed had no computers at all compared to only 12.5 percent of urban schools without computer provision. The average computer–pupil ratio was 1:25 although this ratio rose to 1:33 if only operational PCs are taken into account. Twenty-three percent of all PCs in the surveyed schools were non operational. The majority of PCs were either procured by schools themselves or leased from commercial leasing companies. The schools interviewed for the survey had received little guidance from the MOES on the type of hardware to procure or what to do with it. A high proportion of school-based procurement was of secondhand or reconditioned hardware. Only 26 percent of the PCs in the surveyed schools were protected by UPS against power surges or power outages. Not only could these cause potential damage to hardware, but they could also result in lost work and damage to software. Many secondary schools, and particularly the newer, smaller secondary schools located in rural areas, did not have main power connections and no, or very restricted, access to electricity. Most of the secondary schools surveyed had at least one printer, but only 50 percent of schools had an operational photocopier and only 10 percent of the surveyed schools had a workable data projector.

Sixty percent of the surveyed schools used computers to support school administration and management, largely for financial management, examinations, student and staff record keeping, and student assessment. Curiously, only 40 percent of schools made PCs available to teachers for use in lesson preparation. Fourteen percent of teachers in the surveyed schools reported that they had access to a computer at home.

Thirty percent of surveyed schools gave students complete freedom of access to the school PCs during school hours. The remaining 70 percent did not allow students to bring external peripheral storage devices into the classroom. However, it was not evident in most schools visited that this was actively monitored or enforced. A number of computer labs visited had students working unsupervised. Forty percent of the schools claimed that they maintained legal antivirus software. Only 10 percent of schools were Internet connected, but only one school provided Internet access for students. In most cases the Internet access was reserved for the use of the school principal and for school administration. The high costs of Internet access were widely reported to be the most significant constraint on the development of Internet connectivity.

Only 30 percent of schools reported regular data backups. Of these schools none backed up data from student PC's. No schools had tested their "restore" procedure to see if they were backing up the data correctly. To perform regular backups is only half of the process. Regular "restore" test runs need to be performed to ensure data integrity. Very little basic system security (this is available by default on Microsoft operating systems) had been activated on computers within the schools. Basic login restriction and logon privileges were not being enforced, thus allowing students the same computer privileges as the school ICT administrator. This allows students, if they so wish, to do anything to the school computers, such as install their own applications, change settings, and delete files and programs. Even though no surveyed schools had any Internet monitoring software, one school did check the Internet log files routinely and had found students who were accessing illicit web sites. These students were disciplined accordingly.

Despite school investment in PCs only 25 percent of the surveyed schools had created a school local area network (LAN) for students. Even without an Internet connection a student LAN allows students to share files, communicate with each other, and, if the school wished, develop an intranet to show students the look and feel of using the Internet while being restricted by school policy as to what they were allowed to access.

The only schools that had ongoing maintenance support contracts with an ICT company were those using leased hardware from Computers for Schools Kenya (CfSK). A number of schools reported that when PCs were in need of repair, the schools would outsource to a local agent on an individual basis at an average cost of approximately US$100 per computer. Other schools said that they did not have the budget to repair computers so computers were normally dumped when they stopped working. In figure B.1 Kenyan schools list the problems as (a) no Internet connection, (b) high cost of Internet connection, (c) inadequate connectivity, (d) the high cost of consumables, (e) inadequate school budgets to support ICT, (f) insufficient teacher training in the use of ICTs, (g) high-cost maintenance services, and (h) lack of access to ICT support services.

In all of the surveyed schools the dominant use of ICTs was for teaching basic computer skills to students. There was little evidence that ICTs were used as a

Figure B.1 Major Problems with ICT Use in Education

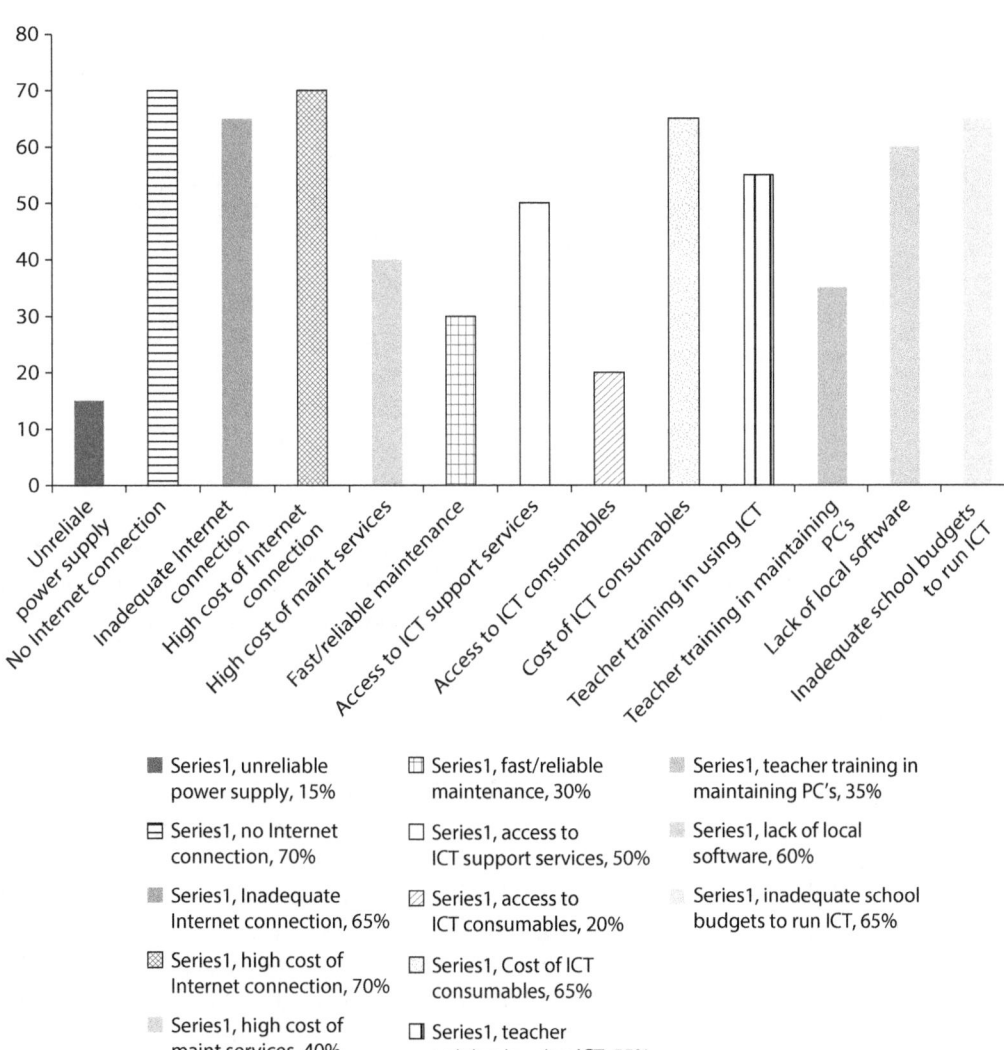

- Series1, unreliable power supply, 15%
- Series1, no Internet connection, 70%
- Series1, Inadequate Internet connection, 65%
- Series1, high cost of Internet connection, 70%
- Series1, high cost of maint services, 40%
- Series1, fast/reliable maintenance, 30%
- Series1, access to ICT support services, 50%
- Series1, access to ICT consumables, 20%
- Series1, Cost of ICT consumables, 65%
- Series1, teacher training in using ICT, 55%
- Series1, teacher training in maintaining PC's, 35%
- Series1, lack of local software, 60%
- Series1, inadequate school budgets to run ICT, 65%

Note: ICT = information and communication technology.

Figure B.2 Means of Procuring Computers

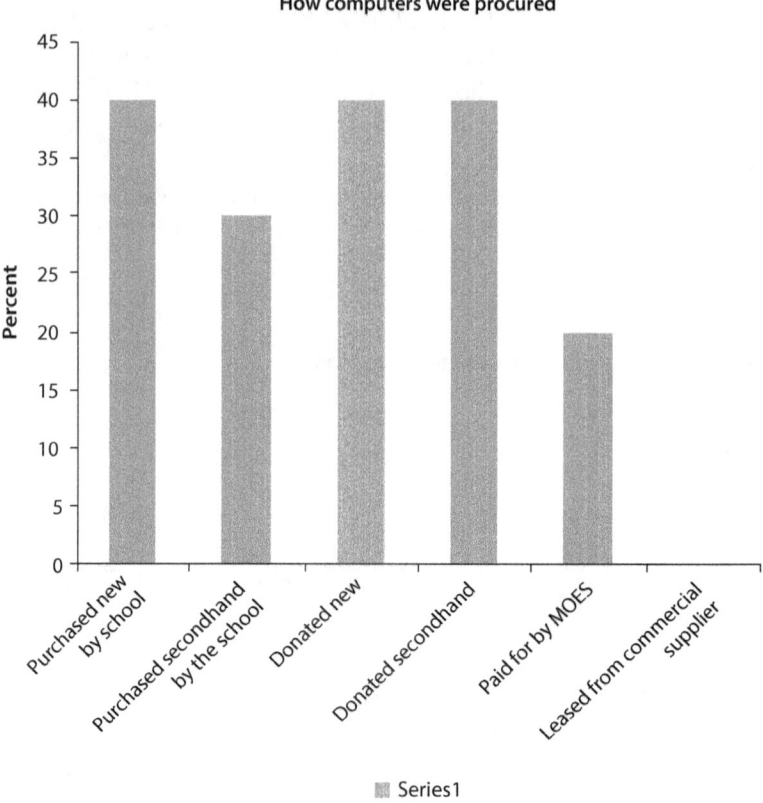

Note: MOES = Ministry of Education and Sports.

teaching and learning tool in other curriculum subjects. Most secondary schools charged parents an annual levy to cover the costs of ICT provision and usage in the schools. Figure B.2 indicates clearly that in Kenya most schools were responsible for their own computer procurement, with government funded supplies in the minority.

Uganda

In December 2007 an ICT survey in 11 secondary schools was conducted as part of the preparation for the Post Primary Education and Training Project (Read 2007). A previous survey conducted in 2002 had indicated comparatively little ICT development in secondary schools with only two out of 35 schools surveyed having any PCs available to students, although 30 percent of schools used computers for administration and school management purposes. By 2007 the situation had changed quite radically. All 11 surveyed schools had PCs for students' use. The numbers varied from eight to 61 for student use. The average was 23 computers per school, representing a 1:40 PC–pupil ratio. Nine out of 11 schools had a dedicated computer room, although not all of these were well designed or met basic health and safety standards. Eighty percent of the PCs were Pentium 3 or better. Seventy percent of computers were purchased by the schools out of operational budgets or parental levies, either new or secondhand, of which 40 percent were purchased new. A further 40 percent of schools had new computers donated, and a further 40 percent of schools had secondhand computers donated. Only 20 percent of schools (three out of 11) had received any computers funded by the MOES. There was no evidence of commercial leasing of computers by schools in 2007 although commercial leasing has been introduced into Uganda since then.

Out of the 7,130 students covered by the survey, 4,364 were attending computer studies classes (61 percent). In nine out of 11 schools, all S1 students received compulsory computer studies classes. Two out of 11 schools provided compulsory classes in computer studies for S2 and S3. Most schools attempted to provide general tuition in Microsoft Office to all students. There was little evidence that ICTs were used for subject teaching and learning outside computer studies. The most basic software available in schools was Microsoft Office, usually procured in pirate editions. Antivirus software was available in only two schools.

Only one of the 11 schools (in Kampala) had effective Internet connectivity via a very small aperture terminal (VSAT) connection donated by an alumnus of the school. Two other schools had dial-up connections using analog telephone lines, which provided limited e-mail access but were of little use for serious data access or downloading from the Internet. School administrators believed that connectivity was expensive, but seven out of 11 schools had never sought pricing information from an Internet service provider (ISP).

Nine of 11 schools had usable printers; only four out of 11 schools had UPS hardware (a dangerous situation when electricity supplies may be liable to power surges and unexpected shut-downs or brown-outs). Only one school had an LCD data projector and only four out of 11 schools had an air-conditioned computer room. Only one school (in Kampala) had a current and operational maintenance and servicing agreement. All other schools lacked local maintenance services and relied upon a combination of computer-interested and trained staff members, alumni or parents with computer skills, or travelling to Kampala with the hardware to consult specialist help. This last was reported to be both expensive and damaging to the hardware on many of the roads in Uganda. The result of the lack of established servicing contracts was a high percentage of nonoperational PCs.

All schools complained of power surges and failures, but only 30 percent of schools had installed UPS and even this did not cover all the computers in the schools. Only one school had a back-up generator and one school appeared to have no power supply at all! Power costs had not been budgeted in any school.

The skill levels of teachers providing instruction in computer studies was very variable and a high proportion of computer studies teachers had no formal ICT qualifications. Most schools wanted more teacher training in ICT skills.

There was no obvious data administration policy in place in any school. Teachers did not have a clear idea of what was being maintained on the computer by teachers or students. No security measures on Microsoft operating systems appeared to have been applied in any school. No school maintained effective computer housekeeping and there was no facility in any school for a media library.

Summary

The four case studies provided above suggest that there are two alternative approaches to ICT developments in education. Jordan, for example, sees the provision of ICT facilities to schools and the development of national ICT strategies and policies as a state-directed and financed activity supported by donor inputs. The African examples quoted in this section see the development of ICT facilities as essentially school and parent financed with greater or lesser support from government and donors.

Although there are two alternative ICT hardware financing strategies many of the problem areas remain the same. Thus investments tend to be hardware led with widespread shortfalls in operational funding. The national and school TCOs are generally not calculated and there is no understanding of the cost implications of ICT provision for either individual school or national system budgets. As a result there are real risks in most countries to the sustainability of effective ICT usage. Lack of maintenance and servicing and the associated costs lead to high levels of hardware downtime in all countries reviewed. Most hardware is provided via computer classrooms, which are widely not available to students or teachers outside formal classes. The hardware profile in most schools is PCs and a printer. Internet connectivity is generally restricted to schools in urban areas and power supplies are a consistent problem in rural areas. School-based management of ICT tends to be poor to nonexistent with a majority of schools unaware of the issues that need to be managed. School-based networks are comparatively rare. ICT facilities are used for school management and administration and for teaching basic computer skills but only rarely as teaching and learning tools for other subjects across the curriculum. Teacher training is generally unplanned, insufficient in duration to make it fit for the purposes to which most MOEs aspire. Often it is conceptually weak and unrelated to effective usage as part of subject learning. Guidance to schools tends to be general rather than specific.

One Laptop per Child and the Future Impact of Low-Cost Laptop Provision on SSA

It is not the intention of this section to make judgments on the benefits—or otherwise—of investments in One Laptop per Child (OLPC) and other low-cost laptop pilot programs[2] for schools in developing countries. The text that follows aims to identify the key issues in the ongoing debate on the OLPC concept and the use of the XO laptop and other low-cost laptops on a 1:1 basis in schools in order to provide DPs and MOEs with basic information to inform future decision making. The OLPC/low cost laptop concept is a subject of intense debate in terms of sustainable cost, potential educational impact, and practicality in many countries and among DP. This debate is made more intense because the OLPC concept is still largely untested in the field over a reasonable period of time and thus cost implications, practical implementation issues, and outcomes on student performance, behavior, attitudes, motivation and attendance are largely a matter of debate and argument rather than of objectively researched impact. The financial implications of OLPC are potentially very significant indeed, particularly for poor countries, and are so large that they could have a considerable impact on many other areas of education provision. As a consequence, in July 2006 the Indian Education Secretary commented that

> [The OPLC] may actually be detrimental to the growth of the creative and analytical abilities of the child.... Even if the idea was acceptable, we cannot visualize a situation for decades when we can go beyond the pilot stage.... We need classrooms and teachers more urgently than fancy tools.... If the Planning Commission has the kind of money that would be required for this scheme, it would be more appropriate to utilize it for universalization of secondary education. (Banerjee 2006)

In effect, India recognized the high cost implications of OLPC on a national scale and preferred to use its available investment and operational finance on improving more traditional components of its education system. Other countries have had different policy viewpoints.

So far as textbook provision is concerned, the problems with using OLPC and the XO laptops are as follows:

- The small screen size is not conducive to modern textbook design and layouts. The XO1 machine has a tiny screen, leading often to screen type sizes smaller than those typically recommended for textbooks and reading books for the same target age group. To save power it typically displays black on grey. Other common criticisms relate to slow operating speeds, an unreliable cursor that regularly freezes or submarines, and short battery life.[3] It is reported that the XO3, when it becomes available, will have much larger screen size (perhaps 7.8 × 11 inches) and an extended battery life.
- The cost of OLPC when supplied on a per pupil basis is high and on a par with the cost of e-readers (see below).
- The mesh network facility is reported to be difficult to operate effectively and downloading textbooks onto individual machines would be problematic in many rural locations where data transmission speeds are substandard. Thus preloading would probably be required.

There has been much debate about the TCO of the OLPC concept and the XO machine, which is still pretty much guesswork because there is no hard evidence available as yet. Nor is there widespread agreement on the cost components to be included in the TCO, nor even how these cost components are to be calculated.[4] Supporters claim as little as US$0.08 per machine per hour. Others estimate US$1,000 per XO over five years. Camfield (2007) has reported as follows:

> At the end of five years of training, continued Internet, and maintenance, the actual cost is USD$972 per laptop, almost quintuple the Libyan estimates, and ten times

the original laptop cost. Of course, a more expensive computer system would just drive all of this upwards.... for the OLPC project to succeed, it needs to accept that it's selling a $100 laptop with an $872 support plan, and find countries that can afford it as such.

India has recently announced a US$60 laptop with a subsidized price for students. It is inevitable that low-cost laptops will fall in price and that affordability will improve. But the TCO of high-density laptop provision will remain high in comparison to disposable education budgets in poor countries, particularly when the impact of OLPC on student achievement is not yet demonstrated.

> Most of the OLPC evaluations to date have been of very small pilots, and given the short duration of these projects it is difficult—if not dangerous—to try to extrapolate too much from the findings from such reports. This is especially true given the 'hothouse flower' nature of most high profile ICT in education pilots in their initial stages, where enthusiasm and statements about expected future changes in behavior, perceptions and impact substitute for a lack of rigorously gathered, useful hard data. (Trucano 2009)

In the United States the states of Maine and California have both had flagship one-to-one laptop projects for primary schools. The evaluation of outcomes in these projects was reported as follows:

> Maine test scores have remained flat through their 1:1 laptop program, and there has been no evidence that laptop programs improve reading or writing skills (or harm them). This can be interpreted either as technology not adding anything to education, or as standardized tests failing to measure the skills learned using technology. (Camfield 2008)

The U.S.-based conclusions listed above tend to support the findings of other country studies that ICT in Education tends to have more impact in "good" schools with adequate infrastructure and operational finance and much less impact in "poor" schools with inadequate infrastructure and operational finance. The widespread distribution of low-cost laptops in developing countries also will raise issues of increased maintenance costs and e-waste disposal.

The current OLPC/low cost laptop profiles make it unlikely that they would be feasible at current costs and specifications as cost-effective and practical vehicles for textbook delivery to schools and students.

Notes

1. For further examples of consistent underfunding of ICT teacher training see Read and Read 2008.
2. There is fairly widespread agreement that there are hardware alternatives to the MIT XO that are at least as effective and cheaper. As a result there are some primary laptop projects that do not use the XO.

3. There is a hand crank to supplement the battery which is specified as 10 minutes play time for each one minute of cranking, but this has been queried when using the Internet or downloading large or complex files, when the play time may be less.

4. For example, should teacher training costs be based on one day or one week per teacher? Should only the first teacher training input be included or should annual refresher training be included in the TCO? How much training is required to enable OLPC (or any other ICT for Education [ICT4E] investment) to reach its potential and how many teachers need to be trained for the purposes of the TCO?

References

Abel, R., L. Humes, L. Mattson, M. McKell, K. Riley and C. Smythe 2007. *Achieving Learning Impact: Annual Report from IMS Global Learning Consortium*. Lake Mary, FL: IMS.

Abuloum, A., and A. Qablan. 2008. *Evaluation of ICT Resources Provision, Access, and Utilization*. Amman: National Center for Human Resource Development.

Banerjee, S. 2006. "The Political Economy of Public Goods: Some Evidence from India." *Journal of Monetary Economics* 53 (5): 1021–26.

Banerjee, A. V. S. Cole, E. Dufflo, and L. Linden. 2007. "Remedying Education: Evidence from Two Randomized Experiments in India." *Journal of Economics* 122 (3): 1235–64.

Barerra-Osorio, F., and L. Linden. 2009. "The Use and Misuse of Computers in Education: Evidence from a Randomized Experiment in Colombia." Policy Research Working Paper 4836, World Bank, Washington, DC.

BECTA. 2010. *The Impact of ICT on Children's Attainment in English: A Review of the Literature*. London: BECTA for Department for Education and Skills.

Camfield, J. 2007. *Edutech* (blog). http://www.joncamfield.com/blog/2006/12/the_true_cost_of_the_olpc.html.

———. 2008. "A Review of One-to-One Laptop Programs in the USA." *Edutech* (blog). http://joncamfield.com/blog/2008/01/a_review_of_one_to_one_laptop_.html.

Condie, R., and B. Munro. 2007. *The Impact of ICT in Schools: A Landscape Review*. Glasgow, Scotland: Quality of Education Centre, University of Strathclyde, for BECTA/DfES.

Cox, M., C. Preston, and K. Cox. 1999. "What Factors Support or Prevent Teachers from Using ICT in Their Classrooms?" Paper presented at British Educational Research Association Annual Conference, BERA, London.

Cristia, J. P. P. Ibarran, S. Cueto, and A. Santiago. 2012. "Technology and Child Development: Evidence from the One Laptop per Child Program." Inter-American Development Bank, Washington, DC.

EdQual. 2011. *Implementing Educational Quality in Low Income Countries: Final Report*. United Kingdom: University of Bristol, http://r4d.dfid.gov.uk/PDF/Outputs/ImpQuality_RPC/EdqualFinalReport.pdf.

Fuchs, T., and L. Woessmann. 2004. "Computers and Student Learning: Bivariate and Multivariate Evidence on the Availability and Use of Computers at Home and at School." CESifo Working Paper 1321, Munich, Germany.

Fullan, J. 1991. *The New Meaning of Educational Change*. London: Cassell Publishers.

Hinostroza, J. E., C. Labbe, M. Brun, and C. Matamala. 2011. "Teaching and Learning Activities in Chilean Classrooms: Is ICT Making a Difference?" *Computers and Education* 57 (1): 1358–67. http://www.sciencedirect.com/science/article/pii/S0360131511000376.

Lynch, O. 1999. "BECTA Speech to Education Conference." London.

Malamud, O., and D. Pop-Eleches. 2008. "The Effect of Computer use on Child School Outcomes." Harris School Working Paper 08.12, Harris School of Public Policy, Chicago, IL.

MOESS (Ministry of Education, Science, and Sport, Ghana). 2009. *ICT Report for the Education Sector Review*. Accra, Government of Ghana.

Power, T., R. Gater, G. Grant, and N. Winters. 2014. *Educational Technology Topic Guide*. London: HEART for DFID.

Read, N. 2007. *Uganda Secondary School ICT Survey*. London: International Education Partners for WB.

———. 2008. *Kenya Secondary School ICT Survey*. London: International Education Partners for MOEST and World Bank.

Read, T. 2005. *Uzbekistan ICT in Basic Education Project: Report and Recommendations to the President*. Manila: Asian Development Bank.

———. 2010. *Ghana Learning and Teaching Materials Policy Review*. Accra: DFID for MOE.

———. 2013. *Ethiopia: The Textbook Component in GEQUIP 1 and GEQUIP 2*. A World Bank Study. Washington, DC: World Bank.

Read, T., and N. Read. 2008. *Regional Report on the Use of ICT in Basic Education in Six Central Asian Republics*. Nice, France: Linpico Sarl for the Asian Development Bank.

Trucano, M. 2005. "Knowledge Maps: ICT in Education." *Edutech* (blog), Washington, DC. http://www.infodev.org/en/Publication.8.html.

———. 2009. "What Have We Learned from OLPC Pilots to Date?" *Edutech* (blog). http://blogs.worldbank.org/edutech/what-have-we-learned-from-olpc-pilots-to-date.

Environmental Benefits Statement

The World Bank Group is committed to reducing its environmental footprint. In support of this commitment, the Publishing and Knowledge Division leverages electronic publishing options and print-on-demand technology, which is located in regional hubs worldwide. Together, these initiatives enable print runs to be lowered and shipping distances decreased, resulting in reduced paper consumption, chemical use, greenhouse gas emissions, and waste.

The Publishing and Knowledge Division follows the recommended standards for paper use set by the Green Press Initiative. Whenever possible, books are printed on 50 percent to 100 percent postconsumer recycled paper, and at least 50 percent of the fiber in our book paper is either unbleached or bleached using Totally Chlorine Free (TCF), Processed Chlorine Free (PCF), or Enhanced Elemental Chlorine Free (EECF) processes.

More information about the Bank's environmental philosophy can be found at http://crinfo.worldbank.org/wbcrinfo/node/4.